Dilemmas of European Integration

Dilemmas of European integration

The ambiguities and pitfalls of integration by stealth

Giandomenico Majone

OXFORD
UNIVERSITY PRESS

OXFORD
UNIVERSITY PRESS

Great Clarendon Street, Oxford OX2 6DP

Oxford University Press is a department of the University of Oxford.
It furthers the University's objective of excellence in research, scholarship,
and education by publishing worldwide in

Oxford New York

Auckland   Cape Town Dar es Salaam   Hong Kong   Karachi
Kuala Lumpur Madrid Melbourne Mexico City   Nairobi
New Delhi Shanghai Taipei Toronto
With offices in
Argentina Austria Brazil Chile Czech Republic France Greece
Guatemala Hungary Italy Japan South Korea Poland Portugal
Singapore Switzerland Thailand Turkey Ukraine Vietnam

Oxford is a registered trade mark of Oxford University Press
in the UK and in certain other countries

Published in the United States
by Oxford University Press Inc., New York

ISBN 978-0-19-955680-9

Printed in the United Kingdom by
Lightning Source UK Ltd., Milton Keynes

Preface to the Paperback Edition
Giandomenico Majone

The text of *Dilemmas of European Integration* was completed two months before the EU governments, assembled in Rome on 24 October 2004, solemnly signed the now defunct Constitutional Treaty (CT)—hence the scattered references, mostly in chapters 1 and 10, to the "new" Constitutional Treaty. The volume was in the bookstores shortly before the French and Dutch voters rejected the same CT in popular referendums which demonstrated how wide was the gap still separating elite from public opinion after half a century of European integration. All the major political parties—on the left and on the right, in government and in opposition–the vast majority of members of the national parliaments, economic leaders (in the Netherlands also trade union leaders), influential media, the European Parliament and the Commission—all supported ratification of the CT. In the Netherlands two-thirds of members of parliament voted for the Treaty, almost the same proportion of voters rejected it. Particularly surprising in both cases were the high voter participation (compared to all previous European elections) and the size of the negative vote: almost 55 per cent against ratification and 45 per cent in favor in France; 61.5 and 38.1 per cent, respectively, in the Netherlands. The rejection of the CT was all the more painful because never before had EU governments tried so hard to make the treaty-making process more transparent and participatory. At their summit in Laeken in 2001, EU leaders decided that a "Draft Treaty establishing a Constitution for Europe" should be prepared by a European Convention–an assembly of 105 full members and 102 alternates, supposedly representing the full spectrum of public opinion. One of the first acts of the Convention secretariat was to set up an internet site where more than 850 documents were eventually posted, as well as material used by the Convention's working groups, and about 6,000 amendments to draft articles submitted during the process of crafting the CT. But even this first (and possibly last) attempt to reproduce at European level the constitutional-convention model of modern democracies failed to impress the majority of voters in two founding members of the European Community.

The rejection of the CT was followed by two years of recriminations, distributive struggles over EU finances, and indecision about how to restart the integration process. Only in the first half of 2007 the German rotating presidency of the EU succeeded in getting a fragile agreement on how to move forward. The "Berlin Declaration" made by Chancellor Angela Merkel on the occasion of the 50th anniversary of the Treaty of Rome, reiterated the commitment to create "a new common foundation" for the EU in time for the 2009 European elections, but the document carefully avoided any reference to a European constitution because of the firm opposition of several countries, including the new members Poland and Czech Republic. In the summit of June 2007, a tentative agreement on a new text could be achieved only by scaling down the Constitutional Treaty to a "Reform" Treaty; granting opt outs to the UK and Poland from the Charter of Fundamental Rights; satisfying Polish demands concerning voting rules in the Council of Ministers; and by carefully avoiding any reference, not only to a European constitution, but to anything smacking of statehood, from the Union flag and anthem to a EU "foreign minister". In spite of all these precautions, in June 2008 the purged version of the CT was rejected by the citizens of Ireland—where a popular referendum is mandatory for amendments to EU treaties. At the time of writing (August 2008), final ratification of the Reform (Lisbon) Treaty remains uncertain, not only because of the Irish 'No', but also because the conclusion of the process still depends on future decisions by the Czech and German constitutional courts, and on the decisions of the Euroskeptic presidents of Poland and of the Czech Republic. Vaclav Klaus, the Czech president, declared the treaty dead, while Mirek Topolanek, his prime minister, was quoted as saying that he would not bet 100 crowns on a Czech 'Yes' to the Lisbon Treaty. Most member states favor a second Irish referendum, but to stage another popular vote the government in Dublin would need some concessions. In his speech to the European Parliament at the beginning of the French presidency of the EU, however, President Sarkozy categorically ruled out any modification of the Reform Treaty. According to him, either it is possible to rescue the Treaty in its present form, or the EU must continue to function under the current Nice Treaty—in which case any further enlargement of the EU would be impossible. Thus it remains to be seen which concessions may be offered for a second referendum. At any rate, the Irish foreign minister ended all hopes of a quick resolution of the crisis when he stated that his government would not be in a position to offer a solution by the next EU summit in October 2008.

Popular referendums have always represented a potential hazard for the elite-driven process of European integration. In June 1992, 50.7 per cent of the Danish voters rejected the Treaty on European Union, proving that after more than twenty years of membership that brought Denmark considerable economic benefits, the nation's elites and ordinary citizens were almost as divided on the question of European integration as they had been in 1972, when Denmark held its first European referendum on whether or not to join the European Community. The Nice Treaty was rejected by the Irish voters in a referendum held in June 2001. In both cases, however, the ratification process in the other member states continued, while in Denmark and Ireland it sufficed to make a few concessions, and to ask again the questions in a somewhat different form, for consent eventually to be granted. The fact that no easy solution could be found after the French and Dutch voters rejected the draft Constitutional Treaty, and that so many uncertainties surround the fate of the Lisbon Treaty, show how much the general situation has deteriorated in recent years.

One paradoxical consequence of the latest manifestations of popular discontent has been to reinforce the elitist nature of the integration project, to the point that a number of EU leaders increasingly perceive popular voting as the main obstacle to the progress of European integration, while some academic commentators are beginning to speak of a "referendum roulette", a "referendum threat", even of a "federalist deficit"—meaning a slowing down or reversal of the federalization process caused by popular referendums (see, for example, the Special Issue: Towards a Federal Europe? of the *Journal of European Public Policy*, Volume 12, Number 3, 2005). The argument is that in an association of twenty-seven member states—whose political, socioeconomic and cultural heterogeneity is probably greater than in any previous, similar free association of states—the probability of a negative popular vote is high. On the other hand, the risk of rejection is not as high at the level of EU's summit diplomacy, where Euro-elites are able to deliberate, bargain, and trade votes. Hence, the real threat to the federalist cause comes from the direct expression of voters' preferences.

I believe that *Dilemmas of European Integration* can help the reader understand why the EU, instead of progressively attracting the loyalty of its citizens, seems to become less popular and less trustworthy over the years. Disappointed expectations are certainly one important reason. As shown in chapter 3, the essence of the Monnet method of integration by stealth consists in pursuing political integration under the guise of economic integration. Monnet hoped that his roundabout strategy would make it possible to advance the integration process even in the absence of popular support—without realizing that poor economic performance over a period of years could undermine the legitimacy of an elite-driven project. Indeed, the attempt to pursue different objectives with the same policy is bound to produce suboptimal results, see chapters 6 and 7. This risk did not appear to be significant in the first years because the foundational period of the European Communities largely overlapped with the three "glorious decades" 1945–1975, when Europe experienced an unprecedented period of growth, macroeconomic stability, and high levels of social protection. Labor productivity was at or above US levels, and most countries reached a situation of full, or nearly full, employment. Although it is known today that these achievements had little to do with the integration process, the impression was created that the same approach could be used to pursue two different objectives: more integration for the elites, and greater prosperity for the masses. This optimistic view was shattered when the "economic miracle" came to an end. After the phase of very rapid catching-up with the United States, convergence in the levels of per capita income stopped at the beginning of the 1980s and has remained unchanged since, at around 70 per cent of the US level. Between 1995 and 2005 productivity in the euro-zone services sector—which accounts for more than 70 per cent of EU GDP and 50 per cent of employment–grew at an average pace of 0.5 per cent a year, against 3 per cent in the US.

In fact, the desire to improve poor economic performance has driven EU policy for more than twenty years: from the Single Market Program, which was meant to provide a response to perceived "Euro-sclerosis" in the mid-1980s, and Economic and Monetary Union (EMU) in the 1990s, to the Lisbon Strategy which promised to boost growth and employment, and to make the EU "the most advanced, knowledge-based economy in the world" by 2010 (see chapter 8). For a long time official rhetoric about the unique benefits of European integration went unchallenged because of the veil of ignorance covering EU policymaking. While the implications of domestic policies are reasonably well understood by the voters, until recently most decisions taken in Brussels were too technical and remote from the daily problems of people to seriously concern public opinion. True, programs like the Common Agriculture Policy have been criticized often enough, but controversies and contestations always remained confined within fairly narrow academic and political circles, or within particular interest groups (see chapter 6). EMU and eastern enlargement have changed all this. Unlike most policy decisions taken in Brussels, the decisions taken by the European Central Bank in Frankfurt are immediately effective and widely advertised, and their consequences, whether on home mortgages, consumer credit, or the availability of publicly-funded services, have a direct impact on the welfare of all inhabitants of the eurozone. Hence some of the costs of a one-size-fits-all monetary policy are plain for everybody to see. Similarly, the implications, true or presumed, of the eastern enlargement on jobs, wages, social standards, and law and order have become part of the daily concerns of many European citizens.

This awareness of the practical implications of European integration is not only a new, but also an ominous development. For half a century Euro-elites could present integration as a positive-sum game. Now everybody can see that the integration project entails not only benefits but also costs—economic, institutional, and not least, in terms of democratic legitimacy (see chapters 2 and 5). Increasingly, European policies are judged, not in terms of their contribution to "ever closer union of the peoples of Europe", but by their ability to tackle everyday issues. Several observers have called attention to the coincidence of the Irish No vote with protests across Europe against rising food and energy costs. Neither the EU summit meeting in Brussels on 19 June 2008 to discuss the consequences of the Irish referendum, nor the European institutions, were able to agree on a common strategy to deal with the situation. This unresponsiveness to popular worries is bound to induce greater popular resistance to new transfers of powers to the European level, as well as a much stronger demand of accountability by results—precisely what is foreign to the political culture of the EU. Chapter 6 is particularly relevant here. It calls attention to the propensity of EU leaders to confuse process and outcome, and to ignore the possibility of failures. EU policies, it argues, are largely epiphenomenal—the by-products of actions undertaken to advance the integration process, to expand European competences, or to facilitate intergovernmental bargaining: incentives to engage in efficient problem solving are largely absent.

The legitimacy of a new polity depends on its capacity to engender and maintain the belief that it is able to resolve the major problems facing society. Conversely, a breakdown of effectiveness in the provision of a satisfactory level of security and economic growth will eventually endanger even a legitimate polity's stability. This connection between effectiveness, legitimacy, and systemic stability is the reason why the unsatisfactory economic performance of the last decades, and the growing security problems of a Union without stable boundaries are so worrisome. Unless the EU can actually demonstrate that it can add value to what individual member states, or subsets of member states, can achieve on their own, it will be impossible to resolve the legitimacy crisis which is currently threatening the stability, and possibly the very survival, of the EU.

G. M.
Villa Lappeggi
Florence
August 2008

Preface

A failed federation, but the successful prototype of post-modern confederation—this is how the concluding chapter of this book summarizes and evaluates half a century of European integration, from the 1951 Paris Treaty establishing a Coal and Steel Community of six member states to the Constitutional Treaty approved by the twenty-five members of the Union in June 2004. A glance at the table of contents suffices to show, however, that this is not another history of European integration. Rather, I rely on a variety of analytical tools and theoretical concepts in order to grasp the basic logic of the institutional architecture designed by the founding treaties, and altered by subsequent amendments. One of the commonplaces of research on the European Community and Union is that these polities are so unique as to require a brand-new terminology, but this view overrates the creativity of the founding fathers. As Alexis de Tocqueville once remarked, the gallery of human institutions contains few originals and many copies. Once the organizing principles of the Community and Union are clearly understood, it becomes possible to relate their modus operandi to other, past if not present, modes of governance. In Chapter 3, for example, the Community method is shown to be a latter-day version of mixed government—a form of governance based on the representation of corporate interests, which was prevalent in preabsolutist Europe.

Another manifestation of the same belief in the uniqueness of the European institutions is the care with which most recent writers on European integration eschew the traditional concepts of federation and confederation, preferring to use new, and apparently more neutral, terms like multilevel governance and intergovernmentalism. However, Occam's razor prescribes not to introduce new terms unless they actually improve our understanding of the processes and phenomena under investigation. This does not seem to be the case in the present context. Early federalists like Jean Monnet, Walter Hallstein, or Altiero Spinelli did not envisage a 'multilevel' system as the ultimate goal of European integration. They knew what they wanted, and that was a full-fledged European federal state—a 'United States of Europe' (see Chapter 10). But also those leaders who did not share the federal vision were aware that they were engaged in something a good deal more significant than the creation of an international organization. The failed Fouchet Plan of 1961–2, which envisaged a confederation of European states with a common foreign and defense policy as well as cooperation on a number of other domains, shows that 'intergovernmentalism' is not an adequate characterization of the position of the minority who opposed the federal vision.

Words do matter. To say that the European Union is not a federation but a confederation has far-reaching consequences. A federation, as the term is generally used today, is a state. A confederation is not a state but a union of sovereign states, which together pool certain powers for mutual advantage; it is a contractual arrangement among otherwise independent partners, not an expression of popular sovereignty. It follows, as I argue in Chapter 2, that the standards of democratic legitimacy that apply to a society of individuals organized in a nation-state become inappropriate when applied to a confederation. Federation and confederation simply belong to different logical categories and cannot be evaluated by the same standards. To complain about the 'democratic deficit' at European level, therefore, only makes sense if one envisages the transformation of the present European Union into a federal state. This is a perfectly legitimate aspiration, of course, but federalists should be more explicit about what a future European federation would be able to do for its citizens. According to the Schuman Declaration, written in 1950, the European Coal and Steel Community was 'the first concrete foundation of a European federation which is indispensable for the preservation of peace'. It is not true, however, that federation is a necessary, much less a sufficient, condition for the preservation of peace—as shown by the tragic experiences of former Yugoslavia and Soviet Union, and perhaps even more clearly by the American Civil War in the nineteenth century. In fact, peace can be maintained quite effectively by other means than federation—for example, by military alliances like the North Atlantic Treaty Organization.

Strange as it may sound, nobody yet has convincingly explicated the value-added of a European federation—what it might realistically do that could not be achieved by less far-reaching commitments. Unlike most other treatments of European integration, this book does not parry such a delicate, but essential, question. On the contrary, it argues that the federalist project was doomed from the start for one basic reason: absent a European demos (see Chapter 2), a European federation would lack the material and normative resources to provide the public goods people have come to expect from the state, whether unitary or federal. In Chapters 9 and 10, I also discuss what such a federation could actually do. It turns out that it is not much more than what the present European Union is already doing—in some respects, it could be even less. Rather than facing squarely such issues, federalists have always preferred to engage in the much easier task of designing alternative institutional architectures for the would-be federation, but such academic exercises are no longer sufficient. To be credible, they will have to explain in detail how a federal state composed of polities separated by deep economic, institutional, cultural, and social cleavages would meet the expectations of European citizens without imposing a politically unacceptable level of centralization; or, alternatively, how the would-be federation could establish and maintain its own legitimacy in spite of being unable to fulfill the basic functions of a modern welfare state, including of course income redistribution.

To revive popular interest in the integration process and restore credibility to the European institutions few things are needed more than putting an end to the present confusion of means and ends. After the collapse of the European Defense Community put to rest all plans for a full-fledged federal union (see Chapters 1 and 2), the 'Monnet method'— the strategy of promoting spillovers from one economic sector to another and eventually from market integration to political integration—came to be accepted as a more roundabout, but safer, path to the ultimate objective of political union. Functional spillovers would create pressure for deepening and widening the scope of supranational policymaking, while political spillovers would set in motion a self-reinforcing process of institution-building. Hence the predictions of a steady progress towards federalism (see Chapter 3). These predictions have not materialized, but what is worse, the Monnet method turned out to be flawed since its votaries never resolved a crucial dilemma: whether European policies should be initiated in order to solve specific problems in the best possible way, or whether they are to serve, first and foremost, integration objectives. Naturally, European policymakers claim that policy and integration objectives can and should be pursued simultaneously, but as will be shown in Chapter 6, the attempt to pursue several objectives simultaneously tends to produce suboptimal policy outcomes. In fact, most of the dilemmas, pitfalls, and outright failures discussed in this book can be ultimately traced to the functionalist approach—the attempt to achieve European integration by stealth rather than by frankly political means.

A notable example of integration by stealth is the use made by the European institutions of Article 235 of the Rome Treaty (now Article 308 EC). As discussed in Chapter 4, this Article has been used all too often to expand the powers of the supranational institutions without following the normal democratic procedures of ratification and approval by national parliaments of formal treaty amendments. As long as the scope of Community competence was limited, and trust in the self-restraint of the supranational institutions was maintained, the simplified procedure for adapting the treaty to new needs had an obvious appeal. Since the Single European Act of 1986 expanded significantly Community powers, however, the member states have been willing to follow the more complex and politically riskier procedure of formal treaty amendment, rather than delegating to the European Commission and Court of Justice the task of deciding whether Community action in a given area is needed, and which form it should take. This explains why since the Single European Act, intergovernmental conferences for the purpose of treaty revision have taken place every three or four years, so that treaty amendment has become almost a routine procedure.

The risks inherent in the Monnet approach to European integration could be significantly reduced by two institutional reforms outlined in Chapters 5 and 7. First, by delegating regulatory powers to bodies independent from both the European institutions and the national governments; and, second, by redirecting the activities of the supranational institutions away from the current emphasis on policy initiation and legal harmonization towards negative integration, that is, a more effective enforcement of European rules.

These, then, are the main themes of this book. Hopefully, enough has been said to suggest that our treatment departs radically from most writings on European integration. As indicated above, the arguments presented here are underpinned by a variety of analytical tools and theoretical concepts, ranging from the economic theory of clubs, used to explain the growing interest in 'enhanced cooperation' between subsets of member states, to decision theory, used to criticize the current EU approach to risk regulation. I have always been careful, however, to define all the technical terms, and to provide examples where needed. Thus the book should be accessible also to undergraduate students and to the nonspecialist reader interested in European integration. The process of ratification of the new Constitutional Treaty, which in a number of countries will include also popular referenda, is bound to increase general interest in many of the issues discussed here. This book is presented as a contribution to the forthcoming public debate, by somebody who deeply believes in the value of integration—not strictly along the lines set in Brussels, however, and certainly not by stealth.

In preparing this text for publication I have been helped by my son Gian Andrea, whose assistance has proved invaluable. I am convinced that his critical assessments have significantly enhanced the clarity of the following pages. I wish to express publicly my gratitude to him.

G. M.
Villa Lappeggi
Florence
August 2004

Contents

From Community to Diverse Union

1.1 The Manifold Path to European Integration

For most of its history, but especially in the period between the peace of Westphalia (1648) and the French Revolution, Europe formed a cultural, economic, even a political unity. Of course, it was a special type of unity that did not exclude frequent, but limited, wars; not the unity of empire, but unity in diversity, embodied in a system of states competing and cooperating with each other. Such a system realized the benefits of competitive decision-making, but also some of the economies of scale of centralized empire, giving Europe some of the best of both worlds (Jones 1987). The search for unity in diversity and competition with cooperation continues to this day along a number of different paths. It is therefore wrong and misleading to reduce the history of European integration after World War II to one particular approach—even one as important as that which has produced, first, the European Communities (ECs) and, then, the European Union (EU) of today. Neither geographically nor functionally or culturally does the 'Europe of Brussels'—even after the latest enlargement—coincide with, or represent, the entire continent.

Take, for example, the Council of Europe established in 1949, which at present has more than forty member countries. The Council may concern itself with all political, economic, and social matters of general European interest and thus has an even broader mandate than the EU. True, it does not have any power to make binding laws. The two instruments at the Council's disposal are nonbinding resolutions and draft conventions, which take effect only between states that have ratified them. The most important convention established under its auspices is the European Convention for the Protection of Human Rights and Fundamental Freedoms (ECHR) of November 4, 1950. The significance of this convention is such that no state can join the Council of Europe unless it agrees to accede to

the ECHR. Furthermore, every person within the jurisdiction of the contracting states is automatically protected by the ECHR, regardless of his or
her nationality or place of residence. With the creation of the European
Court of Human Rights, located in Strasbourg, the ECHR provides an
enforcement structure that subjects the states to a 'European' supervision
of their compliance with the provisions of the Convention. For this reason, it has been argued that the ECHR constitutes a first expression of
supranationalism in the European integration process (Lenaerts and Van
Nuffel 1999). It is at any rate true that levels of compliance with the ECHR
and with the decisions of the Strasbourg Court do not appear to be at all
lower than levels of compliance with EC law (MacCormick 1999).

The Conference for Security and Cooperation in Europe (renamed in 1995
the Organization for Security and Cooperation in Europe, OSCE) is another
cooperative arrangement much broader than the EU framework. The OSCE
has fifty-three member states covering virtually all European countries,
including all the republics of the former Soviet Union, as well as Canada
and the United States. It consists of several institutions, including meetings
of the Heads of State or Government, a Council of Ministers of Foreign
Affairs, a Council of Permanent Representatives to the OSCE, a Parliamentary Assembly, an Office for Democratic Institutions and Human Rights,
and several instruments for dispute resolution. There are many other forms
of European cooperation outside the EU framework, including different but
equally viable policy regimes such as NATO and the European Space
Agency. Of course, the EU itself does not operate within the same legal
framework or in a single policy mode. At the 1991 Intergovernmental Conference the attempt was made of bringing foreign and security policy
within an integrated Community framework. The attempt failed because
most member states felt that the Community did not enjoy sufficient
legitimacy to make policy in areas close to the core of national sovereignty:
a common foreign and security policy, and certain law-and-order matters
should not be delegated to supranational institutions, but made to depend
on the direct cooperation of the national governments. Hence the Maastricht Treaty rejected an integrated model in favor of the three-pillared
structure comprising the EC (first pillar), the Common Foreign and Security
Policy (second pillar), and Justice and Home Affairs (third pillar). The
classical Community method was to apply only to the first pillar and,
eventually, to the 'communitarized' parts of the third one. The new
Constitutional Treaty approved by the member states in June 2004—here
and throughout this book I shall use the expression 'Constitutional Treaty'
since 'Constitution' sounds too pretentious for the outcome of an

Intergovernmental Conference—does away with the pillar structure but this does not imply either the generalization or the rejection of the Community method, which has been maintained, more or less intact, in most policy areas directly related to economic integration. On the other hand, the refusal of the treaty to extend it to foreign affairs and security, as the European Commission and sundry federalists had hoped, reveals a growing feeling that the method, besides lacking democratic legitimacy, is also too rigid to be easily adapted to the new tasks facing the EU today. In subsequent chapters we shall inquire into the reasons why the Community method is increasingly perceived less as the royal road to deeper integration than as an obstacle to institutional and policy innovation. However, such is the historical significance of the method (which will be discussed in detail in Chapter 3) that some authors decompose the entire process of European integration since the end of World War II into a Community and a non-Community integration path—a didactic simplification that may be more misleading than helpful if it induces to underestimate the range and importance of alternative approaches to the former method.

1.2   The Community Path

The European Coal and Steel Community (ECSC) Treaty was the first significant step along this integration path, establishing a novel structure whose independent institutions had the power to bind its constituent member states. The treaty was signed by France, Germany, Italy, and the three Benelux countries (Belgium, the Netherlands, and Luxembourg), in Paris in 1951. It set up four institutions: a High Authority, to be the main executive body with decision-making powers and responsibility for implementing the aims and provisions of the treaty; an Assembly made up of national parliaments' delegates with mainly supervisory and advisory responsibilities; a Council made up of one representative of each of the national governments, given the task of coordinating the activities of the national governments and the High Authority, as well as a consultative role and some decision-making powers; finally, a Court of Justice of nine judges. The Council was given powers of codecision in two specific situations: first, to cope with any decline in demand—the 'manifest crisis' procedure; and, second, 'in all cases not provided for in this Treaty where it becomes apparent that a decision or recommendation of the High Authority is necessary to attain, within the common market in coal and steel . . . one of the objectives of the Community' (Article 95, ECSC Treaty).

Because the High Authority—a body made up of independent appointees of the six member state governments—was empowered to take decisions binding on the member states of the ECSC, and on coal and steel companies, this new form of cooperation among sovereign states was referred to as 'supranational' by the first students of European integration. The notion of supranationalism is intimately related to the particular approach followed in establishing the ECSC. This approach is 'functional' in the sense that the treaty set a specific aim—the establishment of a common market in coal and steel—and transferred genuine legislative and executive powers to the Community in order to achieve it. Unlike the Rome Treaty establishing the European Economic Community (EEC), the ECSC Treaty contains virtually all the rules that the member states deemed necessary for the smooth operation of the common market in those two commodities. These included the prohibition within the Community of all import and export duties, of charges having equivalent effect, and of all measures discriminating between producers, purchasers, and consumers. State aid and restrictive practices were also prohibited.

Jean Monnet, the real father of the ECSC, was hardly interested in the problems of the coal and steel industries as such, and the Community itself achieved a good deal less than the founding treaty had promised. Thus, 'wage harmonization' went nowhere, and also worker relocation and retraining largely failed, despite a generous US loan provided to make it possible. More seriously, the battle over the steel cartels, which were backed by the national governments, was lost (Gillingham 1991). In addition, the ECSC was beset by administrative, personality, and other problems, which eventually induced Monnet to resign from the presidency of the 'first European government'—the ECSC High Authority—in order to work full time for European integration through his 'Action Committee for the United States of Europe'. It seems doubtful that the failures of the ECSC were compensated by its rather unspectacular successes (e.g. in harmonizing certain taxes and unifying railroad rates), but this did not seem to matter much. The openings of the common markets for coal and steel, in February and May 1953, had mainly symbolic significance. For its architects and supporters, it was clear from the beginning that the Community was not merely about coal and steel, but was a first step in the direction of European unity, and the integration process was considered a good deal more important than the substantive policy. We have here the first manifestation of the deep ambiguity of the functionalist approach. Whether European policies should be initiated in order to solve specific problems in the best possible way, or whether they are to serve, first and foremost, integration objectives is a central dilemma that has never been openly faced, let alone resolved. Naturally, European policymakers claim that policy and integration objectives can and should be pursued simultaneously, but, as will be shown in Chapter 6, the attempt to achieve political ends by supposedly technical means tends to produce suboptimal policy outcomes.

A brave attempt to pursue political ends by openly political means was made only one year after the signing of the ECSC Treaty. On May 27, 1952 the six ECSC member states signed the European Defense Community (EDC) Treaty. The treaty defined the EDC as a supranational community, with common institutions, armed forces, and a budget. An overarching political structure was also envisaged. The ECSC's Assembly took the initiative and drafted a treaty for a European Political Community. As discussed in Chapter 2, the draft treaty would have transformed the six members of the ECSC into an actual federation based on the principles of parliamentary democracy and separation of powers. However, the collapse of the EDC Treaty in August 1954 ended all plans for a full-fledged federal union. Since then, no avowedly federalist plan has ever been seriously considered by the national governments. Integration by stealth came to be regarded as the only feasible strategy open to 'good Europeans'. An outstanding example is the Spaak Report, named after the Belgian foreign minister and convinced federalist ('Mr Europe') who chaired the intergovernmental committee launched after the Messina Conference of June 1955, to draft plans for further European integration.

1.3   The Treaties of Rome

The Spaak Report recommended that the two objectives of sectoral integration (atomic energy) and wider economic integration (a common market) be realized in separate organizations, with separate treaties. The resulting European Atomic Energy Community (Euratom) Treaty and EEC Treaty, both signed in Rome in 1957, were politically motivated— 'the Communities are in politics, not business' according to a famous epigram attributed to Walter Hallstein, the first president of the European Commission—but had a specifically economic focus. In accordance with the thrust of the Report, the EEC Treaty carefully avoided the explicit political objectives of the draft European Political Community Treaty and concentrated on the aims of economic integration in the preamble and in Articles 2 and 3. Four of the aims stated in Article 2 are of an economic or social nature (e.g. to promote a harmonious development of economic activities, and an accelerated raising of the standard of living) while the fifth one refers to 'closer relations between the States belonging to [the Community]'. Article 3 lists the activities required to achieve the aims stated in Article 2. These include the elimination of customs duties between the member states; the establishment of a common tariff and a common commercial policy towards third countries; free movement of services, people, and capital; common policies in the spheres of agriculture and transport; a system ensuring that competition in the common market is not distorted; and the approximation of the laws of the member states 'to the extent required for the proper functioning of the common market'.

The declared aim of Euratom was to create the conditions for the speedy establishment and growth of nuclear industries (!). To this end, Article 2 of the Euratom Treaty provided for common policies on research, safety standards, supplies of ore and fuels, right of ownership in fissile materials, and international relations in the field of nuclear energy. Again, the main objective was less to develop a rational strategy to meet the present and future energy needs of Europe than to drive forward the integration process. As Monnet had explained in an interview published by the French newspaper *Les Echos* in 1955: 'The United States of Europe means: a federal power linked to the peaceful exploitation of Atomic Energy' (Lucas 1977: 11). However odd the idea of promoting European unity through nuclear energy may sound today, this was the real objective of Euratom. In the late 1970s a student of energy policy could still write: 'The hope that nuclear energy can promote European unity may... be just as pervasive in the Commission now as in the early days of Euratom' (Lucas 1977: 98)—in spite of the fact that by then it was already clear that Euratom was not going to produce any significant success. When Euratom institutions merged with those of the EEC and the ECSC in 1967 (by the so-called Merger Treaty), Euratom virtually lost its identity. The distrust by the other member states of French motives in supporting the Euratom, an abundance of imported oil—despite the oil crisis in the 1970s—and growing environmental and safety concerns about nuclear energy, eventually resulted in Euratom's marginalization.

The institutional structure of the EEC and the Euratom bears a certain family resemblance to that of the ECSC. It also consists of a Commission (the equivalent of the ECSC High Authority), a Council of Ministers, an Assembly (the precursor of the European Parliament, EP), and a Court of Justice. However, the Rome Treaties located the center of decision-making

powers in the Council. Basically, under the ECSC Treaty, the High Authority decided on the Council endorsement, while under the treaties of Rome,
the Council decides on the Commission's proposal. As noted above, the
ECSC Treaty contains virtually all the rules that the member states deemed
necessary for the smooth operation of the common market in coal and
steel—in the language of international lawyers it is a *traité-loi*. Instead the
EEC Treaty is a *traité-cadre* (or an 'incomplete contract', in the language of
Chapter 4), which designs the institutional framework and decision-
making rules, but leaves many substantive policy choices deliberately
open. Precisely for this reason the member states did not wish to vest
any full legislative powers in the Commission, reserving the ultimate
policy choices to themselves (Lenaerts and Van Nuffel 1999). The Commission's task was confined to making proposal, implementing legislation,
and supervising compliance with Community law. Even so, the powers of
the Commission are quite significant. As explained in Chapter 3, this
institution's monopoly of legislative initiative means that if the Commission does not make a proposal to the Council, then no progress is possible.
This mechanism was conceived as the truly original feature of the Community method. The initiative of the Commission, the response of the
Council, and the synthesis by the Commission—in the days before the EP
was given a power of codecision—was seen as a dialectic that would be the
motive force of the Community (Lucas 1977: 83).

1.4   The Closing of the Foundational Period

Two significant events of what Weiler (1999) has called the foundational
period of the European Community—1958 to the middle of the 1970s—in
fact took place outside the Community framework. Like some scientific
experiments that are seen to have been 'crucial' only *ex post*, the significance of the establishment of the European Political Cooperation (EPC)
and of the European Council (composed of the heads of state or government of the member states) is probably clearer today than it was in the
early 1970s—the EPC as the precursor of today's Common Foreign and
Security Policy (CFSP); the European Council as the core, together with
the Council of Ministers, of the executive of the Union designed by the
new Constitutional Treaty (see Chapter 10).

    After the failure of the European Defense Community and the associ-
ated European Political Community in the 1950–4 period, and after the
abortive Fouchet Plan of 1961–2 (a design, inspired by the French President,

Charles de Gaulle, for a confederation of European states with a common foreign and defense policy), the EPC was the first attempt to achieve a measure of cooperation in the field of foreign policy and some coordination of the member states' international actions. The EPC was the product of the Hague summit of heads of state or government in December 1969, and the ensuing foreign ministers report of November 1970. Institutionally, it was to be completely separate from the EEC, so that during its first years foreign ministers even met at different places depending on whether they were meeting as the Community's General Affairs Council or in the context of the EPC. Only in 1974 the foreign ministers decided to hold EPC meetings at the margin of Council meetings. However, EPC ministerial meetings were not prepared by the Committee of Permanent Representatives of the member states in Brussels (Coreper), but by national foreign ministries' political directors, meeting as the Political Committee (PoCo). Thus, to the extent that EPC was institutionalized, it was definitely not at the level of Community institutions. The institutionalization of EPC was mostly in terms of norms and shared expectations. Norms were established on the need for consultations to precede individual foreign policy initiatives, and generally on the desirability of European solidarity whenever it was possible, in particular at the United Nations. In this way, a habit of foreign policy consultation and coordination began to emerge. Without the processes of socialization and the development of an *esprit de corps* among key policymakers the launch of the CFSP in the early 1990s would have been much more problematic (Joergensen 2002: 213–14, and Chapter 8 in this book).

One of the reasons for the decision to establish the European Council—a decision taken at the Paris summit of 1974—was to provide a platform for EPC discussions at the highest level. In fact, for thirty years (1974–2004) the European Council has exercised significant power, and shaped the integration process like no other institution, without itself being a European institution in the legal sense. Its status has only been changed by Article I-18 of the draft Constitutional Treaty. According to this Article, the European Council *is* now an institution of the Union, along with the EP, the Council of Ministers, the Commission, and the Court of Justice. For the first twelve years of its existence, the Council did not even have a legal basis in the treaties. It has been argued that its power was due precisely to its ambivalence in institutional terms. Unlike other European institutions, the competence, procedures, and decision-making process of the European Council were not determined by the treaty. Hence, it could deal with whatever problem it wished to deal with, in the manner it deemed most appropriate (de Schoutheete 2002). In this way, the Council has been able to counteract the rigidity and legal formalism of the Community method, and also to compensate, at least to some extent, the inadequate democratic legitimacy of the supranational institutions (see Chapters 2 and 3).

The role of the European Council was defined by Article 4, first indent, of the Treaty on European Union (TEU): 'it shall provide the Union with the necessary impetus for its development and shall define the general political guidelines thereof.' Over the years, however, the Council has acquired and exercised a number of other powers and functions: as decision-maker of last resort, when no solutions can be found at the level of the Council of Ministers; as agenda setter and institutional architect; as ultimate negotiator, in the case of the Maastricht, Amsterdam, and Nice Treaties, and of the new Constitutional Treaty; as 'collective head of state' when acting in its external capacity; and as policy initiator. Because the European Council appears to be working effectively, at least by comparison with the rigidity and *lourdeur* of the classic Community method, the temptation to increase its role is strong. Those tempted to follow this course include both federalists like the German Foreign Minister, Joschka Fischer (see Chapter 10), and some, like the British Prime Minister, Tony Blair, who reject the federal vision. It is therefore important to be aware of the weaknesses of the institution, as well as of its strengths. According to de Schoutheete (2002: 43), the limits of the European Council are particularly apparent when it modifies the treaties: 'The structure and *modus operandi* of the European Council [are] well adapted to collective bargaining, to the definition of general guidelines, even to the drafting of political statements. It is not well adapted to the legislative function.' Even in the definition of general guidelines and objectives, however, the Council sometimes tends to equate the desirable with the feasible, as in the case of the overly ambitious 'Lisbon Strategy' discussed in Chapter 8.

Coming back to the foundational period, it seems that the two 'intergovernmental' developments just mentioned—the launch of the EPC and the establishment of the European Council—did not attract anything like the attention devoted to the major 'supranational' developments of the same period. Not only lawyers but also political scientists were especially impressed by the impact of EC law on the legal system of the member states—an impact made evident by the two principles of direct effect and of the supremacy of Community law, introduced by the European Court of Justice (ECJ) in a series of landmark cases starting in 1963. *Direct effect* means the capacity of a norm of Community law to be applied in domestic court proceedings, provided the norm is unambiguous, unconditional, and not dependent on any national implementing rule. *Supremacy* means the capacity of that norm to overrule inconsistent norms in national law. On the strength of such principles the foundational period has been characterized by legal scholars as the time of laying the foundation for a federal Europe (Weiler 1999), but subsequent developments do not support this assessment. Analogies with corresponding principles of the Federal Constitution of the United States are quite misleading. In the case of the EC, neither direct effect nor supremacy has any explicit basis in the treaties, but were developed by the ECJ in order to emphasize its own conception of the autonomy of EC law. Unlike state courts in the United States, most national courts in Europe do not accept the view of the ECJ as regards the principle of supremacy of EC law. While they accept the implications of the principle in practice, most regard this as flowing from their national constitutions rather than from the authority of the European Court, and retain the power of ultimate constitutional review over measures of EC law (Craig and de Búrca 2003; MacCormick 1999). Moreover, these judicial doctrines are not relevant in the most dynamic areas of current Union activities, such as the Common Foreign and Security Policy, where the European Court lacks jurisdiction. Even in the area of Justice and Home affairs, despite the changes made to the third pillar by the Amsterdam Treaty (see Section 1.7), it is unlikely that the Court will find its provisions to have a significant impact, especially since Article 34 of the TEU stipulates that the legislative decisions that may be adopted under those provisions shall not entail direct effect (Craig and de Búrca 2003).

1.5   The Single European Act

The last years of the foundational period were also characterized by a number of official and semiofficial reports suggesting various strategies to accelerate the integration process. The Tindemans Report, presented in January 1976 and named after Leo Tindemans, a Belgian prime minister and convinced federalist, focused less on the goal of a federal Europe than on the need to reform existing EC institutions, for example, by replacing unanimity with qualified majority voting, and lengthening the six-month Council presidency. The report's most controversial aspect was the mention of the possibility of a 'multi-speed Europe', with different speeds of integration depending on the will and the ability of each member state to move forward. Smaller member states disliked the prospect of first-class and second-class (corporate) citizens of the Community, while some of the larger member states were concerned about a further loss of sovereignty, which the idea seemed to entail. The only concrete achievement of the report was that at the Hague Summit of November 1976, the European Council instructed the Commission and the foreign ministers to report once a year on progress made towards EU.

The 'Three Wise Men' Report on the European Institutions, presented at the Dublin Summit of November 1979, was noted mostly for its criticism of the Commission and endorsement of the Council. However, its emphasis on the lack of political will as the main obstacle to the progress of European integration was resented in the national capitals. Hence, after a brief discussion at the Dublin Summit, the Report on European Institutions joined the Tindemans Report and the 1979 Spierenburg Report on reform of the European Commission, in the historical archives of the Communities. The 1981 Genscher–Colombo Draft European Act—which proposed to unify all decision-making procedures of the Communities and EPC by assigning competence for all matters to the European Council and the Council of Ministers, but also to give more powers to the EP—was no more successful than the previous reports.

The Single European Act (SEA), signed in 1986, largely ignored these and other proposals to revive and reform the Community. This is one reason why at the time it was criticized as being too limited or even regressive. In retrospect, it is clear that the SEA succeeded in reviving the Community after the doldrums of the 1970s precisely because it avoided any grandiose institutional reform plans, and instead focused strictly on the completion of the Single European Market. Without altering the objectives or tasks of the Community, as defined in Articles 2 and 3 of the EEC Treaty, the SEA conferred new powers in the areas of social policy, economic and social cohesion, research and technological development, and environmental protection. At the institutional level it simplified Community decision-making by introducing qualified majority voting in the Council. It increased the legislative role of the EP by introducing the cooperation procedure. According to this procedure, at the first reading, the EP issues its opinion and then the Council establishes a common position. At the second reading, if the Parliament rejects the common position by a majority of its members, the Council can adopt the legislation only by acting unanimously.

The single most important innovation of the SEA was Article 100a (now Article 95 EC), dealing with harmonization (or 'approximation') of national laws and regulation, that is, their adaptation to Community requirements. Under the Rome Treaty, the main basis for harmonization activity was Article 100 (Article 94 EC), which provides: 'The Council shall, acting unanimously on a proposal from the Commission, issue directives for the approximation of such provisions laid down by law, regulation or administrative action in Member States as directly affect the establishment or functioning of the common market.' The ECJ has frequently expressed its opinion that directives made under Article 100 deprive member states of competence in that field ('total harmonization'), thus introducing a sort of federal preemption. This federalist interpretation of Article 100 could be accepted by the member states as long as each would have a veto in the establishment of a new European norm. With the SEA, however, the main basis for harmonization became Article 100a, which demands only a quali-fied majority in the Council. In order to restore the balance between national and supranational interests, the member states demanded the inclusion in Article 100a of a fourth paragraph relating to the issue of preemption. Article 100a(4) provides:

If, after the adoption of a harmonization measure by the Council acting by a qualified majority, a Member State deems it necessary to apply national provisions on grounds of major needs referred to in Article 36 [public morality, public policy, or public security; the protection of health and life of humans, animals, or plants; the protection of national treasures ... or the protection of industrial or commercial policy], or relating to protection of the environment or the working environment, it shall notify the Commission of these provisions. The Commission shall confirm the provisions involved after having verified that they are not a means of arbitrary discrimination or a disguised restriction on trade between Member States. . . . [T]he Commission or any Member State may bring the matter directly before the Court of Justice if it considers that another Member State is making improper use of the powers provided for in this Article.

In other words, member states were not prepared to move to qualified majority in the Council without some relaxation of the traditional ap-proach of total harmonization, which leaves no scope for unilateral mem-ber state action. Article 100a(4) recognizes that the fact of Community legislative intervention is not sufficient to exclude the possibility of regu-latory action by the member states, where this is shown to be justified (Weatherill 1995). All measures taken under Article 100a are open to the possibility that one or more member states may choose to invoke Article 100a(4), for example, if they wish to assure their citizens of a higher level of protection than is provided by European regulations. Precisely this possi-bility of unilateral derogation of Community harmonizing measures alarmed influential commentators such as Pierre Pescatore, a former judge at the European Court, who feared that Article 100a(4) represented a serious backward step in the pattern of a uniform Community legal order. Contrary to such doomsday predictions, however, the derogation has been invoked very infrequently—less than ten times in the first ten years since the SEA became effective. The member states seem to be well aware of the damage that could be wrought by recourse to unilateral derogations. Still, Article 100a(4) is important as the first manifestation of the phenomenon of 'flexibility' in European law, which has been playing an increasingly significant role since the TEU.

1.6   The Birth of the European Union

The momentum generated by the SEA continued after its adoption. A committee chaired by Commission President, Jacques Delors, on Economic and Monetary Union (EMU) presented a report setting out a three-stage plan for reaching EMU. The European Council decided to hold an intergovernmental conference (IGC) on the subject, and a second IGC on 'political union', supposedly in order to balance economic integration with political integration. On the basis of the IGC negotiations, a draft treaty was presented by the Luxembourg presidency of the European Council in 1991. The TEU was eventually signed by the member states in Maastricht in February 1992. Apart from the detailed commitment to monetary union, the most striking feature of the TEU was the 'three-pillar' structure for what was henceforth known as the EU, with the EC as the first of these pillars, and the EEC Treaty being officially renamed the European Community (EC) Treaty. The second and third pillars dealt, respectively, with the CFSP, which replaced the EPC, and Justice and Home Affairs (JHA).

The second pillar is strictly 'intergovernmental', and a CFSP act is not binding on Community institutions. On the basis of guidelines from the European Council, the Council of Ministers organizes consultations among the member states, and adopts 'common positions' and 'joint actions' (see Chapter 8). The Commission does not have an exclusive right of initiative, and exercises no supervision over member states compliance with the obligations they enter into, while the EP is entitled only to be consulted and kept informed. Article 46 TEU precludes any review by the Court of Justice. The JHA pillar included policies such as asylum, immigration, and 'third country' nationals, which since the 1997 Amsterdam Treaty have been 'communitarized', that is, have been integrated into the EC Treaty. It also included, and still covers today, police and judicial cooperation in criminal matters (PJCC), both types of cooperation being intended to establish 'an area of freedom, justice and security' (see Chapter 3). The Council of Ministers again was given the role of adopting joint positions and drawing up agreements, acting unanimously except on matters of procedures and when implementing joint actions or agreed conventions.

The TEU brought about a number of legislative and institutional changes to the EC Treaty, as well as a concrete timetable for EMU with provisions for a European System of Central Banks and European Central Bank. The aims of the Community, as defined in Article 2 EC were amended to include EMU, environmental concerns, convergence of economic policies, social protection, and economic and social cohesion. Article 3, which lists the activities of the Community, now included also policies on research and technological development, trans-European networks, health protection, consumer protection, education, energy, civil protection, and tourism. A concept of European citizenship was introduced, a Parliamentary Ombudsman and a 'Committee of the Regions' were established. The most significant change made by the TEU to the Community institutions was the codecision procedure for the EP, which adds a third stage to the two stages that existed under the earlier cooperation procedure, and gives the EP a veto over proposals of which it does not approve. A number of protocols were also signed, including a Social Protocol with an Agreement on Social Policy, and a protocol that preserved the right of Denmark and the United Kingdom to opt out of the third and final stage of EMU.

The ratification process revealed a good deal of public dissatisfaction with the substance of the treaty and with the process of its negotiation. In the words of Craig and de Búrca (2003: 22): 'The ambiguities and tensions inherent in the European Community project from its earliest days, far from being resolved by the new treaty, were positively enshrined in its provisions.' These ambiguities and unresolved tensions explain why both political and scholarly opinions varied so widely in their assessments of the TEU. If the then British Prime Minister, John Major, chose to see the treaty as a victory for intergovernmentalism, more radical Euroskeptics, led by Sir James Goldsmith, viewed 'Maastricht' as a big step towards a full-fledged European federation. Both views, and several intermediate ones, could find plausible support in the final text or in the deliberations that preceded it. Turning to academic opinion, for professor Alan Dashwood, a major result of the treaty was a new precise delimitation of Community powers. According to him, the principles of attributions of powers, sub-sidiarity, and proportionality enacted in Article 3b TEU (now Article 5 EC) marked a shift in the Community's deep structure. The Article 'effectively rules out of court the notion of a Community continuously moving the boundary posts of its own competence' (Dashwood 1996: 113). In fact, the more cautious attitude of the member states towards the delegation of regulatory powers to the supranational institutions is revealed by the fact that the TEU defined new competences in a way that actually limits the exercise of Community powers (see Chapter 4).

Other legal scholars assessed the treaty rather differently. Thus, profes-sor Deidre Curtin (1993: 67), in a much-quoted paper titled 'The Constitu-tional Structure of the Union: A Europe of Bits and Pieces', concluded that: 'The Maastricht summit is an umbrella Union threatening to lead to constitutional chaos; the potential victims are the cohesiveness and the unity of and the concomitant power of a legal system painstakingly con-structed over the course of some thirty odd years... at the heart of all this chaos and fragmentation, the unique *sui generis* nature of the European Community, its true world-historical significance, is being destroyed.' Those who, like professor Curtin, believe that European integration can only move along a single path, presumably towards a federal destination, were naturally disappointed by the final result. It is now clear, however, that the differentiation or flexibility that appeared in several forms in the TEU was no momentary aberration—a sort of *à la carte* integration—but the clear indication of an emergent strategy for achieving progress in politically sensitive areas, even at the price of a loss of overall coherence of the system.

1.7   Differentiated Integration Since Maastricht

Flexibility, variable geometry, opt-outs, derogations are some of the labels used to express the idea that some states may participate in certain policies while others will not, or will only partially. Variable geometry, in particu-lar, is used to denote a division—possibly permanent—between a hard core of member states, which are willing to proceed more rapidly towards 'ever closer union', and the remaining integration 'laggards'. Several com-mentators have pointed out that the examples of flexibility introduced by the Maastricht Treaty—such as the opt-out from monetary union for Denmark and the United Kingdom, or the exemption from defense policy provisions of member states that are neutral—were not new, but had appeared in various forms in earlier Community history, including the SEA, which made possible for the first time opting out of Community harmonizing measures. It will be recalled that this possibility was regarded by some as a serious backward step in the pattern of a uniform Community legal order. In fact, the idea of a common market structured by uniform European rules had to be given up already by the early 1970s. As we shall see in Chapter 4, experience had shown that total harmonization confers on the Community an exclusive competence, which, because of lack of expertise and institutional resources, the supranational institutions are ill-equipped to discharge (Weatherill 1995). Another type of flexibility is represented by a so-called 'extra-EU solution', such as the Schengen system, under which in the early 1990s a core of countries have proceeded under a separate international treaty to remove substantially all the internal borders between themselves.

The aim of greater flexibility was given official recognition and constitutional status by the Amsterdam Treaty (signed in 1997) and by the Nice Treaty (concluded in December 2000, after an exceptionally acrimonious and lengthy European Council Summit). Both treaties include a separate Title on closer or 'enhanced' cooperation among subgroups of member states. The Amsterdam Treaty provided, for the first time, the possibility of closer cooperation within the single institutional framework, subject to a number of strict conditions: such cooperation may not apply to areas of exclusive Community competence; it may not restrict intra-Community trade; it must concern at least a majority of member states and is open to all members of the Union wishing to join. Subject to these and other conditions, member states may establish closer cooperation in the first and third pillar, within the institutional framework of the EU. In granting authorization the Council acts by qualified majority on a Commission proposal, after consulting the EP. However, a member state may veto a request from other members wishing to establish such closer cooperation by declaring that it opposes the authorization 'for important and stated reasons of national policy'. In such a case, the Council may by qualified majority refer the matter to the European Council for unanimous decision (the 'emergency brake' clause). These provisions were never actually used before being amended by the Nice Treaty, but the insertion of the new Title VII, 'Provisions On Closer Cooperation', conclusively demonstrated that differentiated integration should no longer be thought of as an aberration within the EC and EU legal order, nor as a temporary solution until all member states may be accommodated into a uniform system (Craig and de Búrca 2003).

The issue of closer (henceforth called 'enhanced') cooperation was the one where most progress was made during the negotiations leading to the Nice Treaty. A few changes to the Amsterdam Treaty deserve special mention. First, the minimum number of countries required to initiate enhanced cooperation was changed from a majority of member states to an absolute figure of eight. This was of course the majority in a Union of fifteen members, but the change seemed to suggest that in an enlarged Union a majority of member states would no longer be required for enhanced coordination. This interpretation has been confirmed by the new Constitutional Treaty (see later). Second, in the Community pillar and in the new third pillar (PJCC), the 'emergency brake' clause has been taken away, or at least concealed, in the sense that a matter may still be referred to the European Council before a decision is taken, but now there is no mention of unanimity. Finally, the possibility of enhanced cooperation was explicitly extended to the second pillar (CFSP), but military and defense matters were excluded, apparently due to pressure during the IGC from the British Government. This exclusion was the consequence of deep disagreements concerning the independence of Europe's military capabilities with respect to the North Atlantic Treaty Organization (NATO), with Germany and France favoring an independent European military capability, which the United Kingdom opposed.

Other provisions in the Nice Treaty stipulate that any enhanced cooperation must respect the *acquis communautaire*—the body of Community law built up over the years—as well as the competences and rights of non-participating states; that areas where the Community has exclusive powers must be preserved; that the Internal Market must not be affected; and that the mechanism must be open to all member states. Furthermore, enhanced cooperation may be engaged in only as a last resort, when it has been established that it is impossible to achieve, within a reasonable period, the objectives of the Union by following the normal procedures provided by the treaty; the relevant operational expenditures should in principle be borne by the participating countries; and consistency with Union policies must be guaranteed. In sum, the provisions of the Amsterdam and Nice Treaties attempt to constitutionalize and legitimate a mechanism for allowing different degrees of integration and cooperation between different groups of states, and provide a general legal basis for situations, such as the Social Protocols and the EMU opt-outs of the Maastricht Treaty, which had been individually negotiated in response to various political deadlocks in the past (Craig and de Búrca 2003). Since Amsterdam, the tendency has been to make the use of enhanced cooperation more feasible and operational, and the new Constitutional Treaty actually reinforces this tendency. According to Article I-43, one-third of the member states is now sufficient to establish enhanced cooperation, as long as authorization is granted by the Council. Authorization to proceed is granted when it has been established within the Council that the objectives of such cooperation 'cannot be attained within a reasonable period by the Union as a whole'. The same Article imposes less stringent conditions on member states intending to establish enhanced cooperation than the corresponding Articles 43, 43a, and 43b of the Nice Treaty. The drafters of the Constitutional Treaty, like the framers of the Amsterdam and Nice Treaties before them, were aware that in an increasingly inhomogeneous Union enhanced cooperation may offer the only hope of avoiding stagnation while preserving key elements of the traditional framework. An optimistic school of thought tends to focus attention on the potential of enhanced-cooperation clauses to regulate diversity in a principled way, in the sense that any uses of these provisions must adhere to the objectives of the Union (Shaw 2003).

1.8   The Future of Enhanced Cooperation

A more pessimistic school argues that, far from furthering the objectives of the Union, the various forms of voluntary cooperation among member states will in fact undermine the basic assumption of the Community method—that all countries would move together along the same integration path. This pessimistic view of interstate cooperation explains why the Commission's first Communication to the Constitutional Convention— *A Project for the European Union*—was rather hostile to the whole question of flexibility. It argued, *inter alia*, that the enhanced cooperation provisions offer only theoretical answers to the problems of diversity, and that it is time for a critical reappraisal of all derogations. A second Communication on institutional architecture did not even discuss flexibility, while the Commission's informal contribution to the debate on the Constitutional Treaty, the so-called Feasibility Study (codename: Penelope), proposed a structure for the EU's new constitutional framework that excludes the possibility of enhanced-cooperation arrangements. Member states may conclude arrangements among themselves, however, as long as they do not make use of the institutions and procedures of the Union. While the Amsterdam and Nice Treaties encouraged the member states to work within, or as closely as possible to, the framework of the Union when cooperating among themselves, the aim of the Commission's proposal was to separate sharply such voluntary arrangements from the mainstream integration process. In fact, the proposal seems to admit the possibility that the objectives of enhanced cooperation could be unrelated to the objectives of the Union: 'The Member States may establish closer cooperation between themselves in so far as the objectives of such cooperation cannot be attained under the Constitution' (Article 5(2) of the Feasibility Study, cited in Shaw 2003: 189). This is very different from the position taken by the framers of the previous treaties. According to Article 43 of the Nice Treaty, for example, enhanced cooperation 'is aimed at furthering the objectives of the Union and of the Community, at protecting and serving their interests and at reinforcing their process of integration'. Also Article 43 of the Constitutional Treaty states: 'Enhanced cooperation shall aim to further the objectives of the Union, protect its interests and reinforce its integration process.'

The lowering of the participation threshold by the draft Constitutional Treaty could only strengthen the Commission's fears that in a greatly enlarged Union, enhanced cooperation must eventually lead to the demise of the principle of a single institutional framework for the process of European integration. It is true that the possibility of enhanced cooperation has never been used so far, but this is presumably due to the strict conditions imposed by Amsterdam and Nice, in particular the requirements that enhanced cooperation must involve a majority of member states and that it must be open to all members of the Union. But if these conditions are relaxed at the same time that national preferences become more varied as a consequence of enlargement, the temptation to form smaller, more homogeneous groupings may become irresistible. The economic theory of clubs, which will be applied in Chapter 5 to a more specialized context, suggests a scenario that in a sense supports the Commission's fears. Unlike the Commission, however, the theory views the multiplication of voluntary associations as a positive, welfare-enhancing, development. A few key definitions and concepts will suffice for the present purpose. *Pure public goods*, such as national defense or air quality standards, are characterized by two crucial properties: first, it does not cost anything for an additional individual to enjoy the benefits of the public goods, once they are produced (joint supply property); and, second, it is difficult or impossible to exclude individuals from the enjoyment of such goods (nonexcludability). A *club good* is a public good from whose benefits particular individuals may be excluded—only the joint supply property holds. A voluntary association established to provide excludable public goods is a *club*.

Two elements determine the optimal size of a club. One is the cost of producing the club good—in a large club this cost is shared over more members. The second element is the cost to each club member of a good that does not meet precisely his or her individual needs or preferences. This psychic cost is likely to increase with the size of the club. Hence the optimal size is determined by the point at which the marginal benefit from the addition of one new member, that is, the reduction in the per capita cost of producing the good, equals the marginal cost caused by a mismatch between the characteristics of the good and the preferences of the individual club members. If the preferences and the technologies for the provision of club goods are such that the number of clubs that can be formed in a society of given size is large, then an efficient allocation of such excludable public goods through the voluntary association of individuals into clubs is possible. With large numbers of alternative clubs available each individual can guarantee themselves a satisfactory balance of benefits and costs, since any attempt to discriminate against them will induce their exit into a competing club, or the creation of a new one. If optimal club sizes are large relative to the population, however, discrimination is possible and stable equilibria may not exist. With an optimal club size of two-thirds of the population, for example, only one such club is viable (Mueller 1989: 153–4). The important question for us is: what happens as the size (or complexity) of the society increases, perhaps as the result of the integration of previously separate societies? It can be shown that under plausible hypotheses the number of clubs tends to increase as well, since the greater diversity of needs and preferences makes it efficient to produce a broader range of club goods (see Chapter 5).

Think now of a society composed not of individuals, but of independent states. Associations of independent states (alliances, leagues, confederations) are typically voluntary, and their members are exclusively entitled to enjoy certain benefits produced by the association, so that the economic theory of clubs is directly applicable also to this context. In fact, since the property of excludability is more easily satisfied in this case, many goods that are purely public at the national level become club goods at the international level. The club goods in question could be collective security, policy coordination, common technical standards, or tax harmonization. In these and many other cases, countries that are not willing to share the costs are usually excluded from the benefits of interstate cooperation. Now, as an association of states expands, becoming more diverse in its preferences, the cost of uniformity in the provision of such goods can increase dramatically. Hence the theory predicts an increase in the number of voluntary associations, corresponding to the increased demand of club goods more precisely tailored to the different requirements of various subsets of states.

By giving quasi-constitutional status to the principle of enhanced co-operation, the Amsterdam and Nice Treaties acknowledged these implications of the enlargement of the Union, but their framers were even more concerned about the risk of fragmentation of the current EU model. The consequence was a set of conditions so strict as to practically rule out the possibility of establishing associations reflecting the different policy preferences of subsets of member states of the Union. The easing of these requirements by the new Constitutional Treaty, in particular the significant lowering of the threshold necessary to engage in enhanced cooperation, reveals a better understanding of the full implications of enlargement. After having claimed so often that widening and deepening could be pursued simultaneously, the member states now realize that a real dilemma exists, and have decided to resolve it by giving priority to widening, leaving aside concerns about the integrity of the standard model of European integration—a model that is at any rate rather incoherent, having been developed in bits and pieces over a period of several decades. There is a third, more realistic, position between the overly optimistic view of enhanced cooperation as a mechanism to 'further the objectives of the Union, protect its interests and reinforce its integration process' and the position of those who, like the European Commission, would completely exclude such voluntary arrangements from the integration process. As was stressed at the beginning of this chapter, European integration has always followed many different paths, and any attempt to force the process into a single institutional pattern has always ended up in failure. The alternative model—discussed in greater detail in Chapter 10—consists in preserving the integrity of the Single European Market, while allowing subgroups of member states to satisfy their preferences for a variety of club goods, as long as they do not create serious and unjustified obstacles to the smooth functioning of the common market. The model rests on two key ideas. First, economic integration is the basic public good produced by the Union, and the optimal club size for this good includes the entire membership of the Union. However, and this is the second point, the risks of market fragmentation are not as great as the defenders of orthodoxy pretend. Recent research has shown that market integration is possible with much less harmonization than was thought to be necessary in the early days of the Communities (see in particular Chapters 5 and 7). In fact, 'negative integration' (discussed in Chapter 7) may be sufficient to preserve the integrity of the Single European Market. Much harmonization effort of the past was motivated, not by objective functional needs of an integrated market, but by a more or less latent federalist bias. The same bias—the desire to steer the process of European integration in the direction of a unique, potentially federal structure—explains the incessant drive to expand the competences of the supranational institutions. As argued in Chapter 2, the continuous expansion of supranational competences is largely responsible for the widespread perception of a serious democratic deficit at the European level.

Integration and Democracy: the Big Trade-off

2.1   An Apparent Paradox

Membership in the EU is conditional on the acceptance by each member state of 'the principles of liberty, democracy, respect for human rights and fundamental freedoms, and the rule of law …' (Article 6(1) of the EC Treaty). According to Article 7(2) EC, serious and persistent breach of these principles may entail the suspension of 'certain rights deriving from the application of this Treaty to the Member State in question, including the voting rights of the representative of the government of that Member State in the Council'. These treaty articles give quasi-constitutional status to principles that have long been acknowledged by the EC/EU. Already in 1978, for example, the European Council held in Copenhagen declared emphatically that respect and preservation of representative democracy and human rights in every member state are essential conditions of membership in the EC.

Yet, neither the EC nor the EU fully satisfy the criteria of representative democracy they impose on their members. In fact, since the late 1980s the continuous growth of European competences, combined with the extension of majority voting in the Council, has given rise to increasingly vocal complaints of a serious 'democratic deficit' in the EU. According to some commentators this democratic deficit is paradoxical—if the EU were a state it could not be a member of the Union!—or at least an egregious example of double standards: for example, how can the Union impose on the countries of Eastern Europe conditions which itself is unable to satisfy?

This chapter argues that, contrary to widespread beliefs, this democratic *deficit*—not a total absence but an incomplete development, at the European level, of the practices and institutions of representative democracy—is not at all paradoxical. Rather, it is the necessary consequence of the preference of a large majority of European voters and, more fundamentally, of the nonexistence of a European demos, not to say, a European nation. Actually, to argue that the Union should be governed democratically because every member state is democratic is to commit the normative equivalent of the logical fallacy of composition: inferring the property of a whole from a property shared by its component elements (the pitfall consists in treating the EU and its member states as if they were members of the same class) (see Section 2.2). The democratic deficit is sometimes explained by the fact that the EU is not (yet?) a state, but also this argument is unconvincing without further elaboration. After all, many nonstate associations are, or are supposed to be, governed democratically by the members of the association: political parties, trade unions, churches; indeed, according to some advocates of participatory democracy, all associations should be democratic. But even the most ardent supporters of participatory democracy must realize that there are problems in extrapolating democratic principles from the individual to the corporate level—from the collective choices made by individuals as members of a given group to decisions taken by a community comprised not of individuals but of corporate members. It is well known, for example, that the basic democratic principle of 'one person, one vote', when applied to corporate bodies of unequal size, would enable 'a minority... to give law to the whole', as James Madison complained, in the course of the debate on the election of the Senate at the federal convention in Philadelphia (cited in Rakove 1997: 64).

2.2   Category Mistakes

From the perspective of both democratic theory and legal theory, individuals and corporate bodies belong to different categories; and as philosophers tell us, concepts or standards that may be legitimately applied to one category become meaningless, or seriously misleading, when applied to a different category. A category mistake, according to Ryle (1949), consists in discussing certain facts as if they belonged to one logical type or category, when they actually belong to another. Thus it is a category mistake to discuss an institution like a university, in the same terms in which one discusses its departments, professional schools, or administrative offices: the university is not identical with any one of these units; rather, it is the way the units are organized. The pitfall consists in thinking of the university as if it stood for an extra member of the class of which department, schools, and offices are members.

A similar category mistake consists in discussing the EU with the same concepts we use for its component units—as if the Union were a state rather than an organization of corporate bodies: the member states and the European institutions. The principle that Alexander Hamilton considered 'the great and radical vice' of the American Confederation—namely, 'the principle of *legislation for states or governments* in their *corporate* or *collective capacities*, and as contradistinguished from the *individuals* of which they consist' (cited in Rakove 1997: 191, emphasis in the original)—still prevails at the European level. Judicial doctrines of direct effect and supremacy, and the fact that European law can create rights and duties for citizens of the member states—rights that can be enforced only by national courts—do not change this basic fact, which the new Constitutional Treaty has again acknowledged. True, there is also a citizenship of the Union, but only for persons already holding the nationality of a member state: 'Citizenship of the Union shall complement and not replace national citizenship' (Article 17 EC). In other words, citizenship is not an autonomous concept of European law, but is defined exclusively by the legislation of the member states. Again, since 1979 we have a directly elected EP, consisting of 'representatives of the peoples of the States brought together in the Community' (Article 189 EC), but its competences do not include those essential powers of a truly legislative body: the power to tax and spend, to initiate legislation, and (in parliamentary systems) to form a government. Moreover, the EP is seriously deficient as a system of representation of individual interests. These interests are still largely rooted at the national level and hence find their natural expression in national parliaments and political parties. Above all, the EP cannot represent a (nonexistent) European people in the same sense in which national democratic institutions represent a historically defined demos (see also Chapter 9). James Madison, the father of American federalism, understood very well the category mistake discussed here. Unfortunately, the innovation that allowed him to overcome the difficulty is not available to the European leaders of today.

2.3 'We the People'

The preamble to the US Constitution of 1787 opens with the celebrated lines: 'We the People of the United States, in Order to form a more perfect Union . . . do ordain and establish this *Constitution* for the United States of America.' At that time, the vast majority of the inhabitants of the former

English colonies considered themselves, first and foremost, Virginians, Pennsylvanians, New Yorkers, or New Englanders. Madison's 'invention' of an American People, distinct from, and superior to, the peoples of the separate thirteen states, was a decisive conceptual innovation in the struggle to replace the Articles of Confederation by a strong federal constitution. The historical significance of this innovation, and the impossibility of replicating it in the present European context, provide the most intuitive demonstration, *a contrario*, of the practical consequences entailed by the absence of a European demos.

Even before the Philadelphia Convention met in the summer of 1787 some federalists had perceived the political and constitutional importance of founding the new constitution directly on the people rather than on the state governments. The direct appeal to the sovereign people was meant to discredit the states' pretensions of sovereignty. Under the Articles of Confederation, indirect administration was the necessary consequence of the reservation of sovereignty to the states. It followed that the necessary premise of direct administration by the federal government was national sovereignty, derived from the American People. Madison, in particular, saw clearly that the new federal government, if it were to be truly independent of the states, must obtain 'not merely the ratification of the Legislatures, but the ratification of the people themselves' (citation in Wood 1998: 532). The immediate problem was how to circumvent the Articles of Confederation whose amendment required the unanimous consent of the state legislatures. The solution consisted in appealing over the heads of the states directly to the constituent power—the American People. As Madison put it, 'the people were in fact, the fountain of all power, and by resorting to them, all difficulties were got over. They could alter constitutions as they pleased' (cited ibid.: 533).

Beyond ratification, the fundamental issue was how to correct the 'radical vices' of the Confederation. According to the Federalists, one reason for the Confederation's weakness was the central government's lack of adequate authority, especially in matters of finance, defense, and trade. They also realized that a formal reallocation of authority would not bring about a real centralization unless it also dealt with the inability of the Confederation to regulate directly the actions of individuals, in particular by taxing them. The new federal Constitution did expand the power of the federal government and made it directly applicable to individuals. However, the reallocation of authority set out in Article 1 could not accomplish its purpose of bringing about a shift of actual power unless that grant of authority was given a new and stronger basis of legitimacy (Beer 1993).

Madison's invention of popular sovereignty provided the requisite normative foundation. With his invention of the 'American People', distinct from the peoples of the thirteen states, Madison managed to avoid the kind of category mistake discussed above, since a federal government based on popular sovereignty would belong to the same political and constitutional category as the state governments. The implications of this novel notion of the sovereignty of the people of the United States as a whole did not escape the anti-Federalists, who, in the words of Patrick Henry, objected that the attribution of constituent sovereignty in the Preamble to the Constitution, should read 'We the States' rather than 'We the People'.

To many of Madison's contemporaries, but also to later political thinkers like John C. Calhoun (1782–1850), the idea of an American People to whom belonged the constituent power appeared a myth contrived for political purposes. At least, the myth had some plausibility: a common language; legal systems derived from, and still very much influenced by, English common law; similar political and administrative systems at state level; a fairly homogeneous population, largely of English, Scottish, or Irish stock; above all, a war fought together for eight years against the former colonial power. None of these conditions is even remotely approached in contemporary Europe, so that the Madisonian solution to the problem of legitimating a significant centralization of powers is simply unavailable to the political leaders of the Union. The very way in which the citizenship of the Union has been derived from the possession of nationality in one of the member states implicitly denies the existence of a 'European People'. Opinion surveys tell a similar story. Eurobarometer data reveal that there is no long-term increase in European identity among citizens of the EU (Duchesne and Forgnier 1995; Kelemen 2003). Whether we like it or not, the EU remains, to speak with Madison (*Federalist 20*), a 'government over governments, a legislation for communities'. In such a system, the notions of popular sovereignty and popular representation, and hence the idea of direct democratic legitimation, are highly problematic. In spite of the occasional references to a double source of legitimacy, that is, the governments *and* the peoples of the member states, the only concrete form of legitimacy available to the European institutions today is indirect—being derived from that of the national governments—and thus remains fragile and contestable. It follows that arguments about Europe's democratic deficit, to the extent that they are at all meaningful, must be about the assumed finality of the integration process, rather than about the present system. But ideas and aspirations about the final outcome of the process—and thus the standards by which the nature and extent of the 'democratic deficit' are assessed—differ widely.

2.4   A Question of Standards

To clarify such differences it may be useful to classify arguments about the democratic deficits into three main groups, according to the standards of legitimacy on which they rely (Majone 1998). Arguments in the first group, which may be called arguments by analogy, use *national* standards, that is, standards distilled from the theory and practice of parliamentary democracy. Hence, they tend to equate European institutions with national institutions—the category mistake discussed above—or at least to assume that the former will eventually converge towards the model of the latter. The analogy with national institutions leads to the claim that the EP should have an independent power of legislative initiative because national parliaments are so empowered. A stronger version of the same argument holds that the EP is the only (or at least the principal) repository of democratic legitimacy in the EU. Hence increased powers to this institution, directly elected by universal suffrage, would substantially reduce the democratic deficit and restore legitimacy to the Union. The EP was also the central institution for federalists like Altiero Spinelli and his followers. For them, the relevant model was the bicameral system of a federal polity such as Germany. This would require transforming the present EP into a first chamber representing, like the German *Bundestag*, the citizens of the federal union, and the Council into a second chamber (corresponding to the *Bundesrat*) representing territorial interests. For its part, the European Commission (which has no exact equivalent at national level) would lose its independence from the other European institutions and its monopoly of legislative initiative, both being crucial features of the Community method (discussed in Chapter 3). No one today advocates this model in its pure form, not even the EP; yet it remains very influential in more attenuated versions, for example in the neofederalist vision of the German Foreign Minister, Joschka Fischer (see Chapter 10).

Arguments in the second group rely on *derived* standards of legitimacy: the democratic legitimacy of the process of European integration, and of the institutions which drive the process forward, proceeds from the democratic character of the member states. From this perspective, the veto power of each member state is, in Weiler's words, 'the single most legitimating element' of European integration, since it excludes the possibility that the preferences expressed by a majority of voters in a member state may be overrun by decisions taken at European level. It follows that it is the shift to majority voting since the SEA, rather than the incomplete implementation of democratic principles, which is at the root of Europe's democratic deficit. Majority voting weakens national parliamentary control of the Council without increasing the power of the EP (Weiler 1999: 77–86). This argument may be strengthened by the observation that the usual criticism of the unanimity rule—namely that it allows a minority to impose their preference for the *status quo* on the majority of voters— presupposes that majority and minority belong to the same, preexisting, democratic polity. Only in such a case can it be reasonably argued that majority rule maximizes the number of persons who exercise self-determination in collective decisions (Dahl 1989). Such misconceptions about the implications of different voting rules (about which more will be said in Chapter 3) are another instance of the logical problems involved in transferring concepts from the national and individual levels to the transnational and corporate levels.

The third group of legitimacy arguments relies on *social* standards. While such arguments are ostensibly about the democratic deficit, they are in fact driven by a different agenda: dissatisfaction with the slow pace of political integration and/or concerns about the future of the national welfare state in an integrated European market and in a globalizing world economy (see Chapter 9). According to this school of thought, the EU lacks democratic legitimacy not only because it lacks a true legislative body, politically accountable executives, and a truly pluralistic system of interest representation but also, or even primarily, because of its failure to provide sufficient equality and social justice. By the social standards prevailing in the member states, the Union is a 'welfare laggard' and thus cannot count on the popular acceptance enjoyed by the national welfare states. What is more, European rules set increasingly strict constraints on the ability of the member states to provide the services their citizens demand—the 'diminished democracy' syndrome (see Chapter 9). To reduce this double democratic deficit, therefore, it is necessary for the Union to play a much stronger role in social policy than at present, even if this requires a substantial increase of the Union budget. This particular argument will be evaluated later on, but some critical comments may be usefully introduced at this point.

To begin with, it should be noted that the very modest role of social policy in the process of European integration is largely due to the reluctance of the member states, including the national parliaments, to surrender control of such a politically sensitive area of public policy, and to transfer the necessary powers and resources to the European level. This reluctance is clearly expressed by the Rome Treaty. The enumeration of matters relating to the social field in Article 118, and the limited role given to the European Commission in Title III of the treaty, indicate that the social policy domain, with a few exceptions such as the social security regime for migrant workers, was originally considered to be beyond the competence of Community institutions. None of the subsequent treaty revisions have provided true legislative powers in the area of social policy. On the contrary, harmonization of national laws and regulations is often explicitly excluded in this area. Again, integration of health and social security is opposed not only by national executives and parliaments but also by a majority of citizens in the member states who are net contributors to the Union budget. Popular opposition to a supranational policy regime in the social field is understandable. On the one hand, the welfare state represents the unique combination of national traditions and political compromises that formed the basis of the social democratic consensus in many West European countries after World War II. On the other hand, the delicate value judgments about the appropriate balance of efficiency and solidarity that social policy expresses can be made legitimately only within fairly homogeneous polities. Advocates of a 'social Europe' must face the fact that in several countries even *national* redistribution in favor of poorer regions is increasingly challenged in the name of fiscal federalism and regional autonomy. It is difficult to see how politically acceptable levels of income redistribution could be determined centrally in a polity like the EU, where economic, social, political, and legal conditions are still so different. We may conclude that the attempt to legitimate the Union by developing a 'European social model' is bound to fail because it goes against the clearly expressed preferences of the governments and the citizens of the member states. In fact, a large-scale development of welfare policies at European level would likely aggravate the legitimacy problem, reinforcing the popular image of a centralized and bureaucratized Union.

2.5   The Argument by Analogy

Of the three groups of arguments mentioned above, those appealing to standards derived from the theory and practice of democracy at the national level are by far the most popular. For this reason analogical arguments deserve to be examined more carefully. Although, as noted above, they are logically suspect and normatively misleading, they seem to appeal both to opponents and to advocates of political integration. Thus, professor Vaubel, a severe critic of Brussels' centralizing tendencies, finds that the democratic deficit of the EU is actually twofold. First, the executive (the Council of Ministers and the Commission) rather than parliament is primarily responsible for legislation; and, second, within the executive, the bureaucratic branch (the Commission) is unusually strong with respect to the political branch (the Council) whose members are at least subject to the control of national parliaments. Furthermore, because of the supremacy of European law over national law, the governments of the member states, meeting in the Council, can control their own parliaments rather than be controlled by them. To reduce the mismatch between European and national institutions it is proposed to deny the Commission any role in the legislative process, and to assign the right of legislative initiative to the EP or, at least, to the EP and to the Council (Vaubel 1995). Also, Juliet Lodge—no opponent of political integration—assesses Europe's democratic deficit by analogy with national standards. Policymaking processes at European level, she notes, are largely dominated by bureaucracies and governments that provide little scope for parliamentary institutions—whether national parliaments or the EP—to exercise roles traditionally believed to be the hallmarks of legislatures in liberal democratic polities (Lodge 1989). Even more explicitly, Williams (1991: 155) defines the democratic deficit 'as the gap between the powers transferred to the Community and the efficacy of European Parliamentary oversight and control'.

The obvious objection to the normative implications derived from the analogy with national institutions is that the peculiar architecture of the EU has been designed by treaties duly ratified by all national parliaments, and in some cases approved by national referenda. As will be seen in greater detail in Chapter 3, one of the striking features of this institutional architecture is the impossibility of mapping functions onto specific institutions. Thus the Community has no legislature but a legislative process in which different political institutions have different parts to play. Similarly, there is no identifiable executive, since executive powers are exercised for some purposes by the Council acting on a Commission proposal; for other purposes (e.g. competition matters) directly by the Commission; and overwhelmingly by the member states in implementing European policies on the ground (Dashwood 1996). Such institutional arrangements are certainly unusual by the standards of parliamentary democracy, or of the classical separation-of-powers doctrine, but they do serve important functions. Thus, the fact that the treaties make the policymaking powers of the Council and the EP dependent on the proposals of the Commission may be interpreted as a form of precommitment to the process of European integration (see Chapter 4). If the Council had a right of legislative initiative, it could undo previous prointegration legislation any time this appeared to be advantageous in terms of domestic politics. By the same logic, the right of legislative initiative is denied also to the popularly elected Parliament—one of several instances where the goal of integration trumps democratic values. The greatest threat to legitimacy, however, is not the peculiarity of the supranational institutions, but their unrelenting effort to expand their own competence, even at the risk of depleting their limited resources of legitimacy, and of a growing ineffectiveness of European policies (see Chapters 5 and 6). The Union's fragile and contestable normative basis cannot possibly support the expansion of European powers envisaged by some, for example in the area of social policy.

2.6   The Road not Taken

Of course, a system of limited powers and weak democratic legitimacy is not the only conceivable trajectory of the integration process. Instead of opting for such a system, Europeans could have decided to integrate politically, even before having achieved the full integration of their national economies. There is no doubt that in such a case the new European polity would have been organized along strictly democratic principles. In the early 1950s, with the shattering experience of World War II still fresh in people's minds, this possibility seemed concrete enough. The EDC Treaty, signed in Paris in 1952, committed its signatories to examine the nature of the political institutions needed to give direction and democratic legitimacy to the EDC—a truly supranational community with common institutions, an army, and independent taxing powers. The resulting de Gasperi Plan for a European Political Community (Paragraph 38 of the EDC Treaty) would have transformed the six member states of the ECSC into an effective federation, with a European executive accountable to an elected EP.

The plan designed a political community with considerable powers in the areas of defense, external relations, and economic and social integration. As mentioned in chapter 1, the institutions of this community were intended to form the nucleus of a federal union based on the model of parliamentary democracy and the principle of separation of powers: a bicameral Parliament, an Executive Council, a Council of national ministers, a Court of Justice, and an advisory Economic and Social Council. The parliament was meant to be the key institution of the Political Community. Unlike the present EP, this parliament was the legislative branch of a fully developed government, able to exercise effective democratic control over the executive. The Senate, whose members were to be elected by the national parliaments, could censure the Executive Council by electing a new Council president, while the directly elected house of representatives could pass a motion of censure by a majority of three-fifths of its members. The president of the Executive Council was to be appointed by the Senate. Once elected, he/she appointed the other members of the Council, and then the whole Council had to be approved by both houses of parliament. In this plan, the only anomaly with respect to the model of a federal parliamentary democracy was represented by the Council of national ministers—an ambiguous institution, borrowed from the experience of the ECSC, whose function was to coordinate the activity of the European Executive Council with the work of the national governments (Sidjanski 1992).

In the event, the EDC Treaty was rejected by the French National Assembly in August 1954, but its ratification had proved controversial in all the member states of the ECSC. After the Korean armistice and the death of Stalin, European governments were no longer prepared to surrender the political core of national sovereignty. The collapse of the EDC Treaty entailed the collapse of the plan for a political authority to oversee the military organization. A clear indication of the general lack of popularity of federalist solutions is that since the mid-1950s nothing like the Treaty on the European Political Community—not even the already mentioned draft TEU, inspired by the federalist Spinelli Plan and approved by the EP in February 1984—has ever been seriously considered by the national governments.

2.7   The Disjunction of Politics and Economics

After the collapse of the plans for a political union, only a functionalist approach to European integration seemed to offer a realistic hope for the future. Once the decision was taken to postpone political union until an indefinite future, the question was how to integrate the national economies of the member states while preserving national sovereignties essentially intact. In a world of sovereign states, however, international economic integration is feasible only if economics and politics are kept as separate as possible. As shown by the nineteenth century experience of free trade under the gold standard, only the disjunction of *imperium* and *dominium* permits to remove the greatest part of the economic conflicts to which the coexistence of sovereign states is liable to give rise. Hence, the old liberal principle of the separation of state and market, which seemed to have been repealed at the national level at least since the Great Depression of the 1930s, was rediscovered by the EC's founding fathers as a necessary condition for integrating the economies of independent states with different legal orders and systems of administration and citizenship. This liberal principle is firmly embedded in the founding Rome Treaty, although traces of the interventionist philosophy prevailing in the 1950s are also clearly visible. A consistent application of the ideas of economic liberalism could hardly have been expected in a text produced by statesmen raised in the tradition of *dirigisme*. At any rate, the major attempt to transfer to the European level the domestic interventionism of the member states resulted in what *The Economist* of September 29, 1990 called the 'single most idiotic system of economic mismanagement that the rich western countries have ever devised'. I am referring, of course, to the Common Agricultural Policy, to which I shall return in Chapter 6.

Despite the conceptual ambiguities and occasional lapses of the founding treaty, the rejection of any idea of a centralized political control of the nascent European economy turned out to be one of the most striking features of the system created by the 1957 Rome Treaty. In this respect, this treaty is significantly different from the 1951 treaty establishing the ECSC—the original inspiration for much early neofunctionalist theorizing. Although the main objective of the earlier treaty was the elimination of trade barriers and the encouragement of competition in the sectors of coal and steel, many specific provisions were highly interventionist. Thus the supranational executive of the ECSC, the High Authority, was given extensive powers, including the right to levy taxes, to influence investment decisions, and even in some cases to impose minimum prices and production quotas. The Rome Treaty had a much wider scope and greater ambitions than the ECSC Treaty, and for this reason its drafters could not avoid facing directly the issue of state–market relations.

The emphasis on the freedom of movement for persons, services, and capital, and more generally on rules of 'negative integration' (see Chapter 7); the provisions for a forceful European competition policy along the lines of US antitrust policy; the significant addition to the US model of rules on state aids to industry and on national procurement policies having the effect of distorting competition within the common market; the equally significant requirements for the removal of distortions of competition caused by state regulations or resulting from the existence of public-owned companies and companies granted special rights by the member states—all these treaty provisions point in the direction of a far-reaching separation of state power from market power. The desire to depoliticize European policymaking is also revealed by the very limited role given to the EP in areas with clear redistributive impacts such as the Common Agricultural Policy and the Common Fisheries Policy. This is a striking contrast to the way of democratic politics at the national level, where redistributive issues are the lifeblood of majoritarian politics, often determining the fate of governments. Under the treaty, the EP had at most a consultative role in politically sensitive areas, such as social security and the social protection of workers. Even today, agreements reached between management and labor can be transformed into European law without any discussion by the EP. It seems clear that the member states still believe that the integration process must be sheltered from the rough winds of democratic competition.

In spite of their democratic rhetoric, the EP and the Commission tend to agree with this assessment. In the hearings for the appointment of a new Commission, for instance, most committees of the EP appear to be more interested in the integrity, independence, and competence of the Commissioners-designate than in their political positions. In fact, many European parliamentarians see themselves as policy specialists rather than as partisan politicians, and continue to believe that the Commission should be a neutral institution, and that the members of the college should forget their party affiliations, if any (Magnette 2001). This belief was apparently shared by Commission President Romano Prodi when he presented his new team to the Parliament on July 21, 1999. On this occasion he said: 'This new college . . . provides a fair balance between the political complexion of the national governments and the European Parliament, and I welcome this. But let us be clear. The Commission does not function along party lines. This Commission is a college and Commissioners are no more extensions of political groups than they are representatives of national governments' (cited in Magnette 2001: 300). Although this statement is actually contradicted by the increasing politicization of the Commission, it does represent an orthodox interpretation of the original Community model.

In the formative decades of the Community, law and economics—the discourse of legal and economic integration—provided a sufficient buffer to achieve results that could not be directly obtained in the political realm. Not only were national governments required to abstain from measures that would create unjustified obstacles to free movement in the common market. According to the framers of the treaty, the European institutions themselves, in their efforts to bring about the economic integration of Europe rather than mimicking the interventionism of national policy-makers, were to rely primarily on measures of negative integration (see Chapter 7). Things have changed, of course. The idea of reducing the democratic deficit by assigning a larger role to the EP, and, in particular, by involving the Parliament in the appointment of the Commission, is an old one. It featured in the solemn declaration on the EU adopted in Stuttgart in 1983; it has always been high on the list of the EP's demands; and, as already mentioned, it figures prominently in the arguments of those who advocate the development of the Union in the direction of a full-fledged federation. The difficulties surrounding the appointment of the Santer Commission in 1995 showed that the EP intends to influence the distribution of portfolios among Commissioners, and the resignation of the Commission in March 1999 further strengthened these tendencies. Influential members of the EP started to talk of a 'Parliamentary Commission', the composition and programs of which would reflect the will of the parliamentary majority.

Now, an increasing level of politicization of EU policymaking becomes unavoidable as more and more tasks involving the use of political discretion are shifted to the European level. These developments, and the problems connected with the process of enlargement, not only increased the administrative tasks of the Commission but also emphasized the Commission's political responsibilities. In this context, the demand for a greater role of the EP becomes understandable. At the same time, we should not be blind to the risks that politicization entails for the process of European integration and even for the credibility of European policies (see Chapters 5 and 6). The crucial point is that the continuous expansion of the powers of the EP since the 1980s has not been sufficient to improve the legitimacy of an increasingly ambitious integration project. The alternative that suggests itself, therefore, is to reduce the overload of the European institutions to a level compatible with their narrow normative basis. Some suggestions along these lines will be advanced in later chapters.

2.8   Democratic Deficit and Nonmajoritarian Institutions

Before concluding our discussion of the tension between integration and democracy, it may be useful to call attention to a certain ambiguity in the use of the term 'democratic deficit'. Up to now the term was taken to mean an incomplete development of the institutions, policies, and political processes that we take for granted in a representative democracy. However, in the literature and in the discourse on European integration 'democratic deficit' is also used as a label to denote a set of problems that arise whenever important policymaking powers are delegated to politically independent bodies, such as independent central banks and regulatory authorities. These problems, far from being unique to the EU, are increasingly important at all levels of government as the shift from the interventionist to the regulatory state gains momentum throughout Europe (Majone 1996a). Democratic deficit, in this second sense, refers to the legitimacy problem of nonmajoritarian institutions—institutions that exercise important public functions but that, by design, are not directly accountable to the voters or to their elected representatives. For example, when public utilities are privatized, they are subject to rules developed and enforced by specialized agencies, normally established by statute as independent regulatory authorities combining expertise with a rulemaking and adjudicative function. They are independent in the sense that they are allowed to operate outside the line of hierarchical control by the departments of central government, and are granted considerable discretion in the use of the powers delegated to them. While the usefulness of independent regulatory agencies is today widely recognized, it is also felt that the agencies are constitutional anomalies that do not fit well into the traditional framework of democratic controls.

The growing importance of nonmajoritarian institutions in all democratic countries, in spite of persistent doubts about their constitutional status and democratic legitimacy, shows that for many purposes reliance upon qualities such as expertise, professional discretion, policy consistency, fairness, or independence of judgment is considered to be more important than reliance upon direct democratic accountability. But why is the legitimacy problem of nonmajoritarian institutions felt to be more serious at the EU than at the national levels? In addition to the general democratic deficit of the Union, which affects all its institutions, two more specific reasons seem important. First, the regulatory function is, in relative terms, much more important in the EU than in the member states (Majone 1996a). Of the three major functions of modern government in the socioeconomic area—redistribution, macroeconomic stabilization, and regulation—only the latter falls clearly within the scope of Community competence. Now, the major public actors in regulatory policymaking—regulatory authorities and courts—are nonmajoritarian institutions, hence the legitimacy problems of such institutions loom larger at European than at national level.

The second reason becomes clear if we compare the main European regulator, the Commission, with the European Central Bank (ECB). Also the ECB is a powerful nonmajoritarian institution. Its independence, being treaty-based, has a stronger legal foundation than the independence of national central banks, including the old Bundesbank, which usually has only a statutory basis. Actually, Article 88 of the German Basic Law had to be amended expressly to provide for the transfer of the powers of the Bundesbank to the ECB. In this sense, the independence of the ECB forms part of German constitutional law and any attempt to change the status of the ECB by amending the treaty would, in addition to having to be ratified by all the member states, require an amendment of the German constitution (Gormley and de Haan 1996). Not surprisingly, the 'democratic deficit' of the ECB is also becoming a topic of (mostly academic) discussion, but the legitimacy problems of the monetary authority seem to be circumscribed and manageable, more similar to those of the ECJ than to those of the Commission. It is instructive to see why this is so.

The legitimacy of a nonmajoritarian institution depends, in the final analysis, on its ability to generate and maintain the belief of being, of all feasible institutional arrangements, the most appropriate one for solving a certain range of problems. This concept of a *distinctive institutional competence* includes the idea of accountability by result, but goes beyond it to include a judgment of the quality of the institutional design, the general framework of accountability, and the relation of the institution to the other elements of the governance system. It is clear that the role of the ECJ could not be played as effectively by any other European institution. But also a body like the ECB can reasonably claim to enjoy a distinctive institutional competence to manage the common currency, at least under the prevailing conditions. The Bank's high level of independence is meant to compensate the weakness of macroeconomic governance at European level. At the same time, both economic theory and econometric evidence support the belief that an independent central bank is the best institutional arrangement to enhance the credibility of noninflationary policy. Moreover, because price stability is the single overriding objective of the ECB, the performance of the Bank can be measured unambiguously against the rod provided by the regular statistical assessments of inflation in the Eurozone. I should add that to acknowledge the ECB's distinctive institutional competence is not to overlook the risks entailed by the *political* decision to move to monetary union despite the fact that the EU is far from being an optimal currency area (see Chapter 6). Rather, it is to argue that given this political decision, something like the independent ECB was probably the best institutional arrangement that could be devised under the prevailing circumstances.

It is much more difficult to identify the distinctive institutional competence of the European Commission. As noted above, most EU policies are regulatory in nature, and in this respect the Commission may be considered a sort of superagency. However, it has been assigned a variety of other functions: executive, legislative, and quasi-judicial. This multiplicity of functions and objectives expands the scope of the Commission's discretionary choices, and at the same time greatly complicates the task of evaluating the overall quality of the institution's performance. As a result, both political accountability and accountability by results are reduced to vanishing point. In the legislative area, for example, 'success' is measured primarily by the number of Commission proposals accepted by the member states, rather than by the quality of the actual results. Under the Community method only the Commission is entitled to set the legislative and policy agenda, and this monopoly allows it to pursue objectives of political integration and self-aggrandizement while pretending to solve specific policy problems—integration by stealth. Hence the relative indifference to actual policy outcomes, and the importance attached to process *per se* (see Chapter 6).

Precisely because of the multiplicity of objectives the Commission is supposed to pursue, any claim to a distinctive institutional competence is rather implausible. In this respect, the difference with the ECB could not be greater, as shown by the way the leaders of the two institutions respond to their respective legitimacy problems. The executives of the central bank point out the unambiguous definition of the objective assigned to them, the possibility of measuring precisely their performance, and the importance of central bank independence as a guarantee of credible commitment to an anti-inflationary policy. In contrast, the Commission leaders attempt to strengthen the authority and legitimacy of their institution primarily by political means. They do not appeal to criteria relevant to a nonmajoritarian institution, but aspire to the legitimacy of a full-fledged government, even as they strive to maintain all their privileges under the Community method. At some point Commission President Romano Prodi even played with the idea of a popularly elected head of the European executive. By the summer of 2002, however, it was recognized that it would be impossible for a single candidate to fight a meaningful election across twenty-five or more member states. Under a later proposal, the new president would be nominated by the EP and by representatives of the national parliaments, and approved by EU leaders, thus attempting to tap all sources of democratic legitimacy in the EU. But precisely the need to appeal to the legitimacy of the national parliaments is the clearest admission of the continuing absence of a distinctive European political identity—and of the difficulty of legitimating an institution with such varied objectives and extensive political ambitions.

2.9   Reprise

We have seen that Europe's democratic deficit—in the literal meaning of an underdevelopment of democratic institutions and practices—is the unavoidable consequence of a process within which economic and political integration not only move at different speeds but also follow different principles, supranationalism in one case, intergovernmentalism (now changing to 'intensive transgovernmentalism'—see Chapter 8) in the other. The disjunction of politics and economics was a necessary condition of market integration, but it prevented the development of majoritarian politics at European level, hence the tradeoff between integration and democracy. The democratic deficit is the price we pay for pursuing regional economic integration while preserving the core of national sovereignty—in taxation, social security, foreign policy, defense—largely intact. This dual strategy is certainly problematic, but it seems to be supported by the great majority of European voters and by their political leaders. It follows that Europe's 'democratic deficit' is, paradoxically, democratically justified. Recent attempts to increase the legitimacy of the integration process by giving a larger role to the national parliaments—as suggested, for instance, by the new Constitutional Treaty— show that the national institutions remain, for their people, the principal focus of collective loyalty and the real arena of democratic politics. As long as this situation persists, the deficit of democracy will remain endemic at European level, and could only be reduced by reducing the volume of tasks delegated to the supranational institutions.

At the beginning of this chapter it was suggested that arguments about Europe's democratic deficit are really arguments about the finality of the Union. Those who assume that economic integration sooner or later must lead to full political integration tend to apply to the European institutions, seen as the kernel of a future federation, the same standards of legitimacy that prevail at the national level. Full-fledged federalism, however, is an improbable trajectory of the integration process: it never enjoyed popular support, and even elite support seems to be eroding at present. In fact, after the Constitutional Treaty, which maintains the national veto on all matters close to the core of national sovereignty, and after the decision to proceed with a significant enlargement of the Union, the federalist vision seems to recede into an evermore distant and indistinct future. Even assuming a growing demand for greater political union as a result of deepening economic and monetary integration, or of external threats and challenges, there is no reason to think that the political and constitutional arrangements of the future will ever mirror the institutional setup of a federal nation-state. A more likely development is a move toward confederal arrangements of broader scope than at present, as discussed in Chapter 10. A confederation is a union of sovereign states, which together pool certain powers for mutual advantage. It is a contractual arrangement among otherwise independent partners—a 'club' in the language of Chapter 1—not an expression of popular sovereignty. Hence, the standards of democratic legitimacy that apply to the national level would be inappropriate also in the case of a full-fledged European confederation.

The Community Method

3.1 The Dilemma of Supranationalism

'Federalism' and 'functionalism' are recurrent terms in all early accounts of the ECs—the first as the political ideology, the second as the strategy driving the process of European integration. In the late 1950s Ernest Haas (1958) attempted a synthesis of federalism and functionalism with his neofunctionalist theory. This theory provided, *inter alia*, an influential social scientific account of the approach followed by Jean Monnet at the time. Neofunctionalism's central prediction was that economic integration would be self-sustaining and would eventually lead to a unique, potentially federal, political structure in Europe. The theoretical basis of this prediction is the concept of 'spillover', whereby initial steps toward integration trigger endogenous economic and political dynamics leading to further integration. Neofunctionalists identify two kinds of spillovers: functional and political. Functional spillover occurs when incomplete integration undermines the effectiveness of existing policies, thereby creating pressures for new European policies. It is the process of political spillover, however, that is most closely associated with the neofunctionalist approach to the study of European integration. This second type of spillover occurs when the existence of supranational organizations sets in motion a self-reinforcing process of institution-building. Supranational institutions inevitably gain a certain measure of autonomous initiative. Neofunctionalists stressed, in particular, the role of the Commission as a political and policy entrepreneur.

Actually, the original inspiration of the early neofunctionalists was not the Commission of the EEC, but the High Authority of the ECSC (see Chapter 1). Because the High Authority was empowered to take decisions binding on the member states, as well as on coal and steel companies, this new form of cooperation among sovereign states was referred to as 'supranational'. The need to introduce a new term to characterize the ECSC was an indication that the existing terminology was felt to be inadequate to characterize a system which appeared to be closer to a federal or prefederal arrangement, however limited its scope, than to a traditional international organization. Institutions are said to be 'supranational' when they satisfy certain criteria: they enjoy a certain independence from the states that created them; their rules and decisions are directly binding on the member states, and on natural and legal persons; their measures take effective precedence over national ones; and the scope of their powers is such as to result in a qualitative difference from other organizations operating at the international level. In the case of an 'intergovernmental' institution like the Council of Ministers of the EC/EU, which represents the interests of the member states, supranationalism refers to the procedures of decision-making, as when the Council votes by (qualified) majority rather than by unanimity. In such a case, the member states choose, on an ad hoc basis, to forego decision-making under the unanimity rule in favor of a common agreement to pool sovereignty (Moravcsik 1993).

The framers of the Paris (ECSC) and Rome Treaties shared the view that the integration of previously separate national markets was only possible with the help of supranational institutions. This at any rate seemed to be the lesson taught by the history of the American Confederation of 1781, of the Confederate States of America at the time of the Civil War, of the Swiss Confederation and the German *Bund* in nineteenth-century Europe, to mention only some of the best-known cases of failure to achieve market integration for lack of adequate institutions. Hence the conclusion that confederation was no longer a viable form of government, and that strong centralized institutions were needed (see Chapter 10). Such institutions appeared to be especially necessary where the aim was to integrate the markets of West European welfare states accustomed to massive state interventions in the national economies through public ownership of key industries, national planning, aggregate-demand management, and large-scale income redistribution. The delegation of significant regulatory powers to supranational institutions was seen as the means of achieving the separation of politics and economics discussed in Chapter 2. However, such delegation raises a fundamental dilemma: supranational institutions strong enough to liberalize and integrate national markets are also strong enough to overregulate the Single European Market, and, more generally, to abuse their powers. It is interesting to note that neofunctionalists, far from being concerned about this dilemma, actually thought that the very tendency of institutions to expand their powers is an important element of the process by which economic integration leads to political integration. Only by continuously enlarging their competence can supranational institutions play their role as 'agents of integration' (Haas 1958). Different ways of resolving the dilemma of supranationalism will be discussed in the other parts of this book. The aim of this chapter is to understand the method that has allowed the European institutions to play the ambitious role which neofunctionalists assigned to them, and the reasons of its eventual decline.

3.2 The Classical Community Method

As codified by the Commission in its White Paper on *European Governance* (Commission 2001: 12), the Community method, which defines the role of the various European institutions and the modes of their interactions, rests on three principles:

1. The Commission is independent of the other European institutions; it *alone* makes legislative and policy proposals. Its independence is meant to strengthen the ability to execute policy, act as the guardian of the Treaty, and represent the Community in international negotiations.
2. Legislative and budgetary acts are adopted by the Council of Ministers and the EP, always on a proposal made by the Commission.
3. The ECJ guarantees the maintenance of the balance among European institutions, and respect for the rule of law.

Several distinctive features of this scheme should be noted. First, the Commission and the ECJ are major players in areas where the Community method applies—essentially, those connected with the functioning of the Single European Market. Their importance is enhanced by the fact that most European policies are regulatory, as noted in Chapter 2. Second, these major players are nonelected, politically independent bodies—nonmajoritarian institutions—operating within poorly specified accountability structures. For instance, even though the Commission may be submitted to parliamentary censure, in practice censure is often a strategic instrument in the struggle between the EP and the Council, rather than an instrument of control of the Commission by the directly elected institution. The most striking feature of the Community method, however, is its rejection both of the model of parliamentary democracy and of the principle of separation of powers. The Commission's monopoly of legislative and policy initiative—its agenda-setting power—has no analog either in parliamentary or in presidential democracies. In parliamentary systems, legislators introduce relatively few bills; most legislative proposals are instead presented by bureaucrats to the cabinet, which then introduces them as draft legislation to the parliament. Once legislators receive such proposals, however, they are free to change or reject them. This is not the case under the Community method, where as a rule the Council may modify Commission proposals only under the stringent requirement of unanimity. In parliamentary systems, moreover, neither civil servants nor their political masters can preempt the right of initiative of parliamentary parties and individual members of the legislature. Besides, national executives are the expression of the party or coalition that won the elections, and this is certainly not the case of the Commission. In the separation-of-powers system of the United States, not only do legislators have the final word over the form and content of bills but, further, only legislators can introduce bills. In the course of a typical congressional term, members of Congress will introduce several hundred bills on behalf of the president or of executive-branch agencies. During the same period, members of Congress will introduce on their own behalf as many as 15,000 or 20,000 bills (McCubbins and Noble 1995).

It is important to understand clearly what is implied by the Commission's monopoly of agenda-setting. First, other European institutions cannot legislate in the absence of a prior proposal from the Commission. It is up to this institution to decide whether the Community should act and, if so, in what legal form, and what content and implementing procedures should be followed. Second, the Commission can amend its proposal at any time while it is under discussion in the Committee of Permanent Representatives of the member states, or in the Council of Ministers, while, as just mentioned, the Council can amend the proposal only by unanimity. If the Council unanimously wishes to adopt a measure that differs from the Commission's proposal, the latter can deprive the main Community legislator of its power of decision by withdrawing its own proposal. Finally, neither the Council nor the EP or a member state can compel the Commission to submit a proposal, except in those few cases where the Treaty imposes an obligation to legislate. In addition to its monopoly of legislative initiative, the Commission, as guardian of European law, can take autonomous decisions in order to determine whether member states have complied with their treaty obligations, or to permit them in appropriate cases to deviate from their obligations. In some cases the Commission can also take general measures (directives) without Council approval, for example to ensure that state-owned, as well as

private, firms satisfy European rules on competition (Article 86 of the EC
Treaty). The member states have repeatedly, but always unsuccessfully,
challenged the powers of the Commission under this article.

3.3   The Community Method and Mixed Government

As argued in Chapter 4, these peculiar institutional arrangements were
appropriate to the early stages of integration, when the member states had
to find ways of credibly committing themselves to the common aim of
market integration. Here I wish to go beyond mere functional justifications, to probe more deeply into the institutional and political logic of the
method created by the Rome Treaty. Such probing has been impeded by
the oft-repeated assertion that the Community is *sui generis*. It is true that
the principles of the Community method diverge significantly from those
of contemporary democratic states, whether of the parliamentary or the
presidential type. But recall from the preface Tocqueville's remark to the
effect that the gallery of human institutions contains mostly copies. It is
therefore likely that if no relevant contemporary models can be found,
precedents may be discovered in our constitutional past. In fact, the
institutional architecture designed by the Treaty reveals striking similarities to a much older model of governance known as 'mixed government'—a system characterized by the presence in the legislature of the
territorial rulers and of the 'estates' representing the main social and
political interests in the polity. The mixed constitution—already discussed
by ancient political philosophers such as Aristotle and Polybius—was
prevalent in medieval and preabsolutist Europe. According to this philosophy of government, the polity is composed, not of individual citizens
but of corporate bodies balanced against each other and governed by
mutual agreement rather than by a political sovereign.

In practice, these corporate bodies constituting the mixed polity were
interested less in policymaking than in questions of privileges and rights:
rights of the territorial rulers as against the estates, and vice-versa, or the
respective rights of each estate vis-à-vis the others. Hence, the prime
theme of the internal political process was the tug-of-war among autonomous power centers over the extent and security of their respective jurisdictional prerogatives and immunities—the maintenance of 'institutional
balance'. However, the contest was tempered by a high degree of institutionalization. In principle, in the mixed polity law could not be modified
at the will of any one party, since it was not seen as the product of

unilateral will in the first place (Poggi 1978). Although by the nineteenth century the theory of mixed government seemed to have lost its relevance for increasingly complex western societies, in the previous century the theory—through its expression in the English constitution—attained a vitality and prominence that it had not had since antiquity. The result of the Glorious Revolution of 1688–9 was the firm establishment of Crown, Lords, Commons, and Courts of Common Law, each institution possessing rights of its own but dependent upon the others in certain respects, each with a part to play in the government of the realm. Such was the prestige of the English mixed constitution that most Americans set about the building of their new states in 1776 within the confines of such a constitutional model (Wood 1998).

It seems unlikely that the framers of the Rome Treaty were directly inspired by medieval theories of government or by the constitutional discourse of seventeenth-century England and eighteenth-century America. They did, however, make a conscious choice between two distinct constitutional alternatives: either separating the functional branches of government or mixing the 'estates' (or main interests) of the polity in the legislature—where the three political estates are not, of course, the Crown, Lords, and Commons, but the national governments represented in the Council, the supranational institutions—Commission and European Court of Justice, and the 'peoples of the States brought together in the Community' (Article 137 of the Rome Treaty), represented, at least in theory, by the EP.

Jean Paul Jacqué comes close to recognizing the similarity with the model of mixed government when he argues that the organizing principle of the Community is not the separation of powers but the representation of (national and supranational) interests. Each Community institution is the bearer of a particular interest that it strives to protect and promote, and the nature of the prevailing interest determines the structure of decision-making. Thus, where the framers of the Treaty deemed that national interests should have precedence in an area of particular relevance to national sovereignty, such as fiscal harmonization, they required a unanimous vote in the Council. On the other hand, where it appeared that national interests had to be reconciled with the supranational or 'common' interest, it was decided that the Council should legislate by qualified majority, thus enhancing the significance of the Commission's proposals. Again, where it was thought that the common interest should prevail, the Commission was given an autonomous power of decision. In short, under the Treaty each subject matter has its own decision-making procedure according to the nature of the interest receiving special protection (Jacqué 1991).

In the Community, as in all mixed polities, the balance between interests, and between the institutions that represent those interests, has constitutional significance. The principle of institutional balance does not of course imply an equal allocation of power among the various interests represented in the polity. In fact, the dualism between the territorial rulers and the other estates was a structural principle of the preabsolutist system of governance—as is the dualism between the member states represented in the Council and the other European institutions. This notion of dualism, first introduced in the nineteenth century by the great German jurist, Otto von Gierke, suggests that territorial rulers and estates make up the polity jointly, but as separate (and unequal) political centers. They must cooperate while remaining distinct, each exercising powers of its own, and differing in this from the 'organs' of the modern state (Poggi 1978). Thus, the principle of institutional balance refers to the preservation of the relative position of each interest in the relevant domain. In the Community context it is the task of the Court of Justice to ensure the respect of a balance of powers which reflects the basic agreements reached at the 'constitutional' level.

The institutional rigidity, induced by the requirement that the various interests should be balanced, is a key issue discussed at some length later on (see in particular Chapter 5). As argued there, the centrality of the norm of institutional balance has become a serious obstacle to far-reaching reforms in the EU. The rule that 'each institution shall act within the limits of the powers conferred upon it by this Treaty' (Article 4(1) of the Rome Treaty, now Article 7(1) EC), when read in the light of this norm, means that each institution (1) has the necessary independence in exercising its powers; (2) must respect the powers of the other institutions; and (3) may not unconditionally assign its powers to other institutions or bodies. Thus, the principle has been used to exclude the possibility that rulemaking powers may be delegated to independent European agencies, regardless of the advantages of such delegation in terms of policy effectiveness and better accountability. This rigidity is one reason why institutional innovations and new policy developments are taking place outside the Community framework. Being difficult to reform and impossible, at least for the time being, to abandon completely, the Community method is increasingly circumvented.

Several other features of the Community system reveal its deep affinity to the model of mixed government. Thus, the modern notion of indivisible sovereignty is incompatible with the spirit of both the Community method and traditional mixed government. In both systems of governance, sovereignty is shared among the constituents of the polity. For the English of the seventeenth century, for example, sovereignty could reside only in Parliament where the three estates of the realm were 'wonderfully combined'. In analogous fashion, the bits of national sovereignty that the member states decided to transfer to the European level are exercised in common by the Community institutions. Also the limited role assigned to democratic principles and practices in the life of the EC/EU becomes understandable in light of the model of mixed government. In crucial respects this model—grounded in Aristotle, the most notable critic of Greek democracy—is not a variant of, but an alternative to, majoritarian democracy (Dahl 1989). Again, the model of the mixed polity, as reformulated and reinterpreted in seventeenth-century England, was meant to depoliticize governance by curbing factions and political conflicts. After the Civil War, English society was pacified, not by the mechanisms of electoral politics but by the common law. The mixed constitution was the pillar on which the pacified polity rested. Similarly, 'integration through law' served to pacify Western Europe after World War II. After the collapse of the plans for a European Political Community (see Chapter 2), it was realized that economic integration is most likely to occur within a domain shielded from the clash of political interests. This nonmajoritarian stance was inspired by a realistic appreciation of the fact that in the early stages of integration, political conflicts tend to center on divergent national interests rather than on the ideological or party-political issues with which we are familiar at national level. Hence, for several decades, law and economics—the discourse of legal and market integration— provided a sufficient buffer to achieve results at the European level that could not be directly obtained in the political realm.

In modern democracies the main aims of the political struggle are the control of political power and the formulation and implementation of public policy. In contrast, the main theme of political conflict in the mixed polities was the conflict that opposed one estate to another in defense of their respective prerogatives and immunities. Also in this the Community is closer to the premodern systems than to contemporary democracies. On the one hand, in the Community there is no central power to conquer in a competition among political parties; on the other hand, Community policies are not decided upon by a majority government but by a political exchange among the three law-making institutions. Thus, it is not surprising that in the majority of votes the EP does not divide along party lines, but presents a united front against the other institutions—sometimes against the Commission but more often against the Council (Hix 1999). A striking example of the interinstitutional tug of war is the conflict that recently opposed the Council of Economic and Financial Affairs (Ecofin) to the Commission over the interpretation and implementation of the Stability and Growth Pact (see Chapter 8). In sum, political conflict under the Community method consists to a large extent in contrasts about the prerogatives of Council, EP, and Commission, and in questions of institutional balance. The language of majoritarian politics—government and opposition, party competition, left and right—has very limited currency in this context precisely because the prime theme of the internal political process is the contest among autonomous institutions over the extent and security of their respective jurisdictional prerogatives. As shown in Chapter 6, policy emerges as an epiphenomenon from this contest, rather than from opposing ideological positions.

Another characteristic of mixed government was the absence of centralized administration. Since each estate was supposed to take care of its own members, there was no direct link between the general government and the individual members of the estates. Historians of administrative law refer to such a system as 'self-administration of the corporate society' (Mannori and Sordi 2001). In this respect too, the similarity with the Community system is striking. The Community does not have a true bureaucracy, since EC policies are generally implemented by national administrations, while social policy, education, and other welfare-state policies remain in the competence of the member states. It is sometimes argued that even a country like Germany, under what has been called 'cooperative federalism', has only a small central bureaucracy since most of the programs of the federal government are implemented by state or local governments. If these authorities fail to act, however, the federal government has the means for intervening and directly executing its laws, which apply directly to individuals. The situation is quite different in the Union, where the means to enforce compliance by the national governments are very weak. Article 226 EC vests in the Commission the right to invoke an infringement procedure before the ECJ, while Article 227 affords a similar opportunity to the member states. However, the political and administrative costs of attempting to enforce compliance by judicial means are so high that these powers are almost never used by the member states, and relatively infrequently also by the Commission. Recent experience shows that even fines—a possibility introduced by the Maastricht Treaty—may prove illusory. It is the stage of actual implementation, as

distinct from transposition of European law into the national legal systems, that is most problematic for the Commission, which has at its
disposal neither recourse to national courts, nor a general inspectorial
function (Harlow 2002).

A general objection might be raised against the model of the Community as a mixed polity. As already mentioned, by the nineteenth century
the theory of mixed government had lost its relevance for Western political thought because the state and government had become detached from
what was seen as an increasingly complex social structure (Wood 1998). It
could be argued, therefore, that this theory cannot possibly be relevant to
contemporary Europe. Note, however, that European society—as distinct
from the separate national societies of the members of the Union—is still
at a rather primitive stage. The absence of European media, of effective
European political parties, of a genuinely European process of public-
opinion formation, are only some indications of this situation. The archa-
ism of the mixed-polity model reflects the underdevelopment of European
society.

3.4   The Erosion of the Community Method

With its firm commitment to the completion of the internal market,
substantial increase of Community competences, extension of majority
voting, and the first significant enhancement of the powers of the EP, the
SEA represents the zenith of the Community method. After this high
point, decline sets in: most important policy and institutional developments—monetary union and the ECB; the common foreign and security
policy and the office of the High Representative; cooperation in justice
and home affairs and the new agencies Europol and Eurojust—take place,
in whole or in part, outside the rigid framework of the classic Community
method.

September 1991 is a convenient point in time from which to observe the
progressive erosion of the method. This is the date when the Netherlands
Presidency proposed that both the CFSP and JHA were to be brought
within the sphere of competence of the Community. As so often in the
history of the EC/EU, this abortive attempt to establish an explicit commitment to a federal Europe produced a backlash and sharpened conflicts
among the then twelve member states. The proposal of the Dutch
Presidency was supported by the supranational institutions—Commission
and the EP—as one would expect, but was rejected by all the other

countries, except Belgium. As a result, the negotiations leading to the TEU or Maastricht Treaty were pursued on the basis of the Luxembourg scheme of an EU founded on three separate pillars. As already mentioned, in the institutional architecture designed by the TEU the Community method is largely confined to the first pillar. The other two pillars (CFSP and JHA) are smaller, more specific in scope, and are only partly adjusted to the Community method. Here the European Council—the only distinct organ of the EU as a whole—can act without a prior proposal from the Commission, and is not subject to any control by the EP, or to the scrutiny of the ECJ, except indirectly. The Commission is supposed to be 'fully associated' with the tasks in CFSP and JHA, but its power to monitor the fulfillment of treaty obligations by the member states has been explicitly omitted and its power of agenda-setting, severely restricted. The EP is simply informed about decisions taken in CFSP and JHA, and may express its opinion, while the general jurisdiction of the ECJ is explicitly excluded in these areas. Article 34 TEU stipulates that the legislative decisions that may be adopted in the area of police and judicial cooperation in criminal matters shall not entail direct effect—they do not confer rights on individuals that they may enforce before national courts.

Even in the first pillar, the Maastricht Treaty introduced new competences in a way that limits the exercise of Community powers, by explicitly ruling out the harmonization of national laws and regulations (see Chapter 4). Harmonization is one of the most powerful legal instruments available to the Commission. The limits imposed on the use of this instrument are thus a clear indication of the progressive loss of confidence by the member states in the classic Community method, with its tendency to produce binding legislation imposing more or less uniform rules throughout the Community. It should also be noted that the grant of codecision powers to the EP by the TEU, and the extension of those powers by the Amsterdam and Nice Treaties, entailed a nonnegligible cost to the Commission. Under the procedure of Article 251 EC, if the Council accepts all the amendments contained in the EP's opinion, it may adopt the proposed act, as amended, by a qualified majority. This means that the Commission cannot oppose an act on which the Council and EP are in agreement, whereas, in general, the Council can modify a Commission's proposal only by a unanimous vote.

Other signs of erosion of the Commission's monopoly of policy initiation are visible elsewhere also. For instance, the system of social dialogue established by the Maastricht Treaty allows officially recognized representatives of employers and workers to enter into voluntary agreements that are subsequently enacted as directives by the Council. The social dialogue, when successful, conforms with the Community method on the output side, since it leads to a legally binding Council directive, but not on the input side, since the initiative for proposing legislation rests with the social partners, not with the Commission (Scott and Trubek 2002). Arguably the most ominous challenge to the Commission's exclusive power of agenda-setting comes from the growing tendency of the European Council to deliberate on specific policy issues at thematic summits, such as the Lisbon Summit on economic and social policy, the Luxembourg Summit on employment, or the Tampere Summit of October 1999, a true landmark for policy and institutional developments in the area of JHA.

One of the key functions of the European Council is, of course, to define the general policy guidelines of the Union. As mentioned in Chapter 1, however, the Council can deal with whatever problems it wants to deal with, in the manner it judges most appropriate. Not being a European institution (until the new Constitutional Treaty becomes effective) the powers and decision-making procedures of the Council are not determined by the Treaty. This means, in particular, that it is not legally bound to follow the Community method or to respect the treaty-based rights and privileges of the Commission. At the June 2002 Summit in Seville, for instance, the heads of state or government, in order to improve decision-making in Brussels, agreed to extend the time frame in which their key decisions are taken by drawing up annual and three-year programs. According to press reports, the Commission's president was seriously concerned that if the Council decided on such strict planning without previous agreement with the Commission, there would inevitably be practical consequences for his institution's monopoly of legislative initiative.

3.5   A Renewed Community Method?

The introduction to the White Paper on *European Governance* makes clear that the document was produced as the Commission's response to the growing signs of decline of the Community method, as well as to the feeling of alienation of many Europeans from the Union's work. The Community method, according to this document, has served the Union well for almost half a century, and it can continue to do so in the future provided it is brought up to date. The proposed *aggiornamento* would basically consist in drawing a clear separation of powers and functions between the legislature (Council of Ministers and EP) and the executive (Commission), by analogy with the constitutional model prevailing in the member states. The introduction of the principle of separation of powers at the European level would have two important consequences. First, in the growing number of areas where decisions are taken jointly by the Council and the EP, under the codecision procedure, these two institutions should enjoy equal roles, whereas at present the Council is the main legislator. Second, 'this clarification of roles must allow the Commission to assume full executive responsibility' (Commission 2001: 64). In other words, instead of the present system where the executive function is divided between the Council and the Commission—with the national administrations implementing European policies on the ground—we would have a separation-of-powers system with the Commission as the sole European executive.

The problem with this proposal is that the Community system is not based on separation of powers, but on the very different principle of representation of interests. Rather than leading to a 'reinvigorated Community method', therefore, the adoption of the principle of separation of powers would actually amount to its rejection. The explanation of this apparent paradox can only be political. The Commission would like to become the sole executive while at the same time keeping its monopoly of legislative and policy initiation. This accumulation of powers would undoubtedly strengthen the position of the Commission, and in this sense—but only in this sense—it would also 'reinvigorate' the Community method. Unfortunately, the two roles are incompatible: in a system where the legislative and executive powers are separate, the executive cannot have a monopoly, as distinct from a simple right, of legislative initiative. In making their proposal, the authors of the White Paper seem to have overlooked this glaring contradiction. There is reason to believe, however, that if the Commission were forced to make a choice, it would opt for keeping the important power of agenda-setting given by the monopoly of legislative initiative, rather than attempting to mimic the constitutional architecture of the member states.

Another proposed cure to rejuvenate the Community method would consist in generalizing qualified majority voting (QMV) in the Council. In the debate on the draft Constitutional Treaty, the Commission, as well as many independent commentators, have argued that in a Union of twenty-five or more member states, governance will be impossible without extending majority voting to all areas of policymaking, including foreign affairs and security. The rule of unanimity, it is said, is both inefficient and unjust since it gives the possibility to any country, even a very small one, of imposing the status quo on the other members of the Union. Hence, the generalization of QMV is a necessary condition for further advances in the integration process. The link between a generalized QMV and a reinvigorated Community method is explicitly established by the Commission in its unofficial *Penelope* document of December 2002. In order to assess the validity of these claims it is convenient to go back to first principles. As was pointed out in the preceding pages, in the Community system of governance the nature of the prevailing interest determines the structure of decision-making. This means that each subject matter has its own decision-making procedure according to the nature of the interest receiving special protection under the treaties—a unanimous vote in the Council in policy areas of particular relevance to national sovereignty; QMV in matters where national interests have to be reconciled with the common interest; autonomous powers of decision to the Commission when supranational interests should prevail.

That decision rules should be tailored to the nature of different interests deserving protection is also one of the main results of the modern theory of collective choice as developed by James Buchanan and Gordon Tullock. According to this theory, collective activity should *not* be organized through the operation of the same decision rule for all subject matters. At the constitutional stage the individual members of a would-be polity can foresee that collective decisions in such areas as human or property rights may impose quite severe costs on them. For this reason, they may insist that collective decisions in the area of fundamental rights be taken by unanimity or near unanimity. It follows that whether or not a rational individual will support the shift of an activity from the private to the public sector (in the case of a member state of the EU, a shift from the national to the European level) will depend on the decision rule that is to prevail in collective choices concerning that activity. The individual will choose to shift more activities to the public sector the greater the number of individuals whose agreement is required for collective action, with unanimity as the limiting case (Buchanan and Tullock 1962: 63–91).

This analysis shows that the rational choice of rules for collective decision-making depends not only on the time and resources needed to reach a collective decision—the direct costs of decision-making—but also on the costs that the decision may impose on the individual members of the polity. Buchanan and Tullock refer to the latter costs as the 'external costs' of a collective decision. Under the unanimity rule these costs are zero, but the costs of decision-making may be quite high. Hence, there is a trade-off between the external costs caused by a measure to which an individual (or a member state) is opposed and the direct costs of decision-making. Under unanimity any member of the polity can block an agreement until a collective decision emerges, which he or she feels is the best one that can be obtained, or at least one that does not pose an unacceptable threat to his or her basic rights and interests. At the other extreme, any member could decide alone the issue for the entire community. Here decision-making costs will be close to zero but the expected external costs for all other individuals are potentially quite high. The various possibilities can be represented by means of two curves. One curve, call it C, is the *external-cost function* representing the expected loss of utility from the victory of a collective decision to which an individual is opposed. The other curve, D, the *decision-making-cost function*, represents the decision-time costs of reaching agreement, as a function of the size of the required majority: 100 percent in case of unanimity, 85 or 80 percent in case of a supermajority, 50 percent + 1 in case of a simple majority, and so on. The total cost of collective decision-making is C + D, and the optimal decision rule is given by the size of the required majority at which the *sum* of external and decision-making costs is minimized: the reason why one decision rule cannot be optimal for all issues is that the two types of cost represented by the curves C and D vary considerably from issue to issue. When issues of basic human rights (or of national sovereignty in case of the EU) are under discussion, decision-making costs pale in comparison with the external costs that a collective decision can impose on an individual or corporate member of the polity. In such cases, something close to unanimity is the optimal rule. Again, if minorities feel more strongly on particular issues than majorities, then any decision rule short of (near-) unanimity may lead to policies that will produce a net loss of aggregate welfare for the group. Constitutional protection of basic rights against majoritarian decisions embodies this logic of collective decision-making.

3.6   The Practical Case for Unanimity

We can see now that the logical mistake of the advocates of generalized majority voting consists in taking into consideration only one type of cost—the cost in time and other resources required to reach a collective decision—while overlooking the cost imposed on individual members of the Union by a collective decision of which they disapprove. It should also be kept in mind that the achievement of unanimity with respect to a given measure can be greatly facilitated if the winners can compensate the losers. This is the well-known compensation principle (or Kaldor–Hicks criterion) of welfare economics. According to this principle, if a change in policy would result in some persons being better off and some worse off, and if the gainers could compensate the losers in such a way that on balance everybody were better off, then welfare would be increased by implementing that change. Something like this compensation principle has been applied throughout the history of the EC/EU. All major policies requiring the unanimous approval of the member states, from the initial creation of the customs union to the single market to economic and monetary union, have been accompanied by compensatory measures in favor of the poorer member states: the Social Fund, the European Investment Bank, the European Regional Development Fund, the Structural Funds, down to the Cohesion Fund, which the Maastricht Treaty explicitly tied to the adjustments made necessary by monetary union.

Achievement of unanimity in the EU Council of Ministers is also facilitated by Article 205(3) EC, according to which: 'Abstentions ... shall not prevent the adoption by the Council of acts which require unanimity.' Thus, under unanimity an abstention is equivalent to support for a proposal, while under QMV an abstention is equivalent to voting against a proposal, since (under current rules) sixty-two votes are still required to adopt the measure. This way of counting abstentions, an official publication of the Council points out, 'sometimes results in the paradoxical situation where a decision for which a qualified majority cannot be reached ... is taken more easily unanimously as a result of abstention by certain members of the Council who do not wish to vote in favour but who do not want to prevent the Act concerned from going through' (cited in Hix 1999: 69). Additional light on the issue of voting rules in the Council is thrown by a statistical analysis conducted by Golub (1999) on a dataset including all basic proposals for directives for which data were available: 1,262 Commission proposals made during the period 1974–95, as well as fifty six proposals made in previous years that were adopted in that period.

Golub finds that 'decision-making did not accelerate, backlog did not decline, and old proposals were not suddenly unblocked as a result of the 1987 (or 1992) institutional reforms' (ibid.: 743)—reforms that considerably extended the use of QMV. Actually, his statistical analysis suggests that decision-making speed has deteriorated since the passage of the SEA, even more so after the Maastricht Treaty, and that a large, stubborn legislative backlog remains. At least part of the explanation is that while majority voting yields faster decision-making than unanimity, expanding the role

of the EP through the cooperation and codecision procedures has progressively slowed down EU decision-making. The author concludes that while
cooperation and codecision may have conferred greater democratic legitimacy on EC policymaking—a moot point, since the shift to majority
voting weakens control of the Council by the national parliaments (see
Chapter 2)—they have exacted a high price in terms of delays: while
proposals subject to QMV required on average 74 percent less time in
Council before their adoption than did proposals under unanimity, codecision reduced decision-making speed by 174 percent. Such findings challenge the claim that the efficiency gains from majority voting more than
compensate for delays stemming from the enhanced role of the EP. In
addition, one may question the willingness of a member state to implement a European measure against which it voted. Students of the modern
corporation have recognized that taking decisions by consensus may take
a long time, but once a decision is reached, everyone affected by it will be
likely to support it. According to some management experts, the consen-
sual approach to decision-making explains the success of the Japanese
corporation.

In sum, the case for a generalization of majority voting in the EU is a
good deal weaker, both theoretically and empirically, than is suggested by
the Commission. As I tried to show, the greater decision-making efficiency
that majority voting undoubtedly enjoys over unanimity loses some of its
intuitive appeal as soon as one takes a broader, and theoretically more
satisfactory, view of the logic of collective decision-making. Why, then,
the insistence on the need of generalized QMV in an enlarged Union? The
explanation seems to be that, like most political issues, the choice of
voting rules affects different interests differently. QMV enhances the
power of the Commission, and also increases, directly and indirectly, the
influence that the EP can bring to bear on legislation. It will be recalled
that, in general, the Council may amend a Commission proposal only by
unanimity. Under QMV, therefore, if even a single member state agrees
with the proposal, the Council is obliged to reach agreement on the text
that has been submitted, while the Commission can continue to amend it
until it gets the support of a sufficient majority. The asymmetry between
the qualified majority which is sufficient to approve the proposal and the
unanimity required to modify it enhances the Commission's agenda-
setting power. Conversely, the requirement of unanimity deprives the
Commission of the room for maneuver, which it enjoys under a procedure
requiring only QMV. Under unanimity the Commission has to comply
with the wishes of all member states, either by amending its proposal

accordingly or by seeing the Council alter it by a unanimous vote. Although the changes the Council may make must remain within the scope of the act as defined in the original proposal, the Commission's influence over the decision process is significantly reduced. It is ironic, one may add, that the Commission should oppose so radically the veto power that the unanimity rule gives to each member state: with its monopoly of legislative initiative, the Commission also enjoys a power of veto (or at least 'pre-veto') over legislative ideas it dislikes.

I conclude that the proposal to extend QMV to all areas of EU policy-making, far from strengthening the Community method, would actually subvert it. In this respect, this proposal is similar to the one discussed earlier. Just as the transformation of the Commission into the sole European executive—allegedly in the name of the principle of separation of powers—is incompatible with its treaty-based monopoly of legislative initiative, so the generalization of QMV goes against the grain of a method of governance whose organizing principle is the balanced representation of national and supranational interests, and the protection of those interests through differentiated voting procedures.

3.7 New Approaches to Governance

Following Scott and Trubek (2002), I define as 'new governance' any major departure from the classic Community method. While this method tends to give rise to binding legislative and executive acts imposing more or less uniform rules on all member states, the new approaches to European governance are characterized by flexibility, decentralized decision-making, nonbinding coordination, benchmarking, and policy-learning, and by procedural rather than substantive harmonization. In the above-mentioned White Paper on *European Governance*, the Commission gave a very cautious endorsement of these various nonlegislative approaches to European policymaking. With reference to the best known of the new methods, for instance, it argued that 'the open method of coordination should be a complement, rather than a replacement, for Community action.' Furthermore, the Open Method of Coordination (OMC) 'must not dilute the achievement of common objectives in the Treaty or the political responsibility of the institutions. It should not be used when legislative action under the Community method is possible. ... [T]he Commission should be closely involved and play a coordinating role' (Commission 2001: 39–40). The evident lack of enthusiasm for 'soft' approaches to policymaking, and for OMC in particular, is understandable. The OMC and other 'new governance' methods entail a significant loss of influence with respect to the powers that the Commission enjoys under the Community method.

The OMC has been pushed by the European Council in order to favor some convergence of national policies in areas, such as social policy, employment, and pension reform, that are too politically sensitive to be handled by the Community method. The conclusions of the Lisbon Summit of March 23–4, 2000 assert that OMC is a means of spreading best practice, a learning process that should lead to policy convergence in the long run. The same European Council identified the main elements of the approach: general guidelines for the Union, combined with specific timetables for achieving the short-, medium-, and long-term goals set by the member states themselves; quantitative and qualitative indicators and benchmarks derived from best practice worldwide, but tailored to the needs of individual countries and sectors; policy-reform actions of the member states to be integrated periodically into their National Action Plans; periodic monitoring, evaluation, and peer review of the results (European Council 2000). The European Council guides and coordinates the entire process. It sets the overall objectives to be achieved by the Union, while sector-specific committees, operating under the different Council formations, undertake the technical aspects of the work, notably the selection of indicators and benchmarks. The progress made in each area is reviewed annually, during the Spring session of the European Council that is devoted to economic and social questions. The role of the Commission in the entire process is limited. It presents proposals on the European guidelines, organizes the exchange of best practices, proposes indicators and benchmarks, and provides support to the process of implementation, monitoring, and peer review. In essence, the work of an international organization like the Organization for Economic Cooperation and Development is hardly a satisfactory role for a supranational institution that likes to see itself as the kernel of the future government of Europe!

Far more serious than the loss of influence under the OMC, however, is the Commission's diminished role in Treaty-based areas of EU policymaking. As already mentioned, the structure of separate pillars introduced by the TEU had as a practical consequence the virtual exclusion of the Community method from the CFSP, and from cooperation in JHA—an isolation of the Community pillar only partly reduced by the Amsterdam Treaty in the sphere of JHA. Policies concerning asylum, immigration, and 'third country' nationals have been integrated into the EC Treaty ('communitarized'), while judicial and police cooperation in criminal matters remained in the third pillar. The most immediate implications of this institutional design have been sketched in a previous section, but it may be helpful to review the situation in somewhat greater detail, starting with JHA—arguably the fastest-growing policymaking area of the Union since the mid-1990s. The 1985 White Paper on the Single Market included proposals on harmonization in such areas as asylum, immigration, visas, and drugs control. This suggests that already then the Commission considered these matters, now included in JHA, to be fully within its sphere of competence. However, the majority of the member states opposed this interpretation of the Rome Treaty. Fearing to be completely marginalized, the Commission then decided to adopt a low-profile approach in this policy area, associating itself in a pragmatic way with activities by the national governments in JHA—a strategy strongly criticized by the EP as a capitulation to intergovernmental cooperation (Monar 2002).

Perhaps as a result of this low-key approach, the Maastricht Treaty granted the Commission a nonexclusive right of legislative initiative. The Amsterdam Treaty increased somewhat the Commission's powers in JHA, but even in the 'communitarized' portions (Title IV of the EC Treaty) the right of legislative initiative must be shared with the member states during a transitional period of five years. Incidentally, this was the first time in the history of the Community method that the Commission's monopoly of legislative initiative was violated. In this connection, Craig and de Búrca (2003) speak of an infiltration of the Community Treaty by certain third-pillar features. The result is an increasing complexity of the EU constitutional order, and the continuing move away from the clarity and simplicity of the Community legal order of the past. The Commission's capacity to influence the policymaking process was further reduced by the maintenance of the unanimity rule in the Council. Although the Prodi Commission became rather active in this area, it faced a stiff competition from the member states. Since 1999 national governments have made increasing use of their own power of initiative, taking advantage of the fact that in matters related to JHA they possess considerably more expertise than the Brussels bureaucracy. Also, the Council presidency has become quite active in JHA, and this activism further limits the scope of policy initiatives by the Commission. As a result, in many cases the Brussels executive can do little more than base its own proposals on previous initiatives of the member states. The EP and ECJ were largely excluded from the old, pre-Amsterdam, third pillar. The Amsterdam Treaty strengthened somewhat the Parliament's position by granting it a right to be consulted on all legally binding acts both in the communitarized and the noncommunitarized parts of JHA. Codecision was supposed to be introduced for policies on visas, asylum, immigration, and other matters related to free movement of persons, at the end of the transitional period, but still subject to unanimous vote in the Council. In practice, the impact of EP's opinions on final Council decisions seems to be quite limited. Moreover, the Council does not have to consult the EP before it issues documents on strategy, since these are not legally binding. However, such documents often predetermine future EU actions, which are thus subtracted from any parliamentary influence.

The role of the ECJ also was strengthened by the Amsterdam Treaty. However, the Court's role is subject to a number of restrictions, even in the communitarized part of JHA. Thus according to Article 68(2) EC, the Court has no jurisdiction on measures regarding controls on persons at internal borders if such measures relate to 'the maintenance of law and order and the safeguarding of internal security'. This explicitly prevents the Court from reviewing the legality of operations carried out by the police or other law-enforcing agency of the member states. The jurisdiction of the ECJ to give preliminary rulings on the validity or interpretation of acts of Community institutions in connection with matters related to JHA is restricted to requests from national courts 'against whose decisions there is no judicial remedy under national law' (Article 68(1) EC), rather than from 'any court or tribunal of a member state' (Article 234 EC) as is the case under the classic Community method. Thus, the scope of the ECJ's jurisdiction in JHA is significantly more limited than in traditional areas of Community policymaking. In conclusion, it can be said that even after the Amsterdam and Nice Treaties the powers of the Commission, the EP, and the ECJ remain weaker in the area of JHA (including the communitarized parts) than they are under the classic Community method. It has been said that these developments have accentuated the intergovernmental features of the EU (Lenaerts and Van Nuffel 1999; Monar 2002), but as I explain in Chapter 8, the term 'intergovernmentalism' does not really capture the character of policymaking in the new areas of policymaking, including foreign affairs, security, and even monetary policy.

The possibility of extending the scope of the Community method to functions so close to the core of national sovereignty is severely restricted by political constraints—the opposition of the member states—but also by the limited basis of democratic legitimacy on which the method rests. Attempts to expand this normative basis, primarily by increasing the powers of the EP, have largely failed. The direct election of the EP, in 1979, had raised hopes that popular participation would provide true democratic legitimacy to the integration process. Almost three decades later, we must admit that the hope has not been realized. On the contrary, the steady accretion of the powers of the EP since the SEA has been accompanied by a parallel decline in public participation in European elections. In 1999 voter participation dropped below 50 percent for the first time, with minimum values of about 30 percent not only in the United Kingdom but also in the Netherlands—a founding member of the Community. The negative trend accelerated in the elections of June 2004. The average turnout of about 45 percent does not adequately represent a widely dispersed distribution of votes by country, ranging from 73.1 percent in Italy (where European and local elections had been combined) to 20 percent and less in some of the new member states. In most of the older member states the turnout was less that 50 percent, while the drop in turnout between the latest national elections and the European elections was more than 30 percentage points in the Netherlands, Sweden, Denmark, Germany, and Hungary. The main reason for these disappointing results is that elections for the EP are fought not as European elections but as 'national elections of the second order'; that is to say, they are not fought about European issues, much less about the formation of a European government, but about national issues. Typically, such elections, like midterm elections in the United States, are used by the voters to express their opinion concerning the incumbent national government (Hix 1999). Thus, it is not surprising that public participation in European elections is always significantly lower than in national elections. In addition, the EP lacks many of the key powers of national parliaments, for example in taxation and control of the legislative agenda; and being unable to give voice to national concerns, it is regarded as an imperfect instrument of interest representation. In sum, the EP, far from being able to legitimate the Community method, let alone its expansion to new areas of policy-making, suffers itself from a serious legitimacy deficit. The need to involve the national parliaments in EU governance, a need acknowledged also by the new Constitutional Treaty, is the clearest admission of the limited legitimacy of the EP.

Delegation of Powers and the Fiduciary Principle

4.1 Two Modes of Delegation

The Community method is characterized by the extensive delegation of legislative and policymaking powers to the European institutions—in particular to the Commission with its monopoly of agenda-setting. Broad delegation of powers presupposes a fiduciary relationship between the delegating authority and the delegate. Hence the erosion of the Community method discussed in Chapter 3 is the symptom of a deeper crisis: a growing mistrust between the member states and the supranational institutions. Contemporary theories of delegation, but also much older insights of social-contract theorists, can help us understand better the nature of this crisis. Let us start with the general question: Why do political principals choose to delegate some of their powers to agents (or fiduciaries) rather than exercising those powers themselves? A number of reasons have been discussed in the literature, ranging from delivering private benefits to favored constituencies to avoiding the making unpopular choices. However, the most important reasons for delegating powers, and the ones to be considered in this and in the next chapter, are, first, to reduce decision-making costs, for example by taking advantage of executive branch expertise; and, second, to enhance the credibility of long-term policy commitments.

The logic of delegation varies with the reasons for delegating powers. The main difference between the two modes considered here may be stated as follows. In the former case, where the purpose is to reduce decision-making costs, the key problem facing the political principals is bureaucratic drift, that is, the ability of the agent to enact outcomes different from the policies preferred by those who originally delegated powers. This is the only problem considered by most works on delegation and on the principal–agent model, with which delegation theory is often identified (see, e.g. Epstein and O'Halloran 1999). According to this body of literature, the best solution of the delegation problem would be for principals to appoint agents who share their preferences. If this is impossible or too costly, then bureaucratic drift should be reduced with the help of various mechanisms of *ex ante* and *ex post* control. It is recognized that controls are imperfect, so that there will always remain a difference between the policy enacted and what is implemented, and this residual noncompliance is an important component of *agency costs*. To calculate the net benefits of delegation, agency costs are to be subtracted from the gains in decision-making efficiency.

The situation is quite different when credibility is the main reason for delegating powers. In this case the best strategy to enhance the credibility of a long-term policy commitment is often to choose a delegate whose policy preferences differ from those of the delegating principal. For example, if a government wants to credibly commit itself to price stability, it should delegate responsibility for monetary policy to a central banker who values *ex post* inflation less than the government itself, or the average (more precisely, the median) voter. The best-known formalization of this intuitive idea is Rogoff's model (1985) of the 'conservative' central banker. 'Conservative' here means that the banker is more inflation-averse than the government. The government's commitment to a lower average rate of inflation becomes credible precisely because the delegate values *ex post* inflation less than his or her political principals. In Rogoff's model the government has a loss function L_G, which depends on deviations of employment, n, and inflation, p, from their socially desired levels N and P:

$$L_G = (n - N)^2 + g(p - P)^2,$$

where g is the relative weight the government places on inflation stabilization versus employment stabilization. The author proves that the government can improve social welfare by appointing a central banker who is known to value more price stability, relative to unemployment, than the government. The loss function of the conservative banker is:

$$L_B = (n - N)^2 + b(p - P)^2,$$

where $b = g + h$, with $h > 0$ and possibly quite large.

Thus 'it can be entirely rational for society to structure its central bank in such a way that the monetary authorities have an objective function very different from the social welfare function' (Rogoff 1985: 1186). Intuitively this is because if distortions in the labor market cause the rate of inflation to be too high, then society can be made better off by having the central bank place a higher weight on price stability. It should be noted that Rogoff's model does not explicitly assume that the central bank is independent. Rather, independence is implied by the method of selection: if the central banker is not autonomous in monetary policy decisions, his or her policy preferences are obviously irrelevant. Hence, after the parameter g has been selected by the government, the head of the central bank must be free to implement his or her preferred policy.

Alesina and Grilli (1994) have converted Rogoff's model into an explicit voting model—where the voters are the member states of the EU—and applied it to the case of the ECB. In their model, each member state evaluates the consequences of monetary integration according to its own preferences. The authors show that participation in the monetary union can increase national welfare if the preferences of the ECB are more 'conservative' than national preferences. Intuitively this means that monetary union allows countries to credibly commit themselves to anti-inflationary policies. This is the reason why popular support for monetary union was strongest in countries with a historically high inflation bias, such as Italy, Spain, and Greece. Apparently, the political leaders of these countries felt that the credibility for price stability, and the resulting reduction in the cost of servicing the public debt, more than compensated for the potential costs in unemployment.

Similar arguments may be used to explain why members of the Commission tend to be more in favor of European integration than the national governments that choose them. Governments may believe that integration of the national economies is the optimal long-run policy, but they also know that they may be tempted by short-run incentives to renege on their commitment to respect European rules, such as those disciplining state aid to industry. Choosing as commissioners people who are more prointegration than the government is a way for the member states to enhance the credibility of their commitment to economic integration. Again, the logic of the conservative banker model can be extended to such areas of public policy as economic and social regulation. In most countries regulatory policymaking is now delegated to expert agencies operating at arm's length from government. The main purpose of insulating regulators from the political process is to enhance the credibility of long-term policy commitments. Agency heads are chosen not only for their expertise in the relevant area, but also for their proenvironment, proconsumer, or procompetition beliefs. They generally expect, and are expected by others, to have a well-defined agenda, and to measure their success by the amount of the agenda they accomplish. Regulators also know that courts can review their decisions and may overturn them if they seem to depart too widely from the language and aim of the enabling statute. Hence they have an additional incentive to pursue the statutory objectives of the agency, even when those objectives, because of changed economic or political conditions, no longer enjoy popular support. Thus it is reasonable to assume that the head of an independent agency attaches more importance to the agency's long-term objectives than the government or the majority of voters. In this respect the agency head, like Rogoff's independent central banker, is a *fiduciary* rather than a mere agent of his or her political principals. I shall come back to the distinction between agent and fiduciary, and between agency costs and *fiduciary costs*, after discussing the scope of delegation under the Community method.

4.2   Delegation of Powers to the European Institutions

European institutions have no inherent powers; they possess only those powers conferred on them by the member states in the treaties. The important question for us is whether the powers so conferred are limited in scope, or how far they can be expanded by indirect means, such as judicial interpretation or the creation of subsidiary powers under Article 235 of the Rome Treaty. In the euphoria created by the SEA and the highly successful marketing of the 'Europe 1992' program, it became tempting to imagine that there was no effective barrier to the continuous, if incremental, expansion of Community competences. In those days a distinguished jurist could write that 'there is no nucleus of sovereignty that the Member States can invoke, as such, against the Community' (Lenaerts 1990: 220). In thus answering the question about the limits of the delegated powers, European lawyers could point to the broad interpretation given by the ECJ to the theory of implied powers. This theory comes in two versions (Hartley 1991: 102–8). According to the weaker version—or the narrower formulation of a principle that is accepted by international law as well as by most national legal systems—the existence of a given *power* implies also the existence of any other power that is reasonably necessary for the exercise of the former. In the stronger version, the existence of a given *objective* or *function* implies the existence of any power necessary to attain it. The ECJ endorsed the weak version already in the 1950s, while it applied the wide formulation, in favor of the powers of the Commission, only in

1987, in *Germany v. Commission* (Cases 281, 283–5, 287/85). These cases arose out of Article 118 of the Rome Treaty, which gives the Commission a task ('promoting close co-operation between member States in the social field'), but no legislative power to carry it out. In 1985 the Commission, acting under Article 118, adopted a decision that, *inter alia*, obliged the member states to inform the Commission of draft measures and agreements concerning the topic in question. This decision was challenged by some national governments, but was upheld by the Court on the grounds that whenever a provision of the treaty confers a specific task on the Commission, that provision must also be regarded as implicitly conferring on the same institution the powers necessary to carry out that task. At the time, legal commentators thought that this judgment was very significant and that, given the many, far-reaching functions assigned by the treaty to the Commission, it could herald an era of increased Commission law-making. As is shown below, these expectations were, however, not fulfilled.

From the point of view of the theory of implied powers, the most important provision of the Rome Treaty is the above-mentioned Article 235 (now Article 308 EC), which enables the Council to take appropriate measures—acting unanimously on a proposal by the Commission and after consulting the EP—in cases where action by the Community is found to be necessary to attain, 'in the course of the operation of the common market,' one of the objectives of the Community and there is no specific power under the Treaty available for that purpose. Reviewing the effect of Article 235 as a whole, before the Maastricht Treaty, Hartley (ibid.: 108) wrote that 'it confers what can only be termed a general legislative power. For this reason, the theory of limited powers does not seem to be part of Community law, except to the extent that the Community may legislate only within the general area covered by the Treaties.' Indeed, since the early 1970s the Council and the Commission made liberal use of this article to expand Community powers or to broaden the reach of Community legislation in many policy areas such as economic and monetary union, social and regional policy, the free movement of workers and professionals, energy and environment, scientific and technological research and development, and cooperation agreements with third countries. The question whether Community action was in fact necessary was considered by the European institutions as a matter within their complete discretion.

However, such liberal interpretations are no longer tenable in view of the first paragraph of Article 3b of the Maastricht Treaty (now Article 5 EC), which states the principle of conferral in terms of strictly limited powers.

As Dashwood (1996) points out, Article 235 only makes sense post Maastricht if the reference to the attainment of a Community objective 'in the course of the operation of the common market' is taken seriously. This means that subsidiary powers would be created under this article only for matters directly connected with the policies that lie at the very core of the Community, but not for other programs, however worthy their objectives. Thus, the continuous accretion of powers to the Community is no longer on the political agenda. Article 5 EC, which enacts attribution of powers, subsidiarity, and proportionality as organizing principles of the constitutional order of the Community, marks a shift in the Community's deep structure. As already mentioned in Chapter 1, in the words of professor Dashwood, 'the Article effectively rules out of court the notion of a Community continuously moving the boundary posts of its own competence.'

Moreover, the Maastricht Treaty defined new competences in a way that actually limits the exercise of Community powers. For example, Article 126 (now Article 149 EC) adds a new legal basis for action in the field of education, but the measures that can be taken in this field are limited to 'incentive measures' and to recommendations. Any harmonization of national laws and regulations is explicitly excluded. Similarly, Article 129 (now Article 152 EC) creates specific powers for the Community in the field of human health protection, but the competence is highly circumscribed as subsidiary to that of the member states. Harmonization is again ruled out, even though the article states that health-protection requirements shall form a constituent part of the other Community policies. The other provisions of the treaty—defining new competences in such areas as culture, consumer protection, and industrial policy—are similarly drafted. Rather than relying on implicit powers, whose limits seemed out of control, the framers of the TEU opted for an explicit grant that delimits the mode of action and the reach of such powers (Weiler 1999). A similar approach has been followed by the Amsterdam and Nice Treaties, and by the new Constitutional Treaty.

In its *Tobacco Advertising* judgment of October 2000, which annulled for the first time a measure adopted under the codecision procedure, the ECJ showed how strictly the limits of the Community's attributed competence are taken today. Germany, which had been outvoted in the Council, argued that Directive 98/34, prohibiting all forms of tobacco advertising, was a disguised public health measure, while Parliament and Council contended that the Treaty allowed the Community to adopt any measure to regulate the internal market, not just those that liberalize trade. The Court held that the European legislator could not rely on other articles to circumvent the explicit prohibition in Article 152 EC of harmonization of health measures. It argued that measures based on Article 95 EC (on the harmonization of national laws and regulations) must be aimed at improving the conditions of the internal market, not at market regulations in general. As the conditions for recourse to Article 95 had not been fulfilled—the measure neither facilitated trade, nor contributed to eliminating significant distortions of competition—the directive was annulled. As Weatherill (2003) has observed, with this judgment the Court refused to accept that a political majority in the Council, with the support of the Commission, could, in effect, assume responsibility for fixing the reach of the treaty.

Such care in spelling out the limits of the delegated powers has been taken by a number of commentators to reflect a lack of confidence in the capacity for self-restraint of the supranational institutions. There can be little doubt, Dashwood noted more than two decades ago, that in the 1960s 'harmonization tended to be pursued not so much to resolve concrete problems encountered in the course of constructing the common market as to drive forward the general process of integration. This ... was bound to affect the judgment of the Commission, inclining it towards maximum exercise of the powers available under Article 100 and towards solutions involving a high degree of uniformity between national laws' (Dashwood 1983: 194). In fact, from the early 1960s to about 1973 (the date of the first enlargement of the Community) the Commission's approach to harmonization was characterized by a distinct preference for detailed measures designed to regulate exhaustively the problems in question to the exclusion of previously existing national laws and regulations—the approach already referred to as 'total harmonization'. Under total harmonization, once European rules have been put in place, a member state's capacity to apply stricter rules by appealing to the values referred to in Article 36 of the Rome Treaty, such as the protection of the health and life of humans, animals, and plants, is excluded. Clearly, total harmonization reflects a federalist vision of the integration process, corresponding to what in the language of US public law is referred to as federal preemption.

For a long time, the ECJ supported total harmonization as a foundation stone in the building of the common market (Weatherill 1995). By the mid-1970s, however, the limits of the approach had become clear, while mounting opposition to what many member states considered excessive centralization convinced the Commission that this instrument had to be used so as not to interfere too much with the regulatory autonomy of the national governments. The emphasis shifted from total to optional and minimum harmonization—and to mutual recognition. Optional harmonization aims to guarantee the free movement of goods, while permitting the member states to retain their traditional forms of regulation for goods produced for the domestic market. Under minimum harmonization, the national governments must secure the level of regulation set out in a directive but are permitted to set higher standards, provided that the stricter national rules do not violate Community law. Finally, the mutual recognition of national laws and standards does not involve the transfer of regulatory powers to the supranational institutions, but nevertheless restricts the freedom of action of national governments, which cannot prevent the marketing within their borders of a product lawfully manufactured and marketed in another member state.

The realization that total harmonization confers on the Community an exclusive competence that it is ill-equipped to discharge may be considered the first recognition of the limits of positive integration (see Chapter 7). Similarly, the explicit rejection of harmonization in some new areas of Community activity, and the limits on the creation of subsidiary powers not strictly necessary to the functioning of the single market, are clear indications of a growing resistance to the centralizing tendencies of the Commission. A framework agreement like the Rome Treaty has to be adapted to new needs and contingencies, which only infinitely wise and prescient legislators could have foreseen. However, Article 235 of the treaty has been used all too often to practice 'the trick of self-levitation through pulling on its own boot straps' (Dashwood 1996: 123); in other words, to amend the treaty without following the normal democratic procedures of ratification and approval by national parliaments. As long as the scope of European law was limited, and trust in the self-restraint of the supranational institutions was maintained, the simplified procedure for adapting the original agreement had an obvious appeal. However, since the SEA expanded Community powers significantly, the member states have been willing to follow the more complex and politically riskier procedure of formal treaty amendment, rather than delegating to the supranational institutions the task of deciding whether Community action in a given area is needed, and which form it should take. After the SEA, intergovernmental conferences for the purpose of treaty revision have taken place every three or four years. Treaty amendment has become almost a routine procedure, initiated as soon as a new treaty has been accepted by the national governments. Treaties may be thought of as 'incomplete contracts', and this contractual perspective throws additional light on the fiduciary dimension of delegation of powers.

4.3   Incomplete Contracting and Treaty Amendment

In the contracting approach to governance (Williamson 1985), a basic distinction is made between *complete* and *incomplete contracts*—where 'contract' does not necessarily mean a legally binding commitment, but any (explicit or implicit) agreement, between independent parties. A complete contract is an agreement that specifies precisely what each party is to do in every possible circumstance, and arranges the distribution of benefits and costs in each contingency so that each party finds it optimal to abide by the contract's terms. One moment's reflection suffices to show that the conditions involved in reaching and enforcing a complete contract can seldom be satisfied in practice. First, the parties must each foresee all the relevant contingencies that might be important to them in the course of the contract, and to which they might want to adapt the contractually specified actions. They must also be able to know *ex post* which of the particular contingencies considered at the planning stage has actually occurred. Second, they must be able and willing to determine and agree upon an efficient course of action for each possible contingency. Finally, once they have entered the contract, the parties must be willing to abide by its terms (Milgrom and Roberts 1992).

Bounded rationality and opportunism are the basic reasons why the requirements of complete contracting can seldom be fulfilled in practice. Hence all contracts, except for the simplest types, are incomplete. This means that contingencies will arise that have not been accounted for because they were not even imagined at contracting time. Now, incomplete contracting leads to problems of imperfect commitment. There is a strong temptation to renege on the original terms of the contract because what should be done in case of an unforeseen contingency is left unstated or ambiguous, and hence open to interpretation. The root difficulty is that the incentives of contractual partners in the implementation stage may no longer be the same as the incentives in the contract-writing stage. In some circumstances, it could be advantageous for all parties concerned to renegotiate the contract *ex post* because what was efficient when the contract was first stipulated may not be so once actions have been taken or further information obtained. If the parties understand at the time they are defining the original agreement that they will later face these incentives, however, they may not be able to draft the contract in a way that elicits the desired behavior.

One possible response to contractual incompleteness is an arrangement known as *relational contracting*, where the parties do not agree on detailed plans of action, but on general principles, on the criteria to be used in deciding what to do when unforeseen contingencies arise, on who has what power to act and the range of actions that can be taken, and on dispute resolution mechanisms to be used if disagreements do arise. Crucial to this approach is the choice of mechanisms for adapting the contract to unforeseen contingencies, without compromising its credibility. In many transactions one party may be given more authority in saying what adaptation will take place, but if the other contractual partners are to delegate such discretionary authority, they must believe that it will be used fairly and effectively. Milgrom and Roberts (1992) suggest that the party to whom this authority is delegated should be the one with the longer time horizon, the more visibility, and the greater frequency of transactions, and thus the one with the most to lose from a loss of reputation.

A relational contract settles for a general agreement that frames the entire relationship, recognizing that it is impossible to concentrate all the relevant bargaining action at the *ex ante* contracting stage. The Rome Treaty, for example, may be conceived of as a relational contract. With a few exceptions, the treaty only provides general principles and policy guidelines, and delegates to the European institutions the task of specifying the concrete measures to be taken in order to achieve the broad objectives set out in Article 2. In this perspective, Article 235, as discussed earlier, is part of the general response of the member states to the contractual incompleteness that characterizes all treaties and constitutional documents. No such provision would have been necessary if the treaty had been framed by infinitely wise and prescient legislators. In fact, bounded rationality, together with the possibility of imperfect commitment to European integration, suggested to delegate to the Commission and the Court of Justice the task of filling the gaps in the treaty. Thus, for about thirty years the powers of the Community and the reach of European law were expanded, sometimes dramatically, without any formal treaty amendment. The fact that, starting with the Maastricht Treaty, the national governments have taken the initiative in amending the treaties, and have used the amendment process to define new competences in a way that actually limits the exercise of Community powers, shows how serious is the loss of confidence in the self-restraint of the European institutions. This conclusion is supported by the importance the theory of relational contracting attaches to the mechanisms and procedures for updating the original agreement.

It is, however, important to interpret these developments correctly. If it is true that the new assertiveness of the member states denotes a serious loss of trust in the supranational institutions, and in key aspects of the Community method such as the Commission's monopoly of legislative initiative, it does not necessarily follow that the member states have reneged on their commitment to European integration. Rather, a good part of the recent history of the EU is a history of attempts to find credible alternatives both to the classic Community method and to traditional intergovernmentalism (see Chapter 8). Even delegation of powers is still being used as a method of enhancing the credibility of the member states' commitment, as shown by the delegation of responsibility for monetary policy to the ECB. But note that the ECB is not a European *institution* in the sense of Article 7 EC, but a European 'body', and as such largely exempt from the procedural and substantive requirements imposed by the Community method.

4.4   Delegation and Political Property Rights

At the beginning of this chapter two basic modes of delegation were distinguished. In the first, which may be called the *agency mode*, the preferences of the principal and of the agent should be aligned as much as possible, and the delegation structured so as to minimize bureaucratic drift and slippage. However, an agent who simply carries out the principal's directives cannot enhance the latter's credibility. Hence the second mode of delegation—the *fiduciary mode*—implies that the delegate should be independent, although the level of independence will vary with the nature of the task and the seriousness of the credibility problem. Needless to say, the two modes are often combined in practice, as in the case of delegation of powers to the European Commission (see Section 4.5). The difference between these two types of delegation has normative, as well as efficiency, implications. The legitimacy of the principal provides at least prima facie evidence of the legitimacy of the agent's decisions: if the discretion of the agent is suitably controlled, his or her decisions simply implement the principal's prior decisions. The normative position of an independent delegate is more delicate. In this case, the principal can transfer his or her powers, but not legitimacy, to the delegate; hence the latter must find ways of establishing his or her own legitimacy, for example, by demonstrating a distinctive competence in the pursuance of clearly defined objectives (see Chapter 2). To the extent that delegation to an independent fiduciary involves a net loss of legitimacy, we can speak of *fiduciary costs* by analogy with the *agency costs* of principal–agent theory.

While agency costs result from a less-than-complete control of the agent's behavior, fiduciary costs arise from a poorly defined accountability framework. An example is the limited accountability of the European Commission, both in political and policy terms. As was pointed out in Chapter 2, such fiduciary costs contribute significantly to the overall democratic deficit of the EU.

The failure to distinguish between the agency and the fiduciary mode of delegation has led to overlook or misinterpret important aspects of EU governance. For instance, agency theory provides useful insights into the relative effectiveness of various mechanisms to control administrative discretion. The theory has also been applied with some success to the study of the 'comitology' system in areas where the Council delegates implementing powers to the Commission (see Chapter 5). However, the principal–agent model offers no useful insights into the reasons for the treaty-based independence of the Commission in the performance of certain functions, such as agenda-setting or monitoring compliance with European law. At best, agency theory can explain the independence of the Commission as a failure of the control mechanisms established by the member states (see, e.g. Pollack 1997), but this view ignores the fact that this independence is treaty-based. Actually, it is not too surprising that the literature on European integration fails to distinguish clearly between the two main modes of delegation. Even students of corporate law, where the concepts of agent and fiduciary have a long tradition, do not always understand clearly the distinction. This has led a distinguished legal scholar to criticize agency theorists for failing to recognize the complexity of corporate governance, and for having done little 'to explain the concept of the fiduciary, to develop positive theories as to why fiduciary law has developed its particular doctrines and characteristics, and to assess whether particular fiduciary doctrines are efficient or sound' (Clark 1985: 62). Similarly, I suggest, a correct understanding of the governance structure of the EU requires us to go beyond agency theory. Although the key problems of this theory—the agent's hidden actions and hidden information—are present in any relation based on specialization and division of labor, they are not the key to understanding the logic of fiduciary delegation.

When speaking of delegation it is important always to keep in mind that we are not dealing with a binary variable. Rather, delegation should be thought of as a variable, call it D, ranging more or less continuously over a certain interval, say, between $D = 0$ (no delegation) and $D = 1$ (full delegation). The independence of the delegate increases monotonically with increasing values of D. Horn (1995), who introduced this notation in the context of a formal principal–agent model, does not discuss the limiting case $D = 1$, and hence does not specify the meaning of 'full delegation'. The natural meaning to be assigned to this limiting case is that responsibility in a given area is completely transferred to the delegate. More precisely, what is transferred are *political property rights*, these being the rights to exercise public authority in a given policy area. In this terminology, the case $D = 1$ corresponds to a complete, and in some cases irrevocable, transfer of certain political property rights—possibly including some elements of national sovereignty—to some independent institution.

The notion of political property rights allows us to distinguish more clearly the notion of agency from that of a fiduciary or trustee relation (Majone 2001). The agent is not ordinarily the owner of property for the benefit of the principal. Strictly speaking, when property is transferred to a person who is supposed to manage it for the benefit of a third person, we have not an agency but a special type of fiduciary relation known as trusteeship. In Anglo-American law a trust is a situation where the owner of some property, the 'trustor' (or 'settlor'), transfers it to a 'trustee' with the stipulation that the trustee should not treat it as his or her own but manage it for the benefit of the 'beneficiary', who could be the trustor himself or herself. Now, since agency may possess the element of trust and confidence of a fiduciary relation, both agents and trustees can be classed together for many purposes, but the two concepts are distinct. In the legal literature this distinction is sometimes expressed by saying that all trustees are agents but not all agents are trustees: a trustee is an agent and something more (Bogert 1987: 36). The trustee's fiduciary duty is not simply a personal obligation but is attached to a piece of property—the trust assets. To exemplify, a full delegation of authority over monetary policy may be viewed as a transfer of political property rights by the government (the trustor) to an independent central banker (the trustee) for the benefit of the government itself, whose commitment to price stability thereby becomes more credible. In this model the transfer of political property rights is the guarantee of the central bank's independence. The guarantee is particularly strong when the legal basis of the transfer is not a statute, which could be changed by a new parliamentary majority, but a constitutional or quasi-constitutional provision, as in the case of the ECB. Such a transfer is the political analog of the irrevocable character of most ordinary trusts.

In light of the failure of students of European integration, and of contemporary political science more generally, to appreciate the political significance of fiduciary relations, it may be worthwhile to recall that the notions of fiduciary and political trusteeship play a key role in John Locke's philosophy of government. Locke thought in terms of a contract of society, establishing a political (or civil) society, followed by the creation of a fiduciary sovereign under and by a trust deed. In Chapter XIII [149] of the 'Second Treatise of Government', he writes that the legislative, even though it is the supreme power, is 'only a Fiduciary Power to act for certain ends'. Hence (Locke 1965:413; emphases in the original),

there remains still *in the People a Supreme Power* to remove or *alter the Legislative*, when they find the *Legislative* act contrary to the trust reposed in them. For all *Power given with trust* for attaining an *end*, being limited by that end, whenever that *end* is manifestly neglected, or opposed, the *trust* must necessarily be *forfeited*, and the Power devolve into the hands of those that gave it, who may place it anew where they shall think best for their safety and security.

As Barker (1962) has pointed out, when Locke speaks of the government as trustee and of the community as both trustor and beneficiary, he is not using these terms metaphorically, but as technical concepts derived from the English law of trusts as it existed in his time. The relevance of Locke's (and Rousseau's) ideas to the ongoing transformation of EU governance will be discussed again in Chapter 8.

Coming back to the transfer of political property rights, an important example is the transfer of elements of national sovereignty to the European level. In policy areas where the Community is *exclusively* competent, the power to exercise public authority has been irrevocably transferred to the European institutions, and national action is simply impermissible. This, at least, is the doctrine of the ECJ; since the treaties did not contain an explicit list of areas of exclusive Community competence, it has been up to the Court to build up such a list. In a series of landmark decisions the Court decided that the Community enjoys exclusive competence in the area of common commercial policy under Article 113 of the Rome Treaty. In other rulings the Court determined that national action is preempted in the regulation of agricultural markets and fisheries, and in sectors covered by total harmonization. In such areas, the ECJ argued in *Costa v. Enel* (1964), the transfer of powers to the European level carries with it a permanent limitation of the sovereign rights of the member states. Where Union competence is exclusive, member states can advance their interests only through the European institutions, rather than unilaterally or even collectively. The area of exclusive competence is rather limited, but in this area the European institutions enjoy autonomous powers.

4.5   The Dual Nature of the European Commission

The conceptual distinctions drawn in the preceding pages allow us to better appreciate the composite nature of the Commission. It is well known that the treaties assign a variety of functions to this institution, but the implications of this are not always clearly understood. I have argued that the Commission is not an agent but a fiduciary, or trustee, of the member states when it exercises powers expressly granted to it by the treaties, such as setting the legislative and policy agenda, ensuring compliance with Community law, or issuing directives and decisions without the Council's approval under Article 86(3) of the EC Treaty. Although the Commission's monopoly of agenda-setting has been somewhat eroded recently, it is still the case that under the Community method the Commission can decide whether the Union should act and, if so, in what legal form, and what content and implementing procedures the proposal should embody. It may also withdraw its proposal at any time before the Council reaches a decision, while the Council cannot compel the Commission to submit a proposal. Such extensive powers are hardly compatible with the role of a mere agent.

We also saw that as guardian of the treaties, the Commission can take autonomous decisions in order to determine whether member states have complied with their treaty obligations, or to permit them in appropriate cases to deviate from their obligations. Again, in some cases the Commission can take general measures (directives) without Council approval. The member states have repeatedly, but so far unsuccessfully, challenged these autonomous powers of the Brussels authority.

The situation is quite different when the member states, acting in the Council, determine the conditions under which the Commission is to implement the rules that the Council lays down. The Commission *is* an agent when it exercises such implementing powers, as shown by the creation of a system of committees of national representatives who are supposed to control the Commission's discretion in the use of its implementing powers—the so-called 'comitology' system (see Chapter 5). The ECJ has always upheld the legality of these controls, rejecting the argument that the comitology procedures constitute an unwarranted restriction of the decision-making power of the Commission and jeopardize its independence. Precisely the existence of an extensive system of controls makes it possible to delegate to the Commission extensive discretionary powers. The Court's reasoning, especially its refusal to see in the comitology system a threat to the Commission's independence, shows that the logic of delegation in the case of implementing powers is different from the cases considered before.

The purpose of delegating implementing powers to the Commission is to reduce the costs and improve the quality of decision-making in the Council. In fact, the SEA, amending Article 145 of the Rome Treaty, *required* the Council to delegate implementing powers to the Commission. The Council may reserve such powers for itself only in special cases. This requirement—instead of the mere possibility of delegation mentioned by the original Article 145—was part of the same effort to enhance the efficiency of Community decision-making that also introduced QMV for internal market legislation. Nothing like the comitology system of controls is possible in the case of fiduciary duties. According to Article 213 EC, the members of the Commission must be completely independent in the performance of their duties, neither seeking nor taking instructions from any government or from any other body, and 'each Member State undertakes to respect this principle and not to seek to influence the Members of the Commission in the performance of their tasks.' Reality is, of course, more complicated, but the logic of delegation embedded in the treaty is clear.

4.6   Fiduciary Duties and Accountability

We have seen that in relational contracts the task of adapting the contract to unforeseen contingencies is often delegated to somebody who is trusted by the contractual partners to use the delegated authority fairly and effectively. This suggests that the fiduciary relation may be conceived of as a rule for completing incomplete contractual arrangements. What Easterbrook and Fischel (1991: 92) write with reference to corporate law has wider applicability: 'The reason for having a fiduciary principle in the first place is the high cost of specifying things by (express) contract.' The issue of fiduciary duties is central to any analysis of the fiduciary principle. Corporate law again provides some suggestive analogies. Corporate executives often have an affirmative duty to disclose to other corporate decision-makers information that bears on whether the corporation is about to make a good or bad business decision. As Clark (1985) points out, this duty does not arise from the express terms of the employment contract, but depends on the manager's fiduciary status. Again, agents usually have relatively fixed obligations under their employment contract. If their contract does not call for a particular performance, they do not have to do it. By contrast, the company executives' 'duty of care' in the exercise of their functions is open-ended, and their duty of loyalty too is quite open-ended.

Article 10 EC strongly suggests that the fiduciary principle and fiduciary duties play a larger role in EU governance than agency and the normal duties of agents. It must be remembered that the member states, to which the article is addressed, are responsible for implementing Community law, except when the task has been expressly assigned to a European institution. In this capacity they act as fiduciaries or 'trustees of the common interest' as the Court put it in Case 804/79, *Commission v. United Kingdom*. Now, Article 10, as interpreted by the ECJ, imposes a reciprocal duty of loyal cooperation between European institutions and national authorities, and between the national authorities themselves. This duty extends beyond specific obligations imposed by particular legal acts: even when there is no specific obligation, a member state's conduct may nonetheless constitute a breach of the fiduciary duty of loyal cooperation (Lenaerts and Van Nuffel 1999). In particular, the jurisprudence of the Court suggests a general duty of the member states to give the Commission any information that may facilitate the fulfillment of the Commission's tasks, even when the Council has not made use of its powers of setting the conditions under which the Commission may collect information or carry out any checks. Symmetrically, the Commission has a duty of loyal cooperation with national administrations and courts, for example in cases involving the application of the Community's competition rules. Again, Article 10 imposes a duty of mutual cooperation between the Commission and the member states whenever the implementation of Community policies runs into unexpected problems. In sum, among the general rules of the treaty, Article 10 is the one that is most often invoked to fill gaps in European law. Like the fiduciary principle in corporate law, it has been used as a rule for completing incomplete contractual arrangements between the institutions of the EU, and between them and the member states. The importance of fiduciary relations in EU governance makes the current crisis of confidence between member states and supranational institutions all the more worrisome.

For Locke, political trusteeship meant a burden of obligation, the most prominent aspect of which is liability for abuse or neglect of the powers held in trust—a liability that extends to removal for action contrary to the trust. In corporate law, fiduciary duty has both a loyalty component and a care component. As a constraint on directors' pursuit of personal interest, fiduciary duty primarily involves the duty of loyalty. However, in its application to directors' official conduct, fiduciary duty broadens to cover not only selfish actions but also the possibility of negligent behavior (O'Kelley and Thompson 2003). Applying this distinction to EU governance we could say that the duty of loyalty has received much greater attention, both in the treaties and in the jurisprudence of the ECJ, than the duty of care. The reason for the emphasis on 'loyalty' rather than 'care' must be sought in the logic of the Community method, for which the question of institutional balance, rather than system effectiveness, is preeminent.

As in other 'mixed' polities, the prime theme of the internal political process in the EU is the tug-of-war among independent institutions over the extent and security of their respective jurisdictional prerogatives. As noted in Chapter 3, the viability of this mode of governance requires that the contest be tempered by a high degree of institutionalization, and by the duty of reciprocal loyalty. On the other hand, since policies are often initiated less to solve concrete problems than to drive forward the process of European integration, the efficiency of actual outcomes is not considered very important, as is shown in detail in Chapter 6. In addition, the independence of the European institutions, and in particular of the Commission, means that the traditional mechanisms of political accountability are largely absent. As we saw, the Rome Treaty, and all subsequent treaties, emphasize the apolitical character of the Commission, insisting on its complete independence 'from any government or from any other body'. Up to a point, this insulation from the political process makes sense if we think of the Commission as the guardian of the treaties or as an independent regulatory agency. This was indeed what the institution was intended to resemble originally. In the meanwhile, however, it has become a highly politicized body, responsible for decisions involving political judgment and a high level of discretion. In spite of this, the framework of political accountability remains quite weak—the dismissal of the entire Commission is a measure that the EP is understandably very reluctant to use, while there is no possibility of sanctioning an individual Commissioner. At the same time, the limited importance attached to efficiency considerations implies that accountability by results finds limited application under the classical Community method. The parallel drawn in Chapter 2 between the ECB and the Commission is quite instructive in this respect. While the ECB has a single, clearly defined, and measurable objective—price stability—the duties of the Commission not only have greatly expanded over the years but they have also changed in character. This steady increase in the functions and responsibilities of the Commission has several negative consequences: it erodes the narrow legitimacy basis of the institution; it makes objective evaluation of actual outcomes practically impossible because of the absence of clearly defined standards of evaluation; and, not least, the mismatch between the multiplicity and complexity of the tasks and the available resources undermines the credibility of EU programs and policies. Unfortunately, it is hard to see how these defects may be corrected within the framework of the Community method. The difficulty of reforming this rigid framework is the theme of the two following chapters.

Institutional Balance Versus Institutional Innovation

5.1 Delegating Rulemaking Powers

The preceding chapter was primarily concerned with delegation of powers from the national to the European level. Discussing the dual role of the Commission, however, reference was also made to the delegation of implementing ('rulemaking') powers from the Council to the Commission. Such delegation from one European institution to another institution, or body, is the topic of this chapter. Here, too, it will be convenient to start with the general problem of delegation of rulemaking powers from the legislature to administrative agencies, and then consider the special features that this type of delegation assumes in the EU context.

A distinctive feature of the modern regulatory state is the extensive delegation of quasi-legislative powers to bodies operating at arm's length from central government: agencies, boards, commissions, tribunals. The delegation of such powers to policymakers who are neither elected nor under the direct control of elected officials has always been considered problematic from the point of view of democracy. The reason is that this type of delegation creates the 'agency problem' mentioned in Chapter 4: the possibility that the administrative agents will not comply with the policy preferences of their political principals. In spite of such normative concerns, however, the practical case for delegating rulemaking powers to expert agencies has proved to be overwhelming. The case of the United States, the oldest regulatory state, is particularly instructive. Here the initial hostility to delegation, which found expression in the influential 'non-delegation doctrine', was based directly on the key constitutional principle of separation of powers: Congress, rather than administrators or experts, should make the law. While the doctrine has never been repealed,

US courts have not used it to strike down legislation for seven decades. This does not mean that all problems have been laid to rest. The key normative question remains, in Stewart's words, how 'to control and validate the exercise of essentially legislative powers by administrative agencies that do not enjoy the formal legitimation of one-person, one-vote election' (Stewart 1975: 1688). The US polity has grappled with this issue for more than a century. The nondelegation doctrine was the first attempt to resolve the legitimacy problems raised by the emergence of a modern system of administrative regulation. For several decades the doctrine enjoyed such widespread acceptance that it came to be regarded as the traditional model of US administrative law. The model conceives of the regulatory agency as a mere transmission belt for implementing legislative directives in particular cases. Vague, general, or ambiguous statutes create discretion and thus threaten the legitimacy of agency action. Hence, when passing laws, Congress should decide all questions of policy, and frame its statutes in such specific terms that administrative regulation will not entail the exercise of broad discretion by the regulators (ibid.).

The nondelegation doctrine had already found widespread acceptance when the first institutionalization of the US regulatory state, the Interstate Commerce Commission, was established by the Interstate Commerce Act of 1887. The Act, with its detailed grant of authority, seemed to exemplify the transmission-belt model of administrative regulation. However, the subsequent experience of railroad regulation revealed the difficulty of deriving operational guidelines from general standards. By the time the Federal Trade Commission was established in 1914, the agency received essentially a blank check authorizing it to eliminate 'unfair competition'. The New Deal agencies received even broader grants of power to regulate particular sectors of the economy 'in the public interest'. The last time the US Supreme Court used the nondelegation doctrine was in 1935, when in *Panama Refining Co. v. Ryan* (293 US 388) and in *Schechter Poultry Corp. v. United States* (295 US 495) it held the delegation in the National Industrial Recovery Act unconstitutional. However, the US Supreme Court's reiteration of the nondelegation principle, coupled with its very sparing use to strike down legislation, illustrates a continuing judicial effort to harmonize the modern regulatory state with traditional notions of separation of powers, representative government, and the rule of law (Mashaw et al. 1998). The reconciliation of decision-making efficiency with respect to basic constitutional principles has been facilitated by a more optimistic assessment of the possibility of controlling agency discretion. It may be instructive to review some of these recent institutional and theoretical

developments, since they undermine many of the objections raised, especially by the legal service of the European Commission, against the delegation of rulemaking powers to independent European agencies.

5.2   Disciplining Agency Discretion

Before the 1980s, when scholars started to apply principal–agent theory to
political-administrative relations, most research tended to cast serious
doubts on the possibility of effectively monitoring and controlling bureaucratic behavior. However, better theoretical models and more careful
empirical analysis have shown that the variety of control instruments
available to political principals is a good deal greater than traditionally
assumed. Moreover, these various instruments may be combined into an
effective, multipronged scheme of control, creating a situation whereby,
to use Moe's words (1990: 143), 'no one controls the agency, and yet the
agency is under control.' Perhaps the key insight of the new research is
that control is to a large extent a question of good institutional and
procedural design, while the older theories tended to view control as
being exercised from one fixed point (the legislature or the executive)
within a given institutional framework. Consider the two traditional
forms of control of agency decisions: *oversight*—monitoring, hearings,
investigations, budgetary reviews, sanctions—and *procedural constraints*.
Resources devoted to oversight have an opportunity cost, since they
could be devoted to achieving politically more rewarding objectives.
Also, most of the methods for imposing meaningful sanctions for noncompliance create costs for the overseers. Thus, a publicly visible investigation and punishment of an agency may raise doubts in the minds of
citizens about the efficiency and honesty of the principals themselves. In
sum, direct oversight of agency behavior is unlikely to be a completely
effective solution to the control problem; it needs to be supplemented by
more indirect and less costly mechanisms of a procedural nature.

   Outstanding examples of procedural control of agency discretion are the
1946 US federal Administrative Procedure Act (APA), and some later statutes that are mentioned below. The APA still provides the most important
general approach to control agency discretion. Prior to it, procedural
requirements imposed by the courts differed across agencies. These included procedures relating to information gathering and disclosure, and
standards of evidence. The most important effects of the Act, therefore,
were to impose greater uniformity across agencies, and to raise minimum

evidentiary standards to which an agency must adhere. Two provisions are particularly relevant to the present discussion. First, a general notice of proposed rulemaking to be published in the Federal Register. The notice must include a statement of the time, place, and nature of public rulemaking proceedings; reference to the legal basis for the proposed rule; a description of the subjects and issues involved. Second, the agency must give interested persons an opportunity to participate in the rulemaking through submission of written data, views, or arguments, with or without opportunity for oral presentation.

The APA has been followed by the Freedom of Information Act (FOIA) passed in 1966 and amended several times since; the Government in the Sunshine Act (GITSA) of 1976; and the Federal Advisory Committee Act (FACA), enacted in 1972 and amended in 1976 to incorporate the GITSA standards for open meetings. The FOIA gives citizens the right to inspect all agency records that do not fall within any of ten specified categories, such as trade secrets and those files whose disclosure could be expected to constitute an invasion of privacy, or compromise a law enforcement investigation. However, even these exceptions are not absolute. To reduce even further the chances that an agency can manipulate the FOIA to its own advantage, the law requires the agency to prove that it need not release the information, rather than requiring the citizen to prove that it should release it. The FOIA was adopted in response to claims that many core documents and other information underlying important agency decisions were not available to the public, thereby impairing the rights of citizens and of the media to monitor government performance.

The GITSA is similarly designed to prevent secrecy in government, but its reach and impact are more limited than the FOIA's. The GITSA applies to agencies headed by collegial bodies, such as the independent regulatory commissions. It obliges such agencies to provide advance notice of meetings at which agency business is to be conducted, and to meet in public unless the members, by majority voting, decide that the matter falls within one of the statutory exemptions. Yet, Congress recognizes the legitimacy of protecting oral deliberations on issues whose resolution could be undermined by premature disclosure, and thus section 9(B) of the GITSA permits closure if discussion would 'disclose information, the premature disclosure of which would ... be likely to significantly frustrate implementation of a proposed agency action'. The narrow terms of this exception, however, make closure difficult in most cases (Mashaw et al. 1998: 148–52).

The FACA establishes requirements that agencies must follow when consulting groups of individuals who are not federal employees, and it prescribes how such advisory committees shall proceed in rendering their service to the agency. The main requirements for the creation of an advisory committee are the existence of a charter, which must be approved by the General Services Administration; selection of members to ensure diverse views on the issues to be considered; and mandatory expiration, or rechartering after two years. The main obligations of established committees are to publish advance notice of their meetings and to deliberate in public, subject to the GITSA exceptions permitting closure.

In their path-breaking paper on 'Administrative Procedures as Instruments of Control', McCubbins et al. (1987) use the US statutes mentioned above as evidence that procedural rules are not only means of assuring fairness and legitimacy in agency decision-making but they also fulfill important control functions, providing cost-effective solutions to problems of noncompliance by agencies. In addition to reducing the informational disadvantage of political executives, stakeholders, and citizens at large, procedures can be designed so as to assure that agency decisions will be responsive to the constituents that the policy is supposed to favor. For instance, the procedural requirements under the APA, FOIA, and GITSA reduce an expert agency's advantage over its political principals in a number of ways. First, agencies cannot present the political principals with a fait accompli. They must announce their intention to consider an issue well in advance of any decision. Second, the notice-and-comment provisions assure that the agency learns who the relevant stakeholders are, and takes some notice of the distributive impacts associated with various actions. Third, the entire sequence of agency decision-making—notice, comment, collection of evidence, and construction of a record in favor of a chosen action—affords numerous opportunities for political principals to respond when the agency seeks to move in a direction that the principals do not approve of. Finally, the broad public participation, which the statutes facilitate, also works as a gauge of political interest and controversy, providing advance warning about serious distributive consequences of the decisions the agency is likely to make, in the absence of political intervention.

Moreover, by controlling the extent and mode of public participation, legislators can strengthen the position of the intended beneficiaries of the bargain struck by the enacting coalition—the group of legislators that determines the balance of interests represented in the legislation. This has been called 'deck-stacking'. Deck-stacking enables political actors to cause the environment in which an agency operates to mirror the political forces that gave rise to the agency's legislative mandate, long after the enacting coalition has disbanded. The agency may seek to develop a new clientele for its services, but such an activity must be undertaken in full view of the members of the initial coalition, and following procedures that automatically integrate certain interests in agency decision-making. In sum, one important function of procedures is to induce regulatory agencies to take into account broad, politically salient concerns such as environmental quality, or the competitiveness of small and medium-sized enterprises.

5.3   Rulemaking in the EU

In the United States, a realistic appreciation of the functional needs of the modern regulatory state, as well as the influence of theories asserting the possibility of controlling agency discretion by better procedures, contributed to the progressive weakening of the nondelegation doctrine. In the EU, the debate on delegation of rulemaking powers has developed along lines quite different, not only from the US experience but also from that of the member states. The EU equivalent of the US nondelegation doctrine is the *Meroni* doctrine, enunciated by the ECJ in 1958 (Case 9/56 *Meroni v. High Authority* [1957–8] ECR 133). The case relates specifically to the ECSC Treaty, but the doctrine is generally assumed to remain 'good law', applying *mutatis mutandis* to all European treaties and acting as a rigid barrier to the delegation of regulatory responsibilities to institutions or bodies not named within the treaties. In the Court's reasoning, the Commission could, in fact, delegate certain tasks to administrative agencies. However, in line with a 'democratic' concern that continuing and direct oversight need be maintained, such a delegation was subject to strict conditions (Lenaerts 1993):

- delegation might only relate to powers that the Commission itself possesses;
- such assignment must relate to the preparation and performance of executive acts alone;
- as a consequence of this, independent bodies may not be afforded any discretionary powers;
- the Commission must therefore retain oversight over the delegated competence and will be held responsible for the manner in which it is performed;

- finally, such a delegation must not disturb the 'balance of powers' among European institutions.

It is interesting to note that the judicial doctrine of institutional balance ('balance of powers') was formulated for the first time in *Meroni*. According to the Court, such a balance is a characteristic of the institutional structure of the Community and must be seen as 'a fundamental guarantee granted by the Treaty in particular to the undertakings ... to which it applies'. The Court concluded that 'to delegate a discretionary power, by entrusting it to bodies other than those the Treaty has established to effect and supervise the exercise of such power within the limits of its own authority, would render the guarantee ineffective.' Although European courts (the ECJ and the Court of First Instance) continue to consider *Meroni* as good law, doubts about the continued relevance of the doctrine have been raised by several legal scholars who point out that the situation that gave rise to that case—the delegation of certain discretionary tasks to private associations—is quite different from the current issue of delegating powers to European public law agencies. Moreover, the arguments sketched in Section 5.2 show that the Court's view of control is too narrow, and theoretically outdated: accountability and independence are not mutually exclusive. Even admitting the continued relevance of the old doctrine, its conditions would be satisfied as long as the Commission retains certain control powers. For example, a system in which an agency such as the European Agency for the Evaluation of Medicinal Products (EMEA) could autonomously adopt marketing authorizations for new medical drugs would be in line with the doctrine as long as the Commission retained the power to disallow decisions that it found contrary to European law or to the 'common interest'. In other words, other mechanisms of control, more respectful of agency autonomy, might have met the demands of the ECJ. According to the Framework Directive 2002 on telecommunications, for example, National Regulatory Authorities (NRAs) must be independent, but the Commission is authorized to suspend, for a period of two months, draft regulations the NRAs may propose, if such regulations could create barriers to the internal market, or if they appear to be incompatible with European policy objectives, regulatory principles, or law. After two months, the Commission may take a decision requiring the NRA to withdraw its draft regulation. In other words, the Commission can veto an NRA when it regards a draft measure to be incompatible with European rules, and it is hard to see why it could not monitor in the same way an independent European agency. The fact that in the case of the EMEA or of the European Food Safety Authority (EFSA) a much more restrictive option has in fact been chosen is interpreted to show that, in addition to legal concerns, considerations of institutional self-interest played a role in the definition of agencies' powers (Dehousse 2002).

In order to better understand the position of the Commission it should be remembered that since the SEA, the delegation of implementing powers by the Council to the Commission has become the norm (see Chapter 4). As the ECJ ruled in *Commission v. Council* (Case 16/88 [1989] ECR 3457), 'after the amendments made to Article 145 by the SEA, the Council may reserve the right to exercise implementing powers directly only in specific cases, and it must state in detail the grounds for such a decision' (cited in Lenaerts 1993: 36). 'Implementation', according to the Court, includes both rulemaking and adjudication. Hence, once the Council has decided to transfer executive authority to the Commission, it can be expected that the latter will exercise its implementing powers fully and will stubbornly oppose any delegation of powers to independent agencies. Any softening of this position, it is feared, would entail the loss of treaty-based and judicially affirmed competences. The *Meroni* doctrine and the principle of institutional balance provide the crucial rationalization of the Commission's position.

An important reason for the distinction between delegation to the Commission, which may involve wide discretionary powers, and the case covered by *Meroni*, namely, delegation to other bodies (including independent agencies), which may be only of a very limited nature, is the widespread system of committees of national representatives through which the Council can control the exercise of the delegated powers by the Commission. Having made delegation of rulemaking powers to the Commission practically mandatory, Article 145 sought to reestablish the institutional balance between Council and Commission by adding that in delegating implementing powers the Council may impose certain requirements on the exercise of such powers. These requirements were spelled out by a Council Decision of July 13, 1987, the so-called Comitology Decision, and further elaborated in the Second Comitology Decision of June 28, 1999. Under the comitology system, the Council establishes a committee, composed of representatives of national governments, to which the Commission must submit drafts of measures it intends to adopt under the delegated power. There are two main types of such committees: advisory and oversight, the latter being again subdivided into 'management' and 'regulatory' committees. Advisory committees have no formal power to prevent the Commission to act as it wishes, while the other two types can limit the Commission's discretion. Under a management committee procedure, the Commission can enact an implementing measure unless the committee opposes the measure by qualified majority, in which case the matter is referred back to the Council. Under the regulatory committee procedure, of which there are two variants, the Commission can enact the measure only if the committee supports the measure (by qualified majority), otherwise the matter is referred to the Council. In other words, under the management committee procedure it is easier for the national representatives to approve the Commission's proposed implementation measure than to refer it to the Council, while under the regulatory committee procedure the situation is reversed.

The Comitology Decision does not specify the cases in which a particular procedure, or a particular variant of a given procedure, should be adopted. It is therefore up to the Commission to propose the procedure to be followed, and up to the Council to accept, or to reject by unanimity, the proposal. While the Commission and the EP favor advisory committees, particularly for internal market legislation, the Council generally prefers regulatory committees. Even in the case of such committees, however, the Commission is not only in the chair, but has a strong presumption in its favor. Several empirical studies report that Commission officials generally do not think that their comitology committee significantly reduces their discretion, and even less that it has been set up to assure the member states' control, rather than providing information. As a matter of fact, the Council acts only rarely on the complex technical matters dealt with by the committees, but when it does, its decisions mostly support the Commission's original proposal.

The Commission seems to feel that, on balance, the advantages of the comitology system outweigh its disadvantages. The ECJ agrees with this assessment. In *Rey Soda* (Case 23/75 [1975]), for example, the Court pointed out that under the comitology system the Council can delegate exceptionally wide powers of rulemaking, while reserving the right to intervene where necessary. In *Tedeschi v. Denkavit Commerciale* (Case 5/77 [1977]) it argued that even the strictest variant of the regulatory-committee procedure does not necessarily lead to a deadlock in decision-making, since the Commission is always free to submit a new proposal. One final observation before turning to the issue of European agencies: the preference for the Commission over the Council as the institution responsible for the execution of Community legislation may be seen as an imperfect attempt to introduce a kind of separation of powers between the legislature (Council and EP) and the Commission as the executive branch. That the attempt was so half-hearted suggests that the member states are aware of the radical difference between the principle of separation of powers and the philosophy of the Community method (see Chapter 3).

5.4   The Debate on Independent European Agencies

Coming back to the *Meroni* nondelegation doctrine, it should be noted that even within the Commission, not everybody shares the official position. A number of Commission officials now openly advocate the creation of independent European regulatory agencies. Several factors explain the rise of an internal prodelegation faction. First, the advantages of delegation in terms of decision-making efficiency are now widely appreciated, especially by the younger Brussels technocrats. Also, the credibility problems of EU regulation are more clearly perceived after the bovine spongiform encephalopathy (BSE) ('mad cow' disease) crisis. This crisis not only revealed the failure to establish a stable and internationally credible community of scientific experts but also exposed serious inadequacies in the overall coordination of European policies on agriculture, the internal market, and human and animal health. The comitology system, with its division of scientific tasks between committees of national experts dealing with individual issues of animal and human health, has been identified as contributing to the dangerous confusion between the pursuit of market integration, agricultural policy objectives, and the protection of human health. But as interviews I conducted in Brussels between February 2001 and April 2002 have revealed, probably the most important factor is the continuous loss of prestige and influence of the institution, especially since the fall of the Santer Commission in 1999 (Majone 2002). To ambitious technocrats, now working in various services of the Commission and with a long career still in front of them, an independent European agency could represent a safe haven where their expertise would find recognition, without having to sacrifice their privileges as international functionaries.

Partly because of this internal dissent, the issue of regulatory agencies is no longer taboo in Brussels. The Commission's leadership is aware that European regulations suffer from a serious credibility problem. The agency model, which is becoming increasingly popular in the member states, is seen as a promising solution to this problem, but only within the constraints of *Meroni* and of institutional balance, and as long as the Commission's control over the agencies is not only maintained but if possible even increased. True, the refusal to delegate the Commission's regulatory powers is not as absolute as in the past. It is now conceded that agencies may, under some conditions, take individual decisions in specific technical areas; but they cannot adopt general regulatory measures, take decisions 'in areas in which they would have to arbitrate conflicting public interests, exercise political discretion or carry out complex economic assessments', or assume responsibilities for which the treaty has conferred a direct power of decision on the Commission (Commission 2001: 43). In sum, the only formula that seems to be acceptable to the Brussels authorities is an oxymoron: a regulatory agency without regulatory powers. In the meanwhile, the number of European agencies continues to grow, forcing the Commission to elaborate a new doctrine of partial delegation.

5.5 The New Framework

The current official position on delegation is presented in a Communication on *The Framework for European Regulatory Agencies* of December 11, 2002 (Commission 2002). This document is useful not only for understanding the traditional thinking of the Commission's leadership on this specific problem but more generally as further proof of the limited capacity of the Community method to adapt to new tasks and new situations. Hence the attention devoted to the Communication in the following pages.

   At the time of writing (October 2003), there are fifteen agencies created under the EC Treaty—ranging from the European Centre for the Development of Vocational Training and the European Foundation for the Improvement of Living and Working Conditions, both established in 1975, to the three bodies created in 2002: the EFSA, the European Maritime Safety Agency, and the European Aviation Safety Agency. Four more bodies have been established under the second and the third pillar of the EU: the European Police Office (Europol) established by the Convention of July 26, 1995; the European Union Institute for Security Studies (Joint Action of July 20, 2001); the European Union Satellite Centre (Joint Action of July 20, 2001); and Eurojust (the prosecution agency established by Council Decision of February 28, 2002). Of the fifteen Community agencies, the Communication identifies the profiles of two main types: executive and regulatory. Executive agencies are 'responsible for purely managerial tasks, i.e. assisting the Commission in implementing the Community's financial support programmes and are subject to strict supervision by it' (Commission 2002: 3), while '[t]he concept of European Regulatory Agency designates agencies required to be actively involved in exercising the executive function by enacting instruments which contribute to regulating a specific sector' (ibid.: 4). Three groups of such 'regulatory' agencies are identified: (1) agencies, such as EMEA and EFSA, whose function is primarily to provide assistance in the form of opinions and recommendations, which form the technical and scientific basis for the Commission's decisions; (2) agencies, like the European Maritime Safety Agency, providing assistance in the form of inspection reports, in order to enable the Commission to meet its responsibilities as guardian of EC law; and (3) agencies empowered to adopt individual decisions that are legally binding on third parties: the Office for Harmonization in the Internal Market (Trademark Office), the Community Plant Variety Office, and the European Aviation Safety Agency.

Until now, European agencies have been created on an ad hoc basis. The Communication presents several new proposals that, if implemented, would introduce some interesting innovations with respect to current practice. One such innovation concerns the legal basis. In the past, agencies were created using Article 308 EC (former Article 235). It will be recalled that this Article enables the Council—acting by unanimity, on a proposal from the Commission and after consulting the EP—to take measures that should prove necessary to attain one of the objectives of the Community, as long as the Treaty has not provided the necessary powers. Now it is proposed that the legal basis for establishing an agency be the same as that which authorizes the corresponding policy. The argument is convincing: since the regulatory agency is an instrument of implementation of a specific European policy, the legal act creating it should be based on the same provision of the treaty which constitutes the specific legal basis for that policy. This logic has already been followed in the creation of the EFSA and of the two agencies dealing with aviation and maritime safety. It should be noted that this innovation in no way affects the Commission's monopoly of policy initiation—it is always up to the Commission to decide whether an agency is needed in a given policy area—but it changes significantly the role of the EP. Under Article 308 the EP has only to be consulted. Hence its very limited ability to affect the institutional design and powers of the existing agencies. But if the basis of the legal instrument creating the agency is the same treaty provision that authorizes the policy the agency is supposed to (help to) implement, then in all areas of codecision (i.e. in most internal market legislation) the EP should be able to influence the design of the agency, rather than seeing its proposals ignored by the other European institutions. For this very reason, however, this sensible proposal may be opposed by the member states.

Concerning organizational arrangements, the Communication challenges the composition of the management (or administrative) boards of existing agencies. These boards are the steering bodies of the agencies, having responsibility for defining their general operating guidelines and work programs, approving their budgets, and appointing their executive directors. At present, the boards are composed of one or two representatives of each member state and a Commission representative; in some cases, they also include members appointed by the EP or by the social partners. The Commission argues that such arrangements are administratively too cumbersome, especially in view of the enlargements of the Union, and too dominated by the member states. Because of the numerical dominance of the national representatives, it is claimed, the boards fail to take sufficient account of the Community interest. The Communication proposes smaller boards where national and supranational interests are more evenly represented. Concretely, it suggests a fifteen-member administrative board, consisting of six representatives appointed by the Commission, six by the Council, and three, with no voting rights, representing the interested parties.

In an earlier proposal for the organization of the EFSA, the Commission had suggested that the management board of that body should include four representatives appointed by the Council, four by the Commission, four by the EP, and four representatives of consumers and industry, to be designated by the Commission. This proposal, and a similar arrangement for the European Maritime Safety Agency, were rejected by the member states. In the case of the EFSA, however, the member states did draw some lessons from the BSE crisis. They recognized the need to give up, at least in part, the principle of national representation in the board in order to stress its independence and the scientific quality of its advice on food safety. In the end, the member states accepted the idea of rotating management board members from different countries of origin. However, the principle of national representation was again adhered to in the case of the maritime and aviation safety agencies. Hence, it seems doubtful that in the future the member states will accept the idea of smaller boards, with rotating national representatives and an equal number of Commission representatives.

Another new proposal may have better chances of being accepted. While in the past the Commission always pleaded in favor of including EP representatives in the boards, now it argues that appointments by the EP are 'inappropriate in view of the regulatory agencies' work and the fact that the Parliament must be free to exercise external political supervision over their activities, without feeling tied by its membership of the administrative board' (Commission 2002: 9). The point is well taken, since most agencies depend, at least for part of their revenue, on subsidies from the EU budget. As noncompulsory expenditures, these subsidies are ultimately determined by the EP. Discharge for the implementation of agency budgets being given by the Parliament (on the recommendation of the Council), the presence of members of the Parliament in the agency boards could create situations of conflict of interest. Finally, the Communication proposes a procedure for the appointment or dismissal of agency directors that would greatly strengthen the influence of the Commission. At present, the appointment of the director is one of the most important functions of the management boards, which, as we saw, are largely dominated by the member states. The new proposal differentiates between decision-making agencies and those agencies that only assist the Commission in the implementation of regulatory policies. In the former case, appointment (and dismissal) should be by the Commission on the basis of a list of candidates put forward by the board, while in the case of 'executive' agencies the procedure is reversed: appointment by the management board from a list of candidates put forward by the Commission. Making the Commission the appointing authority in the case of the decision-making agencies is necessary, it is argued, if the Commission 'is to assume its responsibility for the executive function at European level effectively while respecting the autonomy of the decision-making agency'. The director must be able to gain and maintain the confidence of the administrative board and, 'especially, of the Commission as the authority ultimately in charge of implementation' (Commission 2002: 10).

5.6   The Limits of Partial Delegation

Although the Commission has modified its traditional stance on a number of points concerning the organization and the functioning of European agencies, on the central issue of the delegation of rulemaking powers its official position has hardly changed: agencies may not be empowered to make rules, i.e. quasi-legislative measures of general applicability. The only exception to a strict nondelegation doctrine—as in the 2001 White Paper on *European Governance*—is the admission that agencies may be allowed to adopt individual decisions in clearly specified areas of Community legislation, 'where a single public interest predominates and where they do not have to arbitrate on conflicting public interests, exercise powers of political judgement or make complex economic assessments' (Commission 2002: 11). The Office of Harmonization in the Internal Market, the Community Plant Variety Office, and the European Aviation Safety Agency have been deemed to satisfy these conditions and hence allowed to adopt legally binding decisions in the adjudication of particular applications. In these three cases, it is claimed, the task is simply to verify that individual applications satisfy certain conditions precisely defined by the relevant European regulations. However, the EMEA and the EFSA seem to satisfy the same conditions: EMEA is exclusively concerned with the safety and efficacy of new medical drugs; EFSA, with the safety of the food we eat. In both cases, the relevant criteria are precisely defined by European regulations. Yet, these agencies have been denied real decision-making power: the Commission makes the final determinations, on the recommendation by the agency and subject to the usual comitology control. It is true that the tasks of the EMEA and of the EFSA are scientifically more complex than those of the three decision-making agencies, but since the Commission has no expertise in scientific matters, it is difficult to see how it could improve the quality of the regulatory process. The only relevant difference between the two groups of agencies seems to be that the EMEA and the EFSA are economically and politically much more significant than the three above-mentioned agencies. Thus the refusal to delegate decision-making powers to the EMEA and the EFSA reveals the Commission's unwillingness to surrender control over these agencies and the activities they are supposed to regulate.

The compromise solutions adopted in these two cases entail costs that a clearer delegation of authority would avoid. As EMEA executives complain, the need to wait for the Commission's formal decision means that precious time is lost before a new, possibly life-saving, product reaches the market. Moreover, the present situation blurs the line of accountability, and because of its ambiguity presents risks for the Commission itself, which some day might be called upon to bear the responsibility of decisions in whose formation it did not play any substantive role. In the case of the EFSA, the tension between the desire to improve the credibility of Community regulation by appealing to independent scientific expertise and the refusal to delegate regulatory powers to the agency has been temporarily resolved by the doubtful expedient of an institutional separation of risk assessment—the task assigned to the Authority—and risk management, which remains the responsibility of the Commission. Such institutional separation has been tried before, usually with disappointing results. For example, the US Occupational Safety and Health Act of 1970 created the National Institute for Occupational Safety and Health (NIOSH), directing it to perform research and risk assessments for the newly established regulatory agency, the Occupational Safety and Health Administration (OSHA). While NIOSH is an independent agency within the Department of Health and Human Services, OSHA has been placed within the Department of Labor—an institutional design largely dictated by political reasons. This organizational separation, however, yielded functional separation to only a limited extent. On the one hand, NIOSH's 'criteria documents' not only provided risk assessments but also recommended occupational standards. On the other, OSHA tended to take on more of the risk assessment function itself. Gradually the agency with regulatory responsibilities asserted control over the entire standard-setting process. The reason: 'despite its separation from OSHA, or indeed perhaps because of it, NIOSH's criteria documents were often found to be deficient as bases for issuing standards. OSHA regulators found them to be little beyond compendium summaries of the literature, with little effort to evaluate the quality of relevant studies or to resolve scientific disputes. The lesson appears to be that such complete organizational separation of functions is counterproductive' (Greenwood 1984: 118).

There are indications that the EU may be experiencing somewhat similar problems. In fact, the new regulatory framework for genetically modified (GM) food and feed keeps to a minimum the involvement of the EFSA in the authorization procedure. The Authority is not consulted systematically on all issues pertaining to the safety of GM food or feed and products. In some cases, decisions are taken by the Commission, in the framework of comitology committees, without consulting the Authority at all. Furthermore, the member states and the Commission can decide on an application to market GM food and feed disregarding the scientific opinion expressed by EFSA, as long as they state the reason for departing from the Authority's opinion. This creates the impression that the Commission and national governments can in practice ignore EFSA's opinions (Poli 2003). Moreover, if it is true that risk assessment and risk management are not separable in practice, then it follows that accountability and efficiency are best achieved when responsibility for the entire regulatory process is concentrated in the head of an expert agency, rather than being diffused in a collegial body of political executives or bureaucratic generalists such as the Commission. As in the case of pharmaceuticals, so in the case of food safety, the refusal to delegate powers to a truly independent agency creates a serious accountability deficit, as well as a growing credibility problem for European regulations.

In the first part of this chapter we saw that many mechanisms to control agency discretion are available. Many countries, in Europe and elsewhere, are today adapting such mechanisms to their constitutional and administrative framework in an effort to reconcile agency independence with accountability. With its stubborn opposition to any significant delegation of regulatory powers, the Commission is trying, like a latter-day King Canute, to stem the tide of regulatory reform that is sweeping the industrialized world. This opposition is perhaps the clearest indication of the difficulty of introducing significant institutional innovations within the framework of the Community method. The root of this difficulty lies in the nature of the method, with interest representation and institutional balance as its organizing principles (see Chapter 3). As Jean Paul Jacqué has argued, it is simply not possible for Community institutions to achieve more than incremental adjustments: 'For a significant evolution to take place it would be necessary that an institution renounces to exercise its prerogatives to align its position on that of another institution. This is hardly conceivable since each institution is the representative of interests which it is its duty to protect' (Jacqué 1991: 252; my translation). This inability to innovate is the main reason why the Community method, which for several decades has been a powerful engine of market integration, is increasingly perceived as too rigid to accommodate the needs of an increasingly complex and diverse polity.

5.7   Regulatory Reform

Given the rigidity of the present legal framework, how is reform of European regulatory policies and institutions possible? Under the Community method only the Commission can set the reform agenda; hence no significant departures from current practice may be expected. But without far-reaching reforms the credibility crisis of European regulation can only deepen. This dilemma can be resolved only by going outside the traditional framework. This could be done following two different strategies, which, if properly implemented, could be mutually reinforcing rather than mutually exclusive.

The key idea of the first strategy is that the growing complexity of policymaking at European level should be matched by greater functional differentiation, in particular, by explicitly assigning an autonomous role to European regulatory networks comprising national, subnational, and EU bodies, operating in the various areas of regulatory policymaking. This autonomous role would be acknowledged in all areas of regulation not assigned by the Treaty to the exclusive responsibility of the Commission. This institution's repeatedly declared aspiration to become the sole European executive makes even more urgent the need of a functional separation of regulation, as a distinctive mode of policymaking, from general executive powers. The operational model, with all the necessary adaptations, is the European System of Central Banks (see below), but the basic idea of a functional differentiation between the executive and the regulatory functions is well expressed by the notion of a 'fourth branch of government'. This expression was introduced by American scholars precisely to emphasize the distinctiveness and underlying unity of the regulatory process, as well as its importance to modern governance. This process, the expression suggests, is not simply an extension, or a subdivision, of the executive power. Rather, to quote one of the most distinguished students and practitioners of regulation in the United States: 'In the grant [to the regulatory process] of that full ambit of authority necessary for it in order to plan, to promote, and to police, it presents an assemblage of rights normally exercisable by government as a whole. Moreover, its characteristic is the concept of governance, limited, of course, within those boundaries derived from its constituent statutory authority' (Landis 1966 [1938]: 15).

At present, the lack of a European administrative infrastructure means that between the supranational level of rulemaking and the national level of enforcement there is an institutional vacuum, which is supposed to be filled by the loyal cooperation of the national authorities. Unfortunately, in many cases such cooperation is not forthcoming, while significant differences in the resources, expertise, and political independence of national regulators—differences that can only increase within the enlarged EU—impede a uniform application of the common rules. One important function of a European 'fourth branch of government' would be to fill this institutional vacuum by straddling the line that still separates the supranational and the national, or subnational, levels of regulatory governance. This would send a clear message to the various economic and social interests, whose plans depend on a reasonably consistent enforcement of European rules, that henceforth they will be able to operate in a predictable environment.

As suggested above, the European System of Central Banks (ESCB), composed of the ECB and the national central banks, provides a heuristically useful model for the network organizations envisaged here. As we know, the ECB is independent from the European institutions as well as from the national governments, while the national banks must be independent from their respective governments as a condition of membership in the monetary union. Although regulatory agencies, for a number of reasons, cannot, and need not, be as independent as central banks, the broad relevance of the ESCB model is increasingly recognized. For example, two well-known financial experts, Jacques de Larosière and Daniel Lébegue, suggested a few years ago that the growing integration of markets in Europe could lead to the creation of a European system of national regulation in the same vein as the ECB, with decisions taken centrally but applied nationally.

In a sense, the ground for such developments has already been prepared. The new European agencies are not designed to operate in isolation, or to replace national regulators. Rather, they are, or are expected to become, the central nodes of networks comprising the national and subnational agencies of the member states in a given area of regulation. Already today some of these networks include the agencies of European countries that are not members of the EU, and have strong links to international organizations. To qualify as full-fledged regulatory networks, however, the European agencies and their national counterparts need autonomous powers of rulemaking, adjudication, and enforcement, and a clear legal basis for their independence from the Commission as well as from the national executives. Independence is important not only to enhance credibility but also to ensure that policies are developed to solve concrete regulatory problems in the best possible way, rather than to pursue integration or other political objectives, as discussed in Chapter 6.

A regulatory agency that sees itself as a member of a network of institutions pursuing similar objectives and facing analogous problems, rather than as part of a general bureaucracy pursuing a variety of objectives, is more motivated to defend its professional standards and policy commitments against external influences, and to cooperate in good faith with the other members of the network. This is because the agency executives have an incentive to maintain their reputation in the eyes of their colleagues from the other member states. Unprofessional, self-seeking, or politically motivated behavior would compromise their international reputation and make cooperation more difficult to achieve in the future. In other words, the function of a transnational network is not only to permit an efficient division of labor and exchange of information but also to facilitate the development of behavioral standards and working practices that create shared expectations and enhance the effectiveness of the social mechanisms of reputational enforcement.

5.8   Self-Regulation

Greater reliance on self-regulation is the second strategy of regulatory reform. This mode of regulation has a long tradition among the crafts and the professions, but in recent times it has extended into many other areas such as technical standardization, industrial safety, and financial services. Self-regulation offers a number of important advantages with respect to government regulation, along with some potential problems to be mentioned in Section 5.9. A self-regulatory organization (SRO) can normally command a greater degree of expertise and technical knowledge of practices within the relevant area than a public agency. What is even more important, as a private 'club' (see Section 5.9), an SRO can tailor its standards to the specific needs of its members in a way that no public agency can do. Also, the rules issued by a private body are less formalized, and this informality reduces the cost of rulemaking, facilitates quick adaptation of the rules to new technical knowledge and changing economic conditions, and permits more flexible enforcement. In terms of speed and efficiency, the superiority of self-regulation over direct government regulation is significant.

These advantages explain why technical standardization has been delegated to SROs in most industrialized countries, with generally good results. Some authors argue that it is not acceptable, either legally or politically, to delegate to private organizations responsibility for the safety of the citizens and the quality of the products they use. However, these arguments assume a distinction between the public and the private sector that in the area of standard-setting is far from being clear. Many technical standards are set through a consensus process that requires government officials as well as industry representatives to be made party to any consensus. From the point of view of citizens' welfare, the efficiency of a standard is much more important than its public or mandatory nature. Even in sensitive areas like occupational health and safety, the superiority of mandatory standards is far from clear. As Mendeloff (1988) has shown in the context of US regulation of the workplace, federal standards are usually too strict and costly relative to the benefits they confer. At the same time, the slow pace of standard-setting by public agencies means that many serious hazards are never addressed at all: overregulation, in the sense of excessively strict or elaborate standards, causes underregulation.

Also, in the EU self-regulation is nothing new. The New Approach to technical standardization—introduced in 1985 after the failure of the attempt to regulate all product-specific details by directives—delegates the task of standard-setting to SROs, the European standardization bodies. Technical specifications worked out by these bodies are not legally binding, but national authorities are obliged to presume that products manufactured in accordance with European standards satisfy the essential health and safety requirements spelled out in the relevant directive. The new strategy has been an undeniable success in terms of legislative output, but by leaving a number of important issues unresolved, it has revealed once more the difficulty of adapting the Community method to the complexity of regulatory tasks. A crucial problem is that in many, perhaps most, New Approach directives the essential requirements are expressed in such general terms that risk assessment is impossible without the support of detailed technical standards set by the European SROs. Thus the Commission is confronted by a dilemma that cannot be resolved within the existing framework. On the one hand, the sharp distinction of (legally binding) regulation and (voluntary) standardization was necessary in order to allow internal market legislation to advance rapidly. On the other hand, the private-law nature of the SROs implies that European standards can only be voluntary, with all the legal uncertainty entailed by a situation where standards that are de jure voluntary often become binding de facto (Previdi 1997). One way out of this dilemma would be the creation of independent regulatory agencies, which, like the Consumer Product Safety Commission and other US agencies, would defer to a voluntary standard if such a standard is being developed by industry, but had the authority to convert a voluntary standard into a mandatory one if they deem that compliance is unsatisfactory. As we know, this solution is rejected by the Commission, but also by many member states.

Even more problematic is the fact that, in spite of the relative success of the New Approach, the Commission does not really believe in the value of self-regulation as such, having delegated certain technical tasks to the European standards organizations only in order to speed up the legislative process. This was made clear by the 1990 Green Paper on the *Development of European Standardization: Action for Faster Technological Integration in Europe*, and by the extremely critical reaction by the SROs and by industry to its proposals. The idea of the Green Paper was to achieve a better control of the standard-setting process by imposing a 'Europeanized' administrative structure on top of the standards organizations (Joerges et al. 1999). The Commission proposed to create a European Standardization System that would define the role of all participants in the standard-setting process, at national and European levels, and ensure the coordination of European standardization by applying common rules to all organizations within the System. The reaction of the standards organizations, which were asked to surrender much of their power in favor of the Commission and of a new layer of Eurobureaucracy, was predictably negative. The proposals to create new sectoral standardization organizations and new bureaucratic controls over the existing SROs were particularly resented.

Other criticisms concerned the Commission's neglect of international standardization, its sole focus on EC-mandated standards, and its basic misunderstanding of operating practices in the standard-setting process—exemplified by the proposal to introduce majority voting instead of the usual consensus approach. The Commission was forced to withdraw most of its proposals, but it is still trying to achieve better control of the European standardization process by other means. Because of the legalistic culture prevailing in Brussels, the Commission finds it difficult to accept the idea that what is important about a standard is less its mandatory or voluntary character than its efficiency, and the ability to satisfy the needs of its users rather than general bureaucratic requirements. These are precisely the properties emphasized by recent economic models of self-regulation.

5.9   Standards as 'Club Goods'

The reluctance to accept the logic of self-regulation is largely due to the belief that, *ex ante*, top-down harmonization of product standards is necessary for the free movement of goods in the Single European Market. In reality, top-down harmonization is less essential to market integration than it was once thought. Research has shown not only that an initial difference in standards need not distort trade but that it is trade itself that leads to their (*ex post*) convergence. This is because standards concerning environmental quality, risk control, or consumer protection are positively correlated with the standard of living. Thus, as wealth grows as a result of free trade, the endogenous demand for higher standards grows as well. It follows that the *ex ante* harmonization of standards as a precondition of free trade can actually be counterproductive since it may prevent or limit trade, and the wealth effects that trade produces (Casella 1996).

Historical traditions may also militate against a full acceptance of self-regulation. There is a strong historical link between standardization and the emergence of the sovereign territorial state (Spruyt 1994), and although the EU is not a state, state- or Euro-centric ideas still prevail in Brussels. Current views of standardization have changed radically, however, as a result of the development of technology and the advance of globalization. Standards are indeed public goods—in the sense that they fulfill specific functions deemed desirable by the community that shares them—but this does not mean that they must be established by government fiat. A good standard must reflect the preferences, resources, and technical constraints of the community of users, rather than some centrally defined vision of the 'common interest'. The fact that in today's integrating world economy the relevant community of standards users need not be territorially defined distinguishes the traditional view from the contemporary understanding of standards as a special class of public goods known as 'club goods'.

As we saw in Chapter 1, the properties of *joint supply* and *nonexcludability* define what the literature of public finance refers to as 'pure public goods'. If only the joint supply property is retained, i.e. it is assumed that exclusion is possible, then we have 'club goods' (Buchanan 1965). A voluntary association established to provide excludable public goods is a 'club'. If many such clubs are available, the risk of discrimination is minimized. If optimal club sizes are large relative to the population, however, discrimination is possible and stable equilibria may not exist. In such a situation, the normative concerns expressed in the past about the delegation of powers to SROs are understandable. Such delegation has been held to be inadmissible for at least three reasons. First, the safety requirements are formulated in such vague terms as to give standard-setting bodies the power to define the level of risk the public is exposed to. Second, there is the practical impossibility of exercising legislative controls over the SROs. Finally, there is the lack of internal democracy within these bodies: industrial interests are said to be overrepresented, while diffuse public interests are not sufficiently represented. As noted above, these criticisms—developed in historical contexts where a few SROs were given near-monopoly powers—lose much of their point where many 'clubs' are available. This tends to be the situation in expanding markets.

It has been shown (Casella 1996) that under reasonable assumptions, the number of clubs increases as the size of the market increases. Two elements determine the optimal number of clubs: one is the cost of producing the standards ('club fees'); the other is the cost of an inappropriate standard (see also Chapter 1). Because a standard represents a public good, its cost is shared by the members of the club producing it, while the cost of an inappropriate standard is borne separately by each club member. As the market expands, for example as a consequence of the merging of different national markets, the number of standards also expands because the increase in the variety of goods makes necessary a more finely tuned targeting of the public goods provided by the standards, such as product quality, safety, or equipment compatibility. The standards required for transactions in a more diverse market are likely to be both more sophisticated and more costly. Because of the larger size of the club, the cost of the standard (the club fee) is shared between more members, but the standard is less precisely tailored to individual needs, hence more costly to the individual club members. This implies that for a sufficiently large increase in market size the optimal number of standard-setting SROs must increase.

The general implication of the model of standards as club goods is that top-down harmonization is desirable only when the market is small and relatively homogeneous. In a large market, harmonization tends to be brought about, not by a policy imposed from the top, but simply through the recognition of similar preferences or similar needs (e.g. for producers in the same industry). This conclusion is supported by empirical evidence. Already some ten years ago, the OECD observed that all industrialized countries tend to converge towards a greater emphasis on self-regulation and nonmandatory standards—hence towards a greater variety of standards and standard-setting organizations. A large market like the United States is remarkable for the high decentralization of its standardization system. There are literally hundreds of organizations involved in the development of standards. The American National Standards Institute (ANSI), a private organization, coordinates private standards, approves standards as American National Standards, and represents the United States in international standards organizations. In practice, however, only about half of all standard-setting organizations participate in the ANSI system, and several organizations that do not participate, such as the American Society of Testing, are as well known internationally as ANSI (Casella 1996).

At the same time, the US regulatory system is characterized by the presence of powerful independent agencies that are perfectly capable of monitoring the activities of the private bodies, as well as filling any gaps in the system. In contrast, we have seen that the Community method represents a serious obstacle to the emergence both of a variety of self-regulatory organizations—corresponding to the expanding size of the Single European Market—and of independent European agencies with real powers of rulemaking and standard-setting. Alternative, more flexible, approaches are needed, and self-regulation has an important role to play in removing the statist bias of the Commission, and in bringing about a better fit between standards and the diverse preferences of the citizens of an enlarged Union.

6

Policy Dilemmas

6.1 Confusing Means with Ends

As already suggested in previous chapters, under the Community method policy is largely epiphenomenal—the by-product of actions undertaken to advance the integration process, of efforts to maintain 'institutional balance', of interinstitutional conflicts and intergovernmental bargaining. Absent an effective system of accountability, there are few incentives to engage in efficient problem-solving. The policy that eventually emerges from the attempt to pursue several objectives simultaneously will typically be the best bargain that can be negotiated politically at a given time. Even then, policy outcomes are uncertain since implementation is largely under the control of the national administrations. What has been said of water policy could be adapted to many other cases: in spite of extensive legislation, 'the EU has consistently failed to improve water quality standards in rivers and lakes to such an extent that 25 years of regulatory activity amounts to a case of regulatory failure' (Grant et al. 2000: 201). Policy failure is of course a well-known phenomenon even at the national level, but there voters can express their dissatisfaction by changing the governing majority at the next elections. European elections are not about policy outcomes, and no clearly identifiable policymaker is accountable for results. Hence policy evaluation, policy learning, even feasibility analysis, play a very limited role in the EU policy process.

Some instructive instances of policy failure are discussed in this chapter. They are meant to provide concrete illustrations of some of the points made in previous chapters, and empirical support to the critical analyses to follow. Before discussing specific examples, however, attention should be called to another, broader, consequence of the absence of electoral accountability: the propensity of EU leaders to confuse process with outcome, and to ignore the risks of failure. Take, for example, the two most significant developments of the 1990s: EMU and eastern enlargement. In both cases, an initial political agreement to proceed in a certain direction was celebrated as the achievement of a result of historical significance. It should be clear, however, that the launch of the common currency, and the eastward (and southward) expansion of the Union are only the initial stages of very complex processes, whose possible—as distinct from the desirable—trajectories have never been sufficiently explained to the citizens of the EU. Monetary union among sovereign states with structurally different economies is always a risky venture—recall the fate of the Latin Monetary Union, established by France, Belgium, Italy, and Switzerland in 1865, which was undermined by the monetary manipulations of some members, and came to a speedy end with the Franco-German war of 1870–1. The EU is far from being an optimal currency area, in the sense of being able to make easy domestic adjustments to external shocks. Areas within which factors of production can move readily or are distributed uniformly can establish a common currency with a reasonable chance of success because balance of payments deficits can be corrected by shifting resources between industries, according to conditions of international demand. In the EU, however, there are no adequate adjustment mechanisms, such as labor flexibility and large budget transfers, to act as effective substitutes for the exchange rate. The EU budget remains very small, with no provisions for a stabilization function, and no indication that the member states are willing to expand it. But a situation where monetary policy is centralized, while fiscal policy is conducted at the national level, may well be unsustainable in the long run.

For these and other reasons, a number of distinguished economists, both European and American, have questioned the wisdom of EMU, which they consider a premature move. A Nobel Prize-winning monetarist has gone as far as predicting that EMU will not last more than fifteen years. It is to be hoped of course that Milton Friedman's dire forecast will turn out to be wrong, but the skepticism of academic experts and the warnings of responsible policymakers should at least have induced EU leaders to make preparations for a number of different scenarios. The possibility of a deflationary bias in the monetary union, and a resulting drag on growth in the United States and the rest of the world, was a fairly constant concern of US policymakers throughout the 1990s. Lawrence H. Summers as deputy secretary of the Treasury explicitly pointed to the danger of deflation in early 1996, while White House, Treasury, and State Department officials reiterated these concerns at the G-7 Summit in

Lyon in June 1996 (Henning 2000). The slow economic growth of the Eurozone since the introduction of the common currency suggests that such fears were not completely unfounded.

Even earlier, the president of the Bundesbank had forcefully reminded European leaders that '[m]ore than a single currency, the emerging single European market needs converging policies, which are still not in place in all participating countries. The repeated references to alleged huge savings in transaction costs for the countries of a single currency area are not in the least convincing' (Poehl 1990: 36). At any rate, Poehl added, a joint monetary policy could turn out to be much more expensive than the conceivable savings in transaction costs. As far as Germany was concerned, it 'would be sacrificing a hard currency on the European altar without knowing what we would be getting in return'. Given the economic realities, the willingness of the German government to transfer responsibility for monetary policy to the European level 'can be accounted for only in a broader political perspective, with the long-term objective of creating a political union' (ibid.: 37). Aside from the ill-fated Stability and Growth Pact, few traces of these concerns can be found in official documents or in public statements by EU leaders. The Maastricht Treaty, although extremely detailed on procedural matters, left a number of fundamental policy questions unanswered. In order to make political agreement possible, the question of measures to coordinate economic policies, or to provide compensatory budgetary transfers, was sidestepped. Also, issues of external monetary policy, unitary external representation of the monetary union, exchange rate policy, and political accountability have been left so far unresolved. In sum, EMU is a high-risk strategy, and there is no easy exit option if things go wrong (Tsoukalis 2000), but all these uncertainties and ambiguities have been carefully concealed from the general public. The chosen strategy simply assumes an irrevocable commitment to the single currency, and accords no place to failure.

Also in the case of enlargement, there is a serious mismatch between the precision of the administrative and technical aspects of the accession process, and the deliberate vagueness about the broader economic, political, and institutional implications of expansion on such a scale. Consider, for example, the uncertainties surrounding such issues as labor mobility within the enlarged Union, or the future of the common agriculture policy and of regional aid. Again, the war in Iraq revealed deep differences between the foreign-policy priorities of the future members in Central and Eastern Europe and the position of those countries that, like Germany, France, Belgium, and the Commission itself, favored a multilateral approach to the problem of terrorism. The foreign-policy priorities of the new member states are quite understandable in light of their history and geopolitical situation. Moreover, such differences are bound to persist as long as the former Soviet satellites view the United States as the only credible guarantor of their national sovereignty against possible military threats from a resurgent Russia. What is less understandable is that their unconditional support of US policy in Iraq should have come as a surprise to leaders in Brussels and in some of the national capitals. It is also clear that the former members of the Soviet bloc are not prepared to surrender to the EU their newly recovered national sovereignty—as shown, for instance, by the incredibly low turnout of East European voters at the European elections of June 2004. Again, it has never been explained how these national sensitivities may be reconciled with the 'deepening' of European integration that many EU leaders claim to be pursuing.

A feature common to both EMU and Eastern enlargement is the willingness of European leaders to increase the risk of failure for political reasons that are never made explicit—in fact, that are often denied. The original plans for EMU envisaged no more than a handful of countries (essentially, the Deutsche Mark bloc, plus France), the structural similarities of whose economies seemed to approach the conditions for an optimal currency area. The final decision to start EMU with eleven, soon to become twelve, countries—a decision made possible by a flexible interpretation of the Maastricht parameters—was indeed dictated by political considerations that were never openly discussed. Similarly, the original plans of opening accession negotiations with no more than five countries from Central and Eastern Europe—five being the number favored by the Commission, while the government of Chancellor Kohl would have preferred to start with only Poland, the Czech Republic, and Hungary—were soon superseded by the decision, taken at the Luxembourg European Council in December 1997, to open formal accession negotiations with all ten CEEC (Central and East European Countries) candidates, plus Malta and Cyprus. The reason was again political, with each incumbent member state pushing for its own favored candidate, and the Commission attempting to present enlargement as feasible without an increase in the budget, and without demanding too many sacrifices from the incumbent member states. As Sedelmeier and Wallace (2000: 453) write, these assurances of the Commission 'implied some optimistic assumptions, notably real growth of the budget through annual growth in EU GDP of 2.5 per cent, but politically the important message was that the reforms needed for enlargement were "yesable".'

The remainder of the chapter is divided into two parts. In the first one, I review three particularly instructive examples of policy failure, while the second part is devoted to a critical review of the so-called precautionary approach to risk regulation. Because of its great scientific and cognitive complexity, this area of regulation reveals most clearly the limitations of the current EU approach, including its unwillingness to learn from best international practice.

6.2   Integration versus Conservation

Our first case study deals with a relatively minor policy sector, but has the advantage of illustrating with particular clarity the dilemma between policy effectiveness and adherence to the principles of European integration. Over its more than twenty-year history, the Common Fisheries Policy (CFP) has largely failed in its aim of conserving fishery resources, notwithstanding its seeming institutional advantages over other international fisheries regimes. In 1997 the Food and Agriculture Organization marked nine important stocks managed by the EU as potentially overexploited or depleted. Indeed, North Sea cod is on the verge of extinction. The problem is that the CFP has been shaped more by concerns about Community powers than about effective conservation measures. According to Symes and Crean (1995, cited in Payne 2000: 312) 'the underlying principles of the CFP... have more to do with reinforcing the concept of European unity and cooperation than with effective management of a seriously depleted, highly sensitive and unstable resource. The CFP is a political statement neatly aligned with the Community's general principles, and designed to avoid rocking the European boat.'

Article 38 of the Rome Treaty stated that the rules of the common market would apply to fisheries products, under the same heading as agricultural products. However, it was not until 1970 that Regulations 2141/70 and 2142/70 introduced the first specific measures for the sector. The initial deadlock was broken when, at the end of the 1960s, the applications for membership of the United Kingdom, Ireland, Denmark, and Norway led to predictions of a quadrupling of fish production within the EC. The original six, led by France—at that time the major producing country— eventually settled on the principle of free access, which guarantees that the vessels of a member state should have the right to fish in the waters of any other member state. This was presented as a necessary application to the fisheries sector of the basic nondiscrimination norm of European law.

This interpretation was hotly disputed by the applicant countries, but eventually an agreement was reached on the basis of derogations limiting the access of foreign boats to sensitive inshore fisheries.

The adoption of 200-mile Exclusive Economic Zones (EEZs) by member states in 1977 required the development of a common conservation policy to manage a scarce, shared resource. This was achieved with the adoption, in January 1983, of Regulation 170/83, which established a Community regime for conservation and management of fisheries resources. This constitutes the cornerstone of the current CFP, which since then has been amended—in particular, to deal with successive enlargements—but not fundamentally altered (Lequesne 2000). The most important feature of the conservation policy was the setting of total allowable catches (TACs) for stocks under threat. It is important to note that responsibility for monitoring and enforcement of conservation regulations lies wholly with the member states. The Commission was granted only minimal authority for enforcement, which left it little power to intervene in the face of divergent levels of enforcement among the member states. Thus, three principles have been developed by the member states to guide the implementation of the CFP: equal access to fishing stocks, relative stability of catches, and individual state implementation. The combination of these principles has produced an ineffective conservation policy (Payne 2000).

Paradoxically, the main culprit for the failure of fisheries conservation under the CFP is the otherwise admirable principle of nondiscrimination on the ground of nationality. The application of the nondiscrimination rule to this sector has produced the equal-access principle, which, in the absence of adequate supranational monitoring, has led to high levels of stock exploitation. From the point of view of conservation, the advantage of the EEZs is that the marine biological resources are changed from an international common property—a situation where resources are not exclusively controlled by a single country and hence can be exploited on a first-come, first-served basis—to a national property. The implementation of EEZs gives states greater control over the resources of the sea, and thus greater ability to deal with the problem of overfishing. This potential advantage has been canceled by the implementation of the equal-access principle. Because all EU fishermen can fish in the offshore waters of any member state, the international commons problem has been perpetuated. In turn, the perception that equal access leads to overfishing has led to the loss of the CFP's legitimacy, especially among British and Irish fishermen. These fishermen are inclined to see the CFP as a policy aimed at redistribution rather than conservation, and fear that their compliance with quotas will simply result in foreign fishermen getting the fish (Payne 2000). In 1988 the UK government attempted to deal with the problem of overfishing by passing the Merchant Shipping Act, which required that vessels operating in British waters had to be largely British-owned, and that their crew be largely British citizens. However, in *Factortame* (Case 213/89), the ECJ accepted the argument of Spanish ship owners that the nationality conditions violated the nondiscrimination provision of the Rome Treaty, and ordered the United Kingdom to lift its restrictions.

In spite of the difficulties that the equal-access principle presents for stock conservation, attempts to end it have been unsuccessful. The absence of any serious discussion of modifying the principle, as it applies to this case, suggests that conservation objectives are not considered as important as upholding a core principle of European law, and preserving the policymaking powers of European institutions. In the summer of 2002 Franz Fischler, the agriculture and fisheries commissioner, proposed a radical reform of the fisheries policies, including the virtual closure of the North Sea cod fishing field, and a substantial reduction in the number of fishing trawlers. However, the member states, led by Spain, succeeded in watering down the Commission's reform plan. The agreement finally reached by the fisheries ministers in December 2003 introduces lower annual catches and new restrictions on how often fishing boats can go to sea, but allows fishermen to increase catches of nonthreatened species. Long-term recovery plans will replace the annual rounds of quota setting, which have proved unable to protect fish stocks. The recovery plans also involve tighter policing to enforce the regime. According to Commissioner Fischler, the agreement takes account of the socioeconomic aspects of the problem—fishermen will continue fishing albeit at a reduced level—but is also justifiable in biological terms. However, marine scientists from the International Council for the Exploration of the Seas (ICES), the body advising the Commission, warned about the possibility of a complete collapse in cod stocks, with no eventual recovery. ICES had called for the total shutting down of cod fishing, rather than the 66 percent reduction agreed by the ministers.

The agreement of December 2003 represents the most far-reaching reform of the CFP to date. It is not, however, sufficient to dispel the doubt that the conservation of marine biological resources may be one of a growing number of areas where better policy results could be achieved by the national governments operating outside the constraints imposed by the Community method. Hence a dilemma, which the political leaders of the Union will have to face with increasing frequency in the future: either to renationalize responsibility over a particular area for the sake of greater policy effectiveness; or give to the European level significantly greater powers to monitor implementation of European rules by national governments and private firms.

6.3   Chronicle of a Failure Foretold

Our next case is, in many respects, the classic example of policy failure in the EU. The story is retold here to illustrate the extreme difficulty of reforming European policies, even when failure is generally admitted. To early students of European integration, the Common Agricultural Policy (CAP) represented a working model of the federal union of the future. Here, wrote Lindberg (1963), 'the Community institutions have the power to legislate for the Union as a whole, without being required to refer back to the national parliaments. The progress made in agriculture will be of definite importance for the integrative potential of the EEC' (cited in Rieger 2000: 181). Forty years later we are more inclined to view agriculture as one of the most divisive issues in the EU. It has been suggested that the CAP is best understood as an integral part of the West European welfare state—a 'welfare state for farmers'. However, even critics of the welfare state find that the analogy is unfair. Whatever their negative consequences in terms of economic growth and market flexibility, national welfare policies at least succeeded in reducing interpersonal income inequality in Europe to a much greater extent than, for example, in the United States. In contrast, calculations of the European Commission show that because of the regressive effect of price support, which favors large production units, the top 20 percent of full-time farmers receive about 80 percent of CAP support.

Article 3d of the Rome Treaty provides that the activities of the EEC shall include 'the adoption of a common policy for agriculture'. Such a policy was to be a means of 'establishing a common market and progressively approximating the economic policies of Member States'. The Commission has repeatedly stressed the 'indispensable role' of the CAP in the process of building a united Europe. However, Article 42 of the treaty effectively excludes the production and trade of agricultural products from the scope of the general provisions on competition contained in Articles 85–94 (now Articles 81–9 EC). This exclusion shows that when the treaty was signed, it was assumed that the CAP's objectives could not be achieved through market liberalization, as in the case of industrial products. These objectives are defined in Article 39 (now Article 33): to increase agricultural productivity; ensure a fair standard of living for farmers; stabilize markets; assure the availability of supply; ensure reasonable prices for consumers.

The details of the policy were worked out at a conference held in Stresa in 1958. In the future, the CAP would be guided by three basic principles: a single product market; 'Community preference'—an extreme form of protectionism, which did not allow any link between Community and world prices of agricultural products; and financial solidarity among the member states, meaning that they would share the overall costs of intervention. It soon became clear that the policy was seriously flawed. The CAP's key policy instrument—the variable levy system and price support for grains—became operational in 1964. Only four years later Commissioner Mansholt presented the first reform plans. Already then prices were well above world levels and several commodity regimes were in surplus, but the reforms were rejected by the national governments and powerful farm lobbies. By the 1980s the CAP was producing consequences that adversely affected international trade negotiations also, but all reforms undertaken before 1992 were limited measures of adjustment to the level of prices, or the introduction of additional instruments—such as quotas in 1984 and automatic stabilizers in 1988—to mitigate the effect of price support. The basic structure of price support and the key principles of the CAP remained unchanged. As a consequence, by 1990 it became clear that the ceilings on agricultural spending imposed by the European Council in 1988 would be breached without strict limitations.

However, the reforms proposed by Commissioner Mac Sharry in 1992 were driven more by international factors than by budgetary considerations. It seems unlikely that the Council of Agriculture Ministers would have been able to agree to the proposed measures without the political pressure emanating from the Uruguay Round of GATT (General Agreement on Tariffs and Trade) negotiations—in particular from the United States and the Cairns Group of agricultural exporting countries—to establish a more transparent and liberal economic order in the agriculture support system. The tying of the CAP reform to the Uruguay Round helped ensure that it would survive. The main features of the 1992 reform—cuts in the support prices of key crops, direct income payments to farmers as compensation for the cuts, and a set-aside scheme where farmers were compensated for taking 15 percent of their land out of production—were the first substantial reductions in support prices in the history of the CAP. Yet, these reforms were considered moderate by most independent experts because farm incomes were only partially decoupled from production, and therefore the incentive for increasing production remained, while the original policy objectives enshrined in the treaty were still in place (Kay 2003). Also, the reform measures increased the bureaucratization of the CAP, since the system of direct payments involves substantial paperwork and on-farm regulation of supply through obligations to set land aside.

The international context—the impending enlargement of the EU to Central and Eastern Europe and the preparation for a new round of World Trade Organization (WTO) negotiations—shaped also the Agenda 2000 proposals. Given the size, nature, and role of agriculture in the new member states, it was obvious that to continue the CAP in its present form would be prohibitively costly. The agreement reached at the Berlin Summit in March 1999 continued along the path of the Mac Sharry reform by further reducing guaranteed prices and increasing direct payments to farmers. Although slightly less ambitious than its own proposal, the agreement was greeted by the Commission as 'the most radical reform since the CAP was first established' (cited in Rieger 2000: 203). In reality, it was a slightly improved version of the status quo that prevailed. The new attempt to decouple income support from production in a more radical way by, *inter alia*, making national governments responsible, did not become part of the agreement. Also the attempt to introduce market forces into the agricultural sector, for example by bringing European prices closer to world prices, failed. Again, it is doubtful whether the new instruments for greening the CAP provide enough incentives to change the production methods of those 20 percent of larger and richer farmers responsible for 80 percent of output, who damage the environment the most.

In conclusion, the CAP has achieved, more or less, a single market for agricultural products—albeit at the cost of high prices for European consumers, dissension among the member states, and constant friction with the EU's major trade partners and with developing countries. It has also helped to close the gap between agricultural and nonagricultural personal incomes, but with perverse redistributive effects in favor of the well-to-do farmers. The other policy objectives have been largely missed, and the overall impact of the CAP has been in many respects disastrous. In spite of all this, all five objectives of the CAP set out in the Rome Treaty have been maintained, word for word, by the drafters of the new Constitutional Treaty: the commitment to a special regime for agriculture remains. Could the reason be that the CAP objectives are so general, and in fact mutually inconsistent, that the Council of Agriculture Ministers and the Commission enjoy an extremely broad discretion in the agricultural sector? At any rate, the history of the CAP, like that of the common fisheries policy, raises serious questions about the ability of the EU to agree to fundamental reform other than under extreme pressure.

6.4   The Greening of Europe?

A Community competence in environmental affairs was explicitly recognized only in 1986, by the SEA. The Maastricht, Amsterdam, and Nice Treaties extended QMV and the codecision procedure to most environmental matters. Even before the SEA, however, the Community had become active in the environmental area. The first measures were justified by concerns that different national regulations could act as trade barriers, but EU policy soon came to embrace environmental protection for its own sake, and for the sake of political integration. Over the years the involvement of the EU in environmental policymaking has become so extensive and intrusive that according to some observers this policy field exhibits strong 'federal' features. It is certainly true that policy developments in the member states cannot be understood without taking European environmental policy into consideration. A number of member states typically introduce environmental regulations only after the Union has become active in a given area. It is also true that for several decades environmental policy was arguably the most popular European policy, despite growing evidence of regulatory failure. Finally, the EU aspires to be recognized as a leader in the establishment of global environmental regimes, an ambition that became particularly evident in the climate-change negotiations (see below). Are these sufficient reasons to justify the powers given to the European institutions in this area?

What is most striking about the development of the EU environmental policy is the amount of legislation that has been enacted in the absence, not only of a firm legal basis until the late 1980s but also of a clear rationale for action at the European level. It is symptomatic of widespread doubts on this score that the principle of subsidiarity was first given treaty status, at Maastricht, in connection with environmental policy. The two most prominent arguments for EU harmonization in the environmental field are the fear of a race to the bottom, and the prevention of segmentation of the single market by different national standards. As Chapter 7 shows in more detail, the race-to-the-bottom argument—European standards are needed because competition for industry would otherwise lead member states to enact suboptimally lax environmental standards—is theoretically unsound. If countries have different preferences for environmental quality, the standards that maximize social welfare will be different rather than harmonized. Related to the race-to-the-bottom argument is the appeal to the principle of 'undistorted competition', also known as the level-playing-field concept. The claim that a well-functioning European market needs a level playing field for the firms operating in it is advanced by companies in countries with high environmental standards. Such companies complain about the advantage supposedly enjoyed by firms in the poorer member states with typically less strict, hence less expensive, standards.

A moment's reflection shows the fuzziness of the notion of 'undistorted competition', which in fact has nothing to do with the competition rules against monopolistic or dominant positions in the European market. The same companies and industries complaining about the 'unfair' advantage provided by lower environmental standards in some member states enjoy a number of competitive advantages, which also create an 'uneven playing field': better infrastructure and a better trained workforce than poorer countries, higher levels of expenditure on research and development, a more efficient bureaucracy. Many other factors could be said to distort competition, such as cross-country differences in energy prices: for instance, businesses pay more than twice for their electricity in Italy and Ireland than they do in Sweden. In sum, it is not at all clear why only environmental standards should be singled out as competition-distorting factors. A level playing field would require the harmonization of all relevant economic, social, perhaps even natural conditions. Similarly, the need to harmonize environmental standards in order to dismantle non-tariff barriers to trade, has been greatly exaggerated. Recent research has shown that diversity of environmental standards can be compatible with free trade under a variety of conditions (Bhagwati and Hudec 1996). In part this is because, as already mentioned, environmental standards are positively correlated with the standard of living, so that as wealth grows as a result of free trade, the endogenous demand for higher standards grows as well. Hence, a good deal of *ex post*, bottom-up harmonization is expected to occur naturally, while the attempt to harmonize the standards *ex ante* may reduce the level of exchange and thus limit improvements in the future. At any rate, a good deal of EU environmental legislation today has less to do with the dismantling of nontariff barriers than with its ability to promote wider integration objectives and institutional aggrandizement. Political motives were particularly evident in the aspiration for environmental leadership on a global scale, and in the ill-fated proposal for a European carbon/energy tax (see below).

The existence of transboundary externalities is often cited as another justification for EU-wide harmonization. For example, the Commission has argued that where there is potential for transboundary pollution there is often justification for the EU to act, but this is far from being obvious. For most environmental problems the EU is not an optimal regulatory area, being either too large or too small. In a number of cases—the Mediterranean, the Baltic Sea, or the Rhine—the scope of the problem is regional rather than EU-wide, and is best tackled through regional arrangements tailored to the scope of the relevant environmental externality. Self-regulatory organizations encompassing only some jurisdictions ('regional compacts', such as the Delaware River Basin Commission) have been used in the United States since the 1960s and in some cases even earlier (Derthick 1974). More recently, organizations including parts of the United States and some Canadian provinces have been created in order to control pollution in the Great Lakes region. By pooling their financial, technical, and administrative resources, such consortia are in a better position to deal effectively with their regulatory problems than either by acting alone or by relying exclusively on centralized regulation that cannot be closely tailored to their specific needs. On the other hand, land-use planning, which is of great importance to environmental policy objectives in relation to the urban environment and protection of the countryside, is a case where the appropriate level of regulation is national or subnational.

In other cases, the scope of the environmental externality is global and hence requires multilateral regulatory cooperation. As already noted, the EU aspires to play a leading role in global environmental affairs, using the window of opportunity opened by the low profile maintained by countries like the United States and Japan in this area. In fact, it is the only regional organization to have signed and ratified the UN Framework Convention on Climate Change (UNFCCC). The demands of negotiating the UNFCCC led the Union to innovate its policymaking process. The member governments committed themselves to a pioneering burden-sharing agreement whereby international commitments are implemented collectively by allocating different responsibilities among the member states. In 1997 the European Council agreed that some member states should reduce their emissions, others should stabilize them, while five countries would be allowed to increase their emissions. This agreement, which effectively treated the EU as a single 'bubble' for the purpose of controlling the emissions of certain greenhouse gases, made it much easier for the EU to adopt a tough stance at the global level. In the run-up to the conference that discussed the Kyoto Protocol, the EU Environmental Council committed the Union to reducing by 15 percent emissions of three important gases by 2010. At the end of 2003, however, thirteen of the fifteen member states seemed likely to miss their individual country targets. The worst performers were Spain, likely to have emissions 30 percent above its target, and Austria, Belgium, and Ireland, each more than 20 percent above. The likely failure of the EU to meet its stabilization targets is especially embarrassing for those member states who signed the UNFCCC with the expectation that their emission growth would be accommodated under the EU 'bubble' target. Indeed, Spain insisted on the EU signing the FCCC as a bloc in order to allow it to increase its own emissions. Article 4 of the Kyoto Protocol makes clear that no member state will be in breach of the protocol as long as the EU as a whole is in compliance. In the event of failure to reach the total combined level of emissions, however, each country will be responsible for its own level of emissions. In practice, the EU's role has been relegated to monitor what the member states decide to do unilaterally, and to estimate the consequences (Grant et al. 2000). Effectively, EU climate policy has been renationalized, so that another possible justification for an EU role in environmental affairs—the advantages of a single European position on major global environmental problems—seems highly implausible today.

A final rationale for a European environmental policy is based on the idea that environmental quality is a 'merit good', which should be available to all the citizens of the Union. Merit goods are goods like elementary education or seat belts in cars that the government compels individuals to consume. The justification usually offered for this kind of paternalism is that the government is entitled to intervene because it knows what is in the best interest of the citizens better than they themselves do. In the EU context, paternalism would imply not only that some member states undervalue the benefits of environmental protection, or overvalue the corresponding costs, but also that the calculus of benefits and costs is more accurate at the European level. Both implications are very doubtful. First, it is arrogant to suggest that the voters in some member states lack the means to make their preferences about environmental quality known to their elected representatives, and to punish them if national policies do not adequately reflect majority preferences. This point deserves to be emphasized because one of the few successes of EU environmental policy, according to many analysts, is precisely the fact of having forced some member states to 'ratchet up' their environmental standards.

As for the ability of the EU to make a more accurate calculus of the benefits and costs of environmental protection than the national governments, the truth is that the fragmented nature of EU policymaking makes any systematic calculus impossible. Consider, for example, an important piece of environmental legislation like Directive 80/778 on Drinking Water Quality. The directive was in part a response to growing public concern about the presence of nitrates and pesticides in drinking water—a form of pollution for which the CAP bears a significant responsibility. The directive set such strict mandatory standards that they effectively prescribed a zero level of pollution. No consideration was paid at the time to the cost implications or the expected health benefits of the regulation. Such concerns emerged in the late 1980s, especially in the United Kingdom where the privatization of the water industry forced the government to critically reexamine what had been decided in Brussels. The UK government advocated a revision of the directive essentially on two grounds: first, that the maximum admissible concentrations of pesticides specified in Directive 80/778 were out of line with scientific evidence currently available; and, second, that the costs of compliance with the 1980 standards exceed the benefits to health from complying with them. The government position was spelled out by the UK permanent representative in Brussels, in a 'non-paper' submitted to the Commission in August 1993 (Matthews and Pickering 1997). According to the UK representative, a revised directive should seek to balance the benefits for consumers with the likely costs of achieving prescribed standards; the opportunity costs of heavy expenditures for limited benefits in one area should be assessed against the benefits of using the same resources to achieve alternative environmental and health goals; and, most important, water quality standards should be set on a sound scientific basis. The UK government's effort to bring about significant changes in the directive faced considerable opposition from the EP, and from a number of member states, led by Germany, which argued that since the precautionary principle is enshrined in Article 130(1) of the treaty (now Article 174(2) EC), there is no place for pesticides in drinking water at all if there remains any scientific doubt about their safety. Matthews and Pickering (1997: 276) conclude their careful analysis of the directive with the following comment: 'To some extent the case against a fundamental revision of the pesticide parameters in Directive 80/778 seems to have been on the emotional argument for "pure" water and hence an apparent unwillingness to take account of new scientific standards no matter how well grounded.... On this evidence, the European Community policy process appears ill-equipped to accommodate subsequent advancements in scientific expertise into EC law.' The example of the 1980 Water Quality Directive is sufficient to show the implausibility of the merit-good rationale as a justification for an EU environmental policy.

Leaving aside the issue of a rational justification of EU competence in this area, what is the practical effectiveness of the policy? There seems to be general agreement that despite three decades of intensive legislative activity, and some evidence that EU policy has assisted the 'ratcheting up' of environmental standards in some member states, the overall impact has been disappointing, to say the least. In 1993 the Fifth Action Program on the Environment acknowledged a continuous deterioration of the general state of the environment. Around the same time, evidence from the European Environment Agency (EEA) indicated that the quality of water in the EU remained below the minimum standards set in the legislation. In 1994 the agency reported that only 10 percent of water in the EU's rivers and lakes met the EEA criteria for good quality. The situation has not significantly improved since then. In the case of air pollution, and especially in the area of climate change, member states have made increasing use of the subsidiarity principle to effectively renationalize environmental policy. In 2000 the EEA reported that ground ozone levels in the EU appeared to have increased over the preceding ten years, and also that a large proportion of Europe's urban population was exposed to particulates above the limits set to protect human health. In the area of waste management, the OECD has predicted that on current rates of growth, the EU will generate nearly twice as much waste in 2020 as it did in 1995. The European Commission is therefore targeting a 20 percent reduction in nonrecycled waste by 2010, but according to the latest available data, the quantity of domestic waste continues to rise. Again, at the beginning of 2004 the targets set for the proportion of renewable energy and of gross consumption of electric energy produced from renewable sources—12 percent and 22 percent respectively, to be achieved by 2010—seemed unlikely to be achieved (Commission 2004).

Part of the explanation of the poor performance of EU environmental policy has to do with the use of outdated policy instruments. Traditionally, EU environmental policymakers have relied on command-and-control mechanisms in the form of legally binding standards prohibiting or directing activities within the member states. This approach generally failed, but attempts to broaden the range of regulatory instruments encounter serious difficulties. Thus, the carbon/energy tax, which was supposed to become the center piece of the EU's climate change policy, met such fierce opposition from member states, from economic interests, and even from the Commission's Directorates General responsible for the internal market and industrial policy that the tax proposal ended up as a mere recommendation to national governments. The European Council meeting in Essen in 1994 did no more than enable member states to apply such a tax if they so desire.

There are other reasons for the low efficiency and effectiveness of the EU's environmental policy, including the limited institutional competence of the Union and the difficulty of adapting European legislation to scientific and technical progress. The major problems, however, are directly linked to the way the Community method operates. First, by the Commission's own admission, the absence of effective implementation and enforcement remains a major flaw of the EU environmental policy process. Late implementation of directives is the norm rather than the exception, and it is rare that more than a handful of member states notify their implementation measures to the Commission within the specified time limit. Thus in 1997 the Commission brought infringement proceedings for nontransposition of environmental directives against every member state, with the Netherlands and Denmark being the only states with a single case brought against them. Infringement proceedings for nontransposition or nonconformity of national legislation with the provisions of European directives are especially significant in the area of water pollution—one of the oldest and most heavily regulated areas in EU environmental policy (Sbragia 2000). The very scale of the phenomenon means that even if the Commission were able to detect a large number of infringements, it would be impossible for the European courts to prosecute them because of the sheer number of cases this would involve.

It has been suggested that the reason that EU environmental legislation is so poorly implemented and enforced is the diffuse nature of the interests it seeks to protect. Protection of the environment is such a general goal that it lacks the commitment of specific groups. At the same time, the costs of the policy are largely concentrated on the regulated industries, which therefore have strong incentives to oppose environmental measures. This diffuse-benefits–concentrated-costs syndrome is not a peculiar aspect of EU policymaking, but a standard feature of environmental policymaking in all industrialized countries. Hence it is not sufficient to explain the abnormally poor record of implementation and enforcement in the EU. Rather, the behavior of the member states, which must not only implement but also finance the measures decided in Brussels, suggests that the benefits of an environmental policy that tends to reflect the preferences of the richer countries of northern Europe are not perceived to be sufficient to compensate the costs its implementation would impose. After the facile enthusiasms of the 1970s, the lack of compelling justifications for EU interventions in this area has contributed to the shift of attention away from ambitious programs for the protection of an ill-defined 'European environment' towards more concrete issues such as the poor performance of the European economy and the new problems raised by monetary union and a greatly enlarged membership. In this respect the failures of the carbon tax proposal and of the quest for leadership in global environmental affairs may have been watershed events. The growing perception that EU environmental policy is designed less to solve concrete environmental problems than to pursue general integration objectives may be another factor contributing to the current loss of dynamism of this European policy, and to the renationalization of some of its important components.

6.5   Dilemmas of Risk Regulation

In the three cases discussed in the first part of the chapter—the CFP, CAP, and environmental policy—the causes of failure are well understood, and the general direction of reform is also reasonably clear, albeit politically difficult to implement. The case of risk regulation is different and requires a rather different treatment. Here the conceptual and scientific problems are at least as serious as the political ones, and desirable reforms would require not only political will but also substantial changes in mental attitudes. The approach to risk regulation currently advocated by the European institutions has considerable popular appeal, but when it is critically examined and compared with the best international practice, it shows that risk regulation in the EU is still at an early stage of development. As is shown below, the consequences of this situation are serious not only in terms of allocative efficiency but also of equity, and of the risk of international isolation. It is, therefore, important to examine critically the logical foundations of the official doctrine. This is the aim of the following pages, including the Appendix where the interested reader may find a simplified presentation of some key concepts of decision-making under uncertainty. The Commission is currently promoting the 'precautionary principle' (PP) as a 'key tenet' of EU risk regulation, and even as a general principle of international economic and environmental law (Commission 2000). The aim is to show that this promotional effort is bound to fail, or to produce unanticipated and undesirable consequences.

6.5.1   An Ambivalent Principle

As a general approach to environmental and risk regulation, the PP suffers from a number of serious shortcomings: it lacks a sound logical foundation; it distorts regulatory priorities; it can have undesirable distributive consequences; not least, it undermines international regulatory cooperation. Above all, the principle is deeply ambiguous. Like the English constitution according to Walter Bagehot, the philosophy behind the PP is composed of two distinct sets of elements: the 'dignified' parts ('those that bring it force'), and the 'efficient' parts ('those by which it, in fact, works'). In its 'dignified' aspect the precautionary philosophy purports to provide a legitimate basis for taking protective regulatory measures even when reliable scientific evidence of the causes and/or the scale of potential damage is lacking. Thus it appeals to many Europeans who are increasingly concerned about the 'globalization of risk'—the transmission of environmental and health risks through the channels of free trade. In its 'efficient' aspect, however, the approach tends to expand regulatory discretion at national and international level—a discretion that can be used for a variety of purposes: to meet legitimate public concerns, but also to practice protectionism, or to reclaim national autonomy in politically sensitive areas of public policy.

   Indeed, the member states of the EU are quickly learning to rely on the precautionary principle as an argument to justify stricter national regulations than those agreed at European level. In theory, the Commission allows member states to rely on the PP only when the Community scientific committees consider that the evidence presented by a member state is justified in light of new data, or by a particular national situation. In practice, the member states seem to be increasingly suspicious of the findings of the European committees, and more inclined to rely on the determinations of their own regulatory bodies. Thus, the French government refused to abide by the decision of the Commission to lift, as of August 1, 1999, the ban on exports of British beef that had been imposed at the height of the first BSE ('mad cow' disease) crisis. The government turned to the newly established French Agency for Food Safety (AFSSA) to justify its refusal. In an Advice of September 30, 1999, AFSSA concluded that the risks associated with beef from Britain were still significant. The Commission requested the opinion of its own Scientific Steering Committee, which concluded that the precautionary position taken by the French agency was unfounded. After AFSSA had once more confirmed its determination, the French government on December 8, 1999 officially declared that it would not lift its ban. At that point, the Commission had no alternative but to submit a complaint to the ECJ, without, however, pushing the case with much conviction. The Commission is well aware that in cases involving genuine scientific doubts, the Court tends to respect the regulatory autonomy of the member states. This episode shows that the PP may be invoked by the national governments against the European institutions as a sword; at the same time, these same institutions use the principle at the international level as a shield to justify measures that are viewed as thinly disguised forms of protectionism by the EU's trading partners (Scott and Vos 2002).

6.5.2   The Precautionary Principle and the WTO: the Beef Hormones Case

The effort to have the PP adopted not only as a 'key tenet' of Community policy but also as a 'full-fledged and general principle' of international law (Commission 2000) has met some limited success in the field of international environmental law. On the other hand, the EU's commitment to, and application of, the principle has been repeatedly criticized by the WTO, the United States, and by many other developed and developing countries. What international organizations and third countries fear is that something as poorly defined as the PP may be too easily misused for protectionist purposes. Such fears are fed by episodes like the aflatoxin standards (to be discussed later on) and the beef hormones dispute, which for years has opposed the EU to some of its major trade partners. In this dispute the European Commission found itself in the position vis-à-vis the WTO that various EU member states have found themselves vis-à-vis the Community, being sanctioned for introducing a public health and consumer protection measure, which was not sufficiently supported by scientific evidence (de Búrca and Scott 2000).

  The controversy over the use of growth hormones in cattle raising has been finally resolved, but it may still be useful to briefly review its historical background for the light it sheds on the current EU approach to risk. The hormones regime stems from Directive 81/602 on the prohibition of 'certain substances having a hormonal action and of any substances having a thyrostatic action'. This directive was amended in 1985 by Directive 85/358, extended in 1988, and consolidated by Directive 96/22. The 1985 directive, which was adopted by qualified majority on the basis of Article 43 of the Rome Treaty dealing with the common agricultural policy, prohibited the use of hormones in livestock farming. Even then the prohibition was controversial. The United Kingdom brought a suit against the directive, arguing *inter alia* that in view of its health objectives the directive should have been based on Article 100 on the approximation of laws. This article requires unanimity and hence would have allowed the UK government to veto the prohibition of growth hormones in cattle-raising and meat products. The effect of the 1985 directive was also to prohibit the importation of American and Canadian beef into the Community, although this point was not addressed in the legal controversy between the United Kingdom and the Community. Instead, the United Kingdom asserted that in enacting the directive the Council should have taken into consideration a report by the Commission's scientific experts, according to which growth hormones used following good veterinary practice would result in no significant harm. This conclusion of its own experts led the Commission to reconsider the ban on growth hormones. However, both the EP and the Economic and Social Council strongly opposed any such policy change. Because of this opposition the Commission canceled further meetings of the group of scientific experts. At the same time the ECJ rejected the complaint of the UK government with a highly formalistic argument (Joerges 2001). In fact, the negative conclusion of the experts led to a change in the rationale of the hormones directive from health safety to 'the interests of the consumers in general'. As Advocate General Lenz put it, this type of consumer protection need not be supported by scientific evidence. Hence, there is 'really no reason to examine the health problem . . . and so the fact that in the preamble to the contested directive the Council did not go into the partial findings of the scientific group . . . cannot be regarded as a failure to give reasons' (cited in Joerges 1997: 309–10). Without citing any empirical evidence, the Advocate General added that 'meat from animals treated with hormones is widely rejected'.

In 1997 the United States and Canada filed complaints with the WTO against the European ban of meat products containing growth hormones, submitting that this measure violates the Sanitary and Phytosanitary (SPS) Agreement. This Agreement allows WTO members to adopt health standards that are stricter than international standards, provided the stricter standards are supported by risk assessment. Unfortunately, the risk assessment conducted by the Community's scientific experts had not established any significant health risk. Hence the Commission was forced to meet the WTO challenge with arguments similar to those used by Advocate General Lenz in rejecting the United Kingdom's complaint against Directive 85/358. In particular, it pointed to various incidents from the early 1980s, when hormones that entered the European food market had allegedly made European consumers wary of beef. The Commission concluded that a ban of beef containing growth hormones was necessary to restore consumer confidence.

The WTO's Dispute Resolution Panel decided against the EC. The Panel raised three objections: first, more permissive international standards existed for five of the hormones; second, the EC measure was not based on a risk assessment, as required by Article 5(1) of the SPS Agreement; third, the EC policy was not consistent, hence in violation of the no-discrimination requirement of Article 5(5). The Appellate Body agreed with the panel that the EC had failed to base its measure on a risk assessment and decided against the EC essentially for two reasons: (1) because the scientific evidence of harm produced by the Commission was not 'sufficiently specific to the case at hand'; and (2) because 'theoretical uncertainty' arising because 'science can never provide absolute certainty that a given substance will never have adverse health effects' is not the kind of risk to be assessed under Article 5(1) of the SPS Agreement. One of the objectives of the Commission, *Communication on the Precautionary Principle* of February 2, 2000, was to respond to the objections raised by these WTO bodies.

6.5.3   Conflicting Objectives

This Communication also serves internal political aims, being a response to pressures originating from the EP and the Council. In a Resolution of March 10, 1998 the EP had invited the Commission 'to anticipate possible challenges to Community food law by WTO bodies by requesting the scientific committees to present a full set of arguments based on the precautionary principle'. On April 13, 1999, the Council of Ministers adopted a Resolution urging the Commission, *inter alia*, 'to be in the future ever more determined to be guided by the precautionary principle in preparing proposals for legislation and in its other consumer-related activities and develop as a priority clear and effective guidelines for the application of this principle' (both citations in Commission 2000: 25).

These political pressures are at least partly responsible for the ambiguity that pervades the document. On the one hand, the Commission is well aware of the danger that the member states may use the PP in order to extend their own regulatory autonomy vis-à-vis the EU. Hence the exhortation to 'avoid unwarranted recourse to the precautionary principle as a disguised form of protection' (p. 3); the insistence that 'the precautionary principle can under no circumstances be used to justify the adoption of arbitrary decisions' (p. 13); the warning that 'reliance on the precautionary principle is no excuse for derogating from the general principles of risk management' (p. 18). On the other hand, there is the desire to accommodate the Council and the EP by using the principle as a means to maximize the EU's regulatory discretion at the international level. Thus on page 3 of the document we read: 'The Commission considers that the Community, like other WTO members, has the right to establish the level of protection... that it deems appropriate. Applying the precautionary principle is a key tenet of its policy, and the choices it makes to this end will continue to affect the views it defends internationally, on how this principle should be applied.' The same demand for maximum regulatory discretion is repeated, in various forms, throughout the Communication. At the same time, the Commission insists that the envisioned use of the PP, 'far from being a way of evading obligations arising from the WTO Agreements', in fact complies with these obligations.

We saw that this is not the opinion prevailing in the WTO. It is true that under the SPS Agreement if a health measure has a scientific basis, there is little other countries can do to challenge it. However, Article 2(2) of the Agreement states, *inter alia*, that members of WTO shall ensure that any SPS measure 'is based on scientific principles and is not maintained without sufficient scientific evidence, except as provided for in paragraph 7 of Article 5'. The exception provided by Article 5(7) applies to cases where relevant scientific evidence is insufficient, in which case a member state may *provisionally* adopt a measure 'on the basis of available pertinent information.... Members shall seek to obtain the additional information necessary for a more objective assessment of risk and review the sanitary or phytosanitary measure accordingly *within a reasonable period of time*' (emphasis added). The requirement of a scientific justification, and of risk assessment as a prelude to standard-setting, puts a limit on regulatory discretion. But for the requirement to have meaning, there must be the possibility of a panel finding the absence of a scientific justification or the inadequacy of a risk assessment. As we saw in the growth hormones case, both the WTO's Dispute Resolution Panel and the Appellate Body determined that the EC's ban on the importation of American beef was unsupported by scientific evidence and by an adequate risk assessment.

One of the undeclared aims of the Communication on the PP is to prevent similar embarrassments in the future—by proposing very elastic interpretations of the requirements of the SPS Agreement, and by making the PP itself, in the words of Scott and Vos (2002: 276), 'infinitely malleable'.

For example, the Communication interprets the requirements of Article 5(7) of the SPS Agreement as follows: 'The measures, although provisional, shall be maintained as long as the scientific data remain incomplete, imprecise or inconclusive *and as long as the risk is considered too high to be imposed on society*' (Commission 2000: 21; emphasis added). It is difficult to see how a panel could apply such subjective standards. Again, the document insists that the PP offers no excuse for derogating from the general principles of risk management, including an examination of the benefits and costs of action and inaction. However, cost-benefit analysis should include not only evaluation of the costs 'to the Community', but also noneconomic considerations such as acceptability to the public. Who should determine public acceptability remains unclear, unless this determination is seen as part of the right of the Brussels authorities to establish the level of protection that they deem to be appropriate for the entire Union at any particular time. Such an adjustable peg can justify any measure, making cost-benefit or risk analysis superfluous. We have here another manifestation of the deep ambiguity of the Communication. This document is also a public relations exercise 'designed to calm the fears of those who perceive that the precautionary principle serves, in the case of the EU, to legitimate decisions which are irrational, other than in terms of their capacity to serve protectionist goals' (Scott and Vos 2002: 278). The exercise is ultimately unpersuasive because all the substantive and procedural constraints on regulatory arbitrariness, set by the WTO rules, are relaxed to the point of becoming nonbinding.

Such is the flexibility of the PP that it may be stretched to include the principle of 'reversal of the burden of proof', according to which it is up to the developer of a new product or process to prove that the product or process poses no health or environmental risk. To quote again the Commission (2000: 21): 'Community rules . . . enshrine the principle of prior approval (positive list) before the placing on the market of certain products, such as drugs, pesticides or food additives. This is one way of applying the precautionary principle. . . . In this case the legislator, by way of precaution, has clearly reversed the burden of proof by requiring that the substances be deemed hazardous until proven otherwise.' In conformity with this strict interpretation of the PP, Article 3.1 of the 'Novel Food' Regulation (Regulation 258/97) states that GM food can be authorized only if 'it does not present a danger to the consumer'. Since no such proof is, strictly speaking, possible, this interpretation of the PP is equivalent to advocating a zero-risk approach, which, if consistently applied, would effectively stop scientific and technical innovation.

But here the Commission is caught in a serious dilemma: on the one hand, it has officially espoused the PP, in the hope of enhancing its regulatory credibility and political legitimacy in the eyes of a skeptical public opinion; on the other hand, it is committed to finding means for increasing the international competitiveness of Europe's biotech industries. Biotechnology is one of the priorities of the EU's sixth research framework program, and significant budgetary resources have been allocated to this area of research. The Commission has sought a way out of the dilemma of precaution versus innovation—which at the institutional level is reflected in severe turf conflicts among several of its Directorates General—by softening the rigorous standard of the Novel Food Regulation. The new regulation for GM food being proposed at the time of writing (December 2003) lowers the threshold: GM food may be authorized if it does not present an *unacceptable* risk for human health or the environment. Moreover, traces of unauthorized GMOs are now acceptable, under certain conditions, whereas previously they were not allowed to circulate in the market under any condition (Poli 2003). As the following section makes clears, the shift from 'no risk' to 'acceptable risk' represents a significant weakening of the precautionary philosophy in the direction of a more reasonable 'balancing approach', which takes the benefits, as well as the risks, of the new technology into account. The Communication on the PP admits that risk regulation cannot be based on a zero-risk approach, but fails to provide an alternative, logically defensible, concept. By contrast, US courts and regulators have been able to move beyond early simplistic approaches to the determination of safety.

6.5.4   Benchmarking

In Chapter 3 reference was made to the Open Method of Coordination (OMC), an attempt to improve policymaking in the EU by indirect means such as policy-learning and the use of benchmarks derived from best practice worldwide. If we were to apply this method to improve risk regulation, we would probably choose current US practice as the relevant benchmark. Indeed, a transatlantic comparison reveals a number of shortcomings of the precautionary approach, of which the most serious is the absence of a methodology for the rational setting of priorities. By focusing the attention of policymakers and the general public on one specific, perhaps only hypothetical, risk the PP ignores the possibility that a different allocation of the same resources might save more lives. Any attempt to control poorly understood, low-level risks necessarily uses up resources that in many cases could be directed more effectively towards the reduction of well-known, large-scale risks, as shown by the following example. In the late 1990s the risks connected with electromagnetic fields (EMFs, 'electrosmog') and towers or masts became a topic of intense political controversy in Italy, involving even the Vatican because of certain radio-transmitters located near Rome. Explicitly appealing to the PP, the then minister of the environment forced the government to approve what are believed to be the most stringent EMF exposure standards in the world. The minister of health of the same government, a highly respected cancer specialist, argued that with the resources needed to implement the new standards it would have been possible to save thousands of cancer patients—rather than the one death from leukemia per year that the new standards for electromagnetic exposure are supposed to prevent—but to no avail.

Similarly, the Communication on the PP makes no reference to the opportunity cost of precautionary measures, so that the issue of a rational setting of regulatory priorities is not even raised in a document that pretends to clarify a 'key tenet' of risk regulation in the EU. But as risks multiply while resources remain limited, the necessity of deciding which risks to regulate can no longer be evaded. Hence, it is instructive to see how the question of regulatory priorities was raised in the United States as part of a slow but steady improvement in the conceptual foundations of risk regulation. This learning process may be traced through a sequence of three regulatory principles: *lowest feasible risk*; *elimination of significant risk*; and *balancing costs and benefits* (for a fuller discussion see Majone 2003). Although this is not a linear sequence—different principles coexist even in the same area of regulation—a trend can be clearly detected towards a broader inclusion of relevant considerations, including the opportunity costs of individual measures.

6.5.4.1 Least-feasible-risk approach

According to the least-feasible-risk principle—the American equivalent of the precautionary approach—human exposure to health risks should be reduced to the lowest possible level. This principle is a sort of second-best rule. The best policy would be one that ensures a risk-free working and living environment, but because of technical and economic constraints a risk-free environment is unattainable; hence the need of a second-best rule. For instance, Section 6b(5) of the 1970 Occupational Safety and Health Act directs the OSHA to set standards that 'most adequately assure, *to the extent feasible,...* that no employee will suffer material impairment of health or functional capacity even if such employee has regular exposure to the hazard ... for the period of his working life' (emphasis added). Trade union representatives claimed that this instruction obliged OSHA to mandate the use of whatever available technology an industry could afford without bankrupting itself. In the 1981 case *American Textile Manufacturers Institute, Inc. v. Donovan*, Justice Brennan of the US Supreme Court agreed that 'Congress itself defined the basic relationship between costs and benefits, by placing the benefits of worker health above all other considerations save those making attainment of the "benefit" unachievable' (cited in Graham et al. 1988: 97). In the EU, the Court of First Instance (CFI) was still holding a similar opinion in 1999, when in *Alpharma* (Case T-70/99R) it emphasized that the requirements of public health must take precedence over economic considerations. Like the precautionary approach, the least-feasible-risk approach, rejects any sort of balancing of costs and benefits, presumably on the ground that the two sides of the basic relationship are incommensurable. In the 1980s and 1990s, however, US courts, regulators, and eventually also legislators, went through a learning process, which convinced them that in the presence of multiplying risks and limited resources, a rational setting of regulatory priorities is impossible without a more sophisticated balancing approach to risk regulation.

6.5.4.2 Significant-risk doctrine

In *American Petroleum Institute v. OSHA* (1978), the Fifth Circuit Court of Appeals invalidated a regulation that reduced the occupational exposure to benzene, a carcinogen, from 10 parts per million (ppm) to 1 ppm. The court found that the competent regulatory agency, OSHA, had not shown that the new exposure limit was 'reasonably necessary and appropriate to provide safe or healthful employment' as required by the relevant statute. Specifically, the court argued that OSHA had failed to provide substantial evidence that the benefits to be achieved by the stricter standard bore a reasonable relationship to the costs it imposed. The court added: 'This does not mean that OSHA must wait until deaths occur as a result of exposure levels below 10 ppm before it may validly promulgate a standard reducing the permissible exposure limit. Nevertheless, OSHA must have some factual basis for an estimate of expected benefits before it can determine that a one-half billion dollar standard is reasonably necessary' (cited in Mendeloff 1988: 116–17).

What the court required was some sort of quantification of benefits as a necessary step to carry out a benefit-cost test of the new standard. Without a quantification of risk, and hence of the expected number of lives saved by the regulation, it is clearly impossible to weigh the benefits against the costs. OSHA, unlike other American agencies involved in risk regulation, had always maintained that quantitative risk analysis is meaningless. Hence, the agency's leaders decided to appeal against the Fifth Circuit Court's decision. In *Industrial Union Department (AFL-CIO) v. American Petroleum Institute* (1980), the US Supreme Court upheld the Fifth Circuit's decision. Justice Powell noted that 'a standard-setting process that ignored economic considerations would result in a serious misallocation of resources and a lower effective level of safety than could be achieved under standards set with reference to the comparative benefits available at a lower cost' (cited in Mashaw et al. 1998: 815). Expressing the view of a four-judge plurality (in a separate opinion, Justice Rehnquist provided the fifth vote for overturning the standard), Justice Stevens explicitly rejected the precautionary, lowest-feasible-risk approach followed by the agency: 'We think it is clear that the statute was not designed to require employers to provide absolute risk-free workplaces whenever it is technologically feasible to do so, so long as the cost is not great enough to destroy an entire industry. Rather, both the language and structure of the Act, as well as its legislative history, indicate that it was intended to require the elimination, as far as feasible, of *significant* risks of harm' (cited in Graham et al. 1988: 100; emphasis added).

Thus was born the 'significant-risk doctrine', a crucial step in the process of learning how to deal with risk regulation in a rational manner. Justice Stevens insisted that 'safe' is not the same as risk-free, pointing to a variety of risks in daily life—ranging from driving a car to 'breathing city air'—that people find acceptable. Hence, before taking any decision, the relevant risk must be quantified sufficiently to enable the agency to characterize it as significant 'in an understandable way'. In fact, OSHA was not required to support its finding that a significant risk exists with anything approaching scientific certainty. So long as the determination is supported by a body of reputable scientific thought, the agency is free to use conservative assumptions in interpreting the data, risking error on the side of overprotection. From the government's generic carcinogen policy the agency had concluded that in the absence of definitive proof of a safe level, it must be assumed that *any* level above zero presents *some* increased risk of cancer. But, as the justices pointed out: 'In view of the fact that there are literally thousands of substances used in the workplace that have been identified as carcinogens or suspect carcinogens, the Government's theory would give OSHA power to impose enormous costs that might produce little, if any, discernible benefit' (cited in Mashaw et al. 1998: 813). The great merit of the significant-risk doctrine is to have raised the crucial issue of regulatory priorities. Most risks are regulated in response to petitions or pressures from labor unions, public-health groups, environmentalists, and other political activists, with little analysis by the agency of other possible regulatory targets. Given that resources are always limited, the real (opportunity) cost of a regulation is the number of lives that could be saved by using the same resources to control other, more significant, risks. By requiring the agency to show significant risk as a prelude to standard-setting, the justices were insisting on some analysis in priority-setting: regulatory priorities should be directed toward the most important risks, which are not necessarily those that are politically most salient.

The significant-risk doctrine places a higher analytical burden on regulators than the lowest-feasible-risk approach, or the PP. Not all potential risks are treated equally; only those substances shown to pose a significant risk of cancer will be regulated, focusing limited regulatory resources on the most important health risks. In addition, the doctrine, without requiring a formal analysis of benefits and costs, does place a constraint on the stringency of standards. If exposure to a carcinogen is reduced to the point that the residual risk is insignificant, then no further tightening of the standard is appropriate. *Industrial Union Department (AFL-CIO) v. American Petroleum Institute* is a landmark case also from the point of view of the methodology of risk analysis. The US Supreme Court not only confirmed the legitimacy of quantitative risk assessment but it effectively made reliance on the methodology obligatory for all US agencies engaged in risk regulation. In most subsequent disputes over regulatory decisions to protect human health, the question has not been whether a risk assessment was required but whether the assessment offered by the agency was plausible. This historical background probably explains US advocacy of science-based risk assessment at the international level, as well as that country's opposition to the PP advocated by the European institutions.

6.5.4.3   Balancing costs and benefits

With the great expansion of environmental, health, and risk regulation in the 1970s, the need to calculate more precisely the benefits and costs of the proliferating regulations became increasingly evident. Important steps to improve the quality of federal regulation were taken under President Carter, when the notion of a 'regulatory budget'—the attempt to assess an acceptable level of regulatory costs for the entire economy—was first introduced. The oversight mechanism was perfected in the late 1980s, during the second term of the Reagan administration. The Office of Management and Budget (OMB), in the president's executive office, was given responsibility for setting the budgets of all regulatory agencies, and for monitoring the rulemaking process. Instead of simply imposing a cost-effectiveness requirement, as previous presidents had done, Reagan moved to a full-fledged cost-benefit test with his Executive Order No. 12291 of 1981: regulatory action is not to be undertaken unless the potential benefits to society outweigh the potential costs; among alternative approaches to any given regulatory objective, the alternative involving the least net cost to society has to be chosen; finally, agencies are required to set regulatory priorities with the aim of maximizing the aggregate net benefits, taking into account the condition of the particular industries affected by regulations, the condition of the national economy, and other regulatory measures contemplated for the future.

As a result of this and subsequent reforms, the quality of rulemaking has improved significantly over the last two decades. The usefulness of the regulatory oversight process designed by the Reagan administration explains why subsequent administrations, democratic as well as republican, have continued to use it in a form that has not substantially changed from the original model. In the meantime Congress was also undergoing a learning process, resulting in a better appreciation of the opportunity costs of risk regulation. In 1995, new regulatory legislation was passed. Its net effect was to strengthen the test that must be passed by new regulations. The key congressional concerns were that regulations be based on an accurate and comprehensive assessment of the risks involved, rather than on worst-case scenarios, and that regulatory agencies proceed with regulations only if the benefits exceed the costs.

6.5.5 What Price Safety?

This brief survey of developments in the United States reveals a steady improvement in the understanding of the subtle dilemmas posed by risk regulation. The progress from the early reliance on outright prohibitions or simple 'feasibility' tests to the application of key principles of decision-making under uncertainty (see Appendix to this chapter), not only to agency rulemaking but also to the enabling legislation, is an outstanding example of policy-learning. It justifies our choice of the US experience as the appropriate benchmark for European regulators.

The Commission's Communication on the PP overlooks not only the issue of opportunity costs and regulatory priorities but also the distributive implications of the principle, in particular the impact of precautionary standards on the welfare of developing countries. The Commission maintains that in considering the positive and negative consequences of alternative risk strategies, one should take into consideration '*the overall cost to the Community*, both in the long- and short-term' (Commission 2000: 19; emphasis added). Such Eurocentrism could perhaps be justified if the cost of precautionary measures was felt only by exporters in rich countries, but what if the cost is borne by very poor countries? The EU claims to be deeply committed to assist, financially and otherwise, developing countries, especially African ones. However, World Bank economists had estimated the serious impact on some of the poorest African countries of precautionary standards for aflatoxins proposed by the Commission in 1997. Aflatoxins are a group of related toxic compounds that contaminate certain foods and have been associated with acute liver cancer in humans. Aflatoxin B_1, the most common and toxic of these compounds, is generally present in corn and corn products, and various types of nuts. The proposed Community standards were significantly more stringent than those adopted by the United States, Canada, and Australia, and also stricter than the international standards established by the FAO/WHO Codex Alimentarius Commission. Brazil, Bolivia, India, Mexico, Uruguay, Australia, Argentina, Pakistan, and other countries, in opposing the proposed measures, demanded to know in detail which risk assessments the EU had used in setting the new standards. As a consequence of consultations with the trading partners about these concerns, the Commission relaxed the standard for cereals, dried foods, and nuts. Even after this relaxation, however, aflatoxin standards for products intended for direct human consumption remain quite stringent: 4 parts per billion (ppb), and 2 ppb for B_1 aflatoxin, against an overall Codex standard of approximately 9 ppb.

Using trade and regulatory survey data for the member states of the EU and nine African countries between 1989 and 1998, the World Bank economists estimated that the new standards would decrease African exports of cereals, dried fruits, and nuts to the EU by 64 percent, relative to regulation set at the international standards (Otsuki et al. 2000). The total loss of export revenue for the nine African countries amounted to US$400 million under EU standards, compared to a gain of US$670 million if standards were adopted according to Codex guidelines. Were these costs imposed on some of the poorest countries in the world justified by the health benefits to Europeans? According to studies conducted by the Joint Expert Committee on Food Additives of the Food and Agriculture Organization and World Health Organization (WHO), the Community standard of 2 ppb for B_1 aflatoxin would reduce deaths from liver cancer by 1.4 deaths per billion, that is, by less than one death per year in the EU. For the purpose of this calculation the Community standard was again compared to a standard that follows the international (Codex) guideline of 9 ppb. Since about 33,000 people die from liver cancer every year in the EU, one can see that the health gain promised by the precautionary standard was indeed minuscule, and certainly out of proportion to the cost imposed to the countries of sub-Saharan Africa.

Appendix: Regulatory Science, the Precautionary Principle, and Decision Theory

In the absence of any generally accepted definition, the PP is often taken to mean that incomplete scientific knowledge is not a valid excuse for regulatory inertia; or, more explicitly, that it is legitimate to take regulatory measures to prevent possible risks even in the absence of strong scientific evidence on causal relationships or the extent of damage. The problem with statements such as these is not that they are wrong, but that they provide no practical guidance for taking regulatory decisions under uncertainty. This is because incomplete scientific knowledge is the rule, not the exception, in risk regulation. Extrapolation—a key element in the establishment of health and safety standards—is inherently an uncertain operation. There is, first, the problem of extrapolating from animal experiments. Scientists have developed several mathematical models expressing the probability of a lifetime response, P, as a function of dosage (or exposure) D: $P = f(D)$. This is the dose-response function. Different choices of the functional form lead to different models. Regardless of the choice of model, however, one has always to extrapolate from data points at high doses (the type of data provided by animal experiments) to the low levels relevant to the regulation of risk to humans. Moreover, the same data points are compatible with a variety of extrapolating functions. Thus, under a threshold (nonlinear) dose-response model it would be possible to establish a 'virtually safe' level of exposure, at the numerical value of the threshold. Instead, if one uses a linear dose-response relationship, adverse health effects are predicted at every level of exposure, so that there is no obvious point at which a reasonable standard could be set. It may be argued—as many advocates of the PP do—that if there is no firm scientific basis for choosing among different dose-response models, then one should prefer the safest or most conservative procedure. The problem with this argument is that it is not clear where one should stop: it is difficult to be conservative in a consistent manner unless one is prepared to propose a zero level of exposure in each case.

The statement that incomplete knowledge is not a valid excuse for regulatory inertia is unhelpful rather than wrong. More problematic are suggestions that precautionary regulation should be based on 'worst-case' scenarios, or that the approach is to be used when the probabilities of adverse events are 'unknown'. All such views, of which more than a trace can be found in the Commission's Communication on the PP, are ultimately rooted in fundamental misunderstandings about the logic of decision-making under uncertainty. The aim of this Appendix is to clarify some basic concepts, in order to demonstrate more precisely the logical inadequacy of the PP. To begin with, risk is a product of the probability of harm times its severity, the 'expected loss'; so risk regulation is a special case of decision-making under uncertainty. Now, according to the fundamental theorem of decision theory, the only consistent decision rule is to choose the alternative that minimizes the expected loss (or maximizes the expected utility) of the decision-maker. Consider a situation where there are various possible events $E_1, E_2, \ldots, E_n$, with corresponding probabilities $p_1, p_2, \ldots, p_n$, and where the feasible alternatives are $A_1, A_2, \ldots, A_m$. Indicate with l_{ij} the loss for each combination of alternative A_i and event E_j, $i = 1, 2, \ldots, m; j = 1, 2, \ldots, n$. The optimal decision consists in choosing the alternative that minimizes the expected loss, that is, the sum of the products of the losses by the corresponding probabilities (formally: the alternative that minimizes $\Sigma_j\, p_j l_{ij}$). Any good textbook on decision theory (e.g. Lindley 1971) provides the proof that any other decision rule—and in particular any rule that does not take into account both the losses and the probabilities of *all* possible events—can lead to inconsistent decisions.

One such potentially inconsistent decision rule is the minimax, which formalizes the worst-case approach mentioned above. The minimax decision rule uses losses but not probabilities, either denying the existence of the latter, or claiming that the method is to be used when they are unknown. This decision rule makes sense in special situations, like zero-sum games where the uncertainty is 'strategic', that is, part of the strategy of a rational opponent, but not in the general case. A formal proof that the rule can produce inconsistent decisions is beyond the scope of the present discussion (the interested reader may consult Lindley 1971: 172–7). The basic problem may be understood with the help of simple examples. Consider first the following decision problem, where the entries indicate losses, for example extra deaths due to exposure to a toxic substance:

$$
\begin{array}{ccc}
 & E_1 & E_2 \\
A_1 & 10 & 0 \\
A_2 & 1 & 1
\end{array}
$$

Following the minimax rule, for each row (i.e. each alternative) we select the maximum loss (10 for A_1 and 1 for A_2), and choose that alternative having the minimum of these values. This is A_2 with value 1. Hence the minimax rule says: always choose $A_{\pm 2}$. The principle of expected loss would assign probabilities p_1 and p_2 to the uncertain events E_1 and E_2, and choose A_2 if $1 < 10p_1$, that is, $p_1 > 1/10$, otherwise A_1 should be selected. To see which of the two rules is more reasonable, suppose that p_1 is quite small (say, $p_1 = 0.001$ or 0.0001) so that $10p_1$ is much less than 1. The minimax rule would still choose A_2, even though it is almost sure that no extra deaths would occur if A_1 is chosen.

The conclusion is even more striking in a second example, where only the loss corresponding to the pair (A_1, E_1) has been changed:

$$
\begin{array}{ccc}
 & E_1 & E_2 \\
A_1 & 1.1 & 0 \\
A_2 & 1 & 1
\end{array}
$$

The minimax rule would still choose A_2, even though the expected loss for A_1 is much smaller for all values of p_1 less than, say, 0.8. In short, the problem with the minimax rule is that, by considering only the worst possible case and disregarding probabilities, it does not take into account all the information available to the decision-maker. The advantage of the expected-loss (or expected-utility) rule is that it takes account of both losses/utilities and probabilities.

As mentioned above, one defense of the minimax is that it is to be used when probabilities are unknown (and perhaps unknowable). This argument is strongly reminiscent of the distinction made by the American economist Frank Knight in the 1920s between 'risk' (when the events are uncertain, but their probabilities are known) and 'uncertainty' (the probabilities are unknown). Knight attached great theoretical importance to this distinction, but modern analysis no longer views the two classes of events as different in kind. Probabilities may be known more or less precisely, they may be more or less subjective, but it is logically difficult to give precise meaning to the statement that certain probabilities are completely unknown. For instance, if we insist that we are 'completely ignorant' as to which of the possible events $E_1, \ldots, E_n$ will occur, it is hard to escape the conclusion that they are all equally likely to occur. But this implies that the probabilities are in fact known, and that $p(E_j) = 1/n$ for all j: the uniform distribution, well known to first-year students of probability and statistics!

A basic, if generally unrecognized, reason for the inability of the advocates of the PP to deal consistently with risk and scientific uncertainty is an outdated understanding of the very notion of probability. The contemporary view of probability as expressing the strength of our knowledge or beliefs is much broader than the old ('objective') view of probability, which only applies to phenomena or experiments that can be indefinitely repeated under essentially the same conditions. But each political or regulatory decision is essentially unique, and hence can be analyzed only by means of the subjective notion of probability. From the newer viewpoint, 'objective' probabilities are only a special case. Fortunately, the same mathematical rules apply to objective as to subjective probabilities. Subjective probabilities, like all other types of knowledge, are fallible, but what is important is the procedure (known as Bayes theorem) by which they can be revised in light of new information. Hence, 'subjective', in the present context, is not at all equivalent to 'arbitrary'. In the modern theory of decision-making under uncertainty, both subjective probabilities and utilities (or losses) are derived according to precisely defined rules that guarantee their internal consistency and logical transparency—all subjective evaluations are explicitly quantified, and then assembled together in a way that guarantees that no inconsistencies between the various evaluations (of probabilities and utilities/losses) will arise.

The theoretical framework sketched here is sometimes criticized for being normative rather than positive or descriptive. For instance, it is said that laboratory experiments, as well as casual observation, prove that people do not choose under uncertainty, or update their beliefs, in the manner prescribed by the theory. However, this criticism overlooks the complex interdependence between the normative and the positive viewpoint in social life. Grammar, logic, arithmetic, and legal codes are all examples of normative systems that are often violated in practice, but are not discarded as a consequence—society could not function without them. What is true is that social practice is guided by norms, which in turn develop under the influence of social practice. For example, normative principles of decision-making have been quite influential in directing the attention of US courts and policymakers to the importance of opportunity costs and the rational setting of regulatory priorities. In turn, this learning process has changed the practice of the regulatory agencies. Again, the normative theory of decision-making under uncertainty casts serious doubts on the wisdom of institutionally separating risk analysis and risk management (see Chapter 5). The fact that in risk regulation, because of the uncertainty of regulatory science, all probabilities are essentially subjective increases the importance of coherence—all parts of the decision-making process must fit together in a consistent and transparent manner. But consistency, transparency, and especially accountability are greatly facilitated if the agency head is responsible for the entire regulatory process, rather than only for the risk analysis or the risk management part.

The point of this digression on the foundations of decision theory was to identify with more precision than would otherwise be possible the logical problems raised by the application of the PP. Like the minimax principle, the PP tends to focus the attention of regulators on some particular events and corresponding losses, rather than on the entire range of possibilities. As a consequence, regulators will base their determinations on worst cases, rather than on the weighted average of all potential losses—the expected overall loss. The Commission's Communication provides several instances of this pitfall. To mention only one example, in examining the benefits and costs of different alternatives '[a] comparison must be made between the *most likely* positive and negative consequences of the envisaged actions and those of inaction' (Commission 2000: 19; emphasis added). Actually, rational decision-making under uncertainty requires consideration of all consequences, not just the most (or, for that matter, least) likely ones.

Positive and Negative Integration

7.1   Integration by Stealth

The two preceding chapters have stressed the difficulty of introducing significant institutional and policy reforms under the classical Community method. This chapter moves the argument one step further by asking which parts, if any, of the Community method are still needed. To answer this question it is necessary to examine the relative merits of positive and negative integration. Repeated policy failures, and the weak incentives to learn from those failures, suggest that the institutional system designed by the treaties is more suitable to the promotion of negative integration— removing obstacles to market integration, but also restraining the discretionary powers of national governments and protecting fundamental rights under European law—than to the development and implementation of effective supranational policies, that is, positive integration. One of the underlying assumptions of the Community method is the efficacy of the functionalist approach to integration. It will be recalled that after the debacle of the EDC the 'Monnet method'—the strategy of promoting spillovers from one economic sector to another and eventually from market integration to political integration—came to be accepted as a more roundabout, but safer, path to the ultimate objective of political union. Functional spillovers would create pressure for deepening and widening the scope of supranational policymaking, while political spillovers would set in motion a self-reinforcing process of institution-building. Hence the neofunctionalist predictions of a steady progress towards federalism (see Chapter 3).

For neofunctionalists, the aim of policymaking is less to find the best feasible solution to a concrete problem than to drive forward the integration process: integration by stealth, as it has been called. Hence, a relative indifference to actual policy outcomes, and to the requirements of accountability. Integration by stealth worked, more or less, as long as Community competences were limited, and the emphasis was on negative integration. As the European policy space became increasingly crowded, however, the limits of the approach became evident. Economists insist that policymaking is more efficient if different instruments are used to achieve different objectives. Applying this prescription to our case leads to the conclusion that objectives of political integration should be pursued by political means, rather than under the guise of technocratic problem-solving. By the same token, policies should be designed and implemented to solve concrete problems, not for the sake of integration.

After half a century of market building and integration by stealth, the idea that economic integration must necessarily lead to a strengthening of the supranational institutions, and eventually to political integration along federalist lines, appears to be increasingly implausible. European competences have certainly expanded, but in a highly selective fashion. While regulatory policies have continued to grow, albeit at a decreasing rate, other policies explicitly mentioned in the treaties—such as transport, energy, and social policy—have remained largely underdeveloped. Key policies of the welfare state, health, social services, and income redistribution, are still made at the national level, while foreign policy and security are developing outside the Community method. Thus, *pace* Monnet and neofunctionalist scholars, the advocates of political union must in the future fight for their ideas in the political arena (see Chapter 10). The disjunction of policymaking and political integration should not only improve the quality of European policies but also enhance the legitimacy of the integration process, by making it more transparent, and more directly linked to the actual (rather than assumed) preferences of the citizens of the Union.

7.2   Positive Integration and the Regulatory Model

The proliferation of Community programs of doubtful effectiveness (see Chapter 6) has been abetted by the mistaken idea of the superiority of 'positive' over 'negative' integration. The distinction between these two approaches goes back to the earliest studies of regional economic integration. The Rome Treaty itself did not attach any normative connotation to the distinction. The common market was to be achieved by both methods, but in fact by greater reliance on negative law—witness the significance of such Articles as 12–17 (elimination of customs duties); 30–7 (elimination of quantitative restrictions to intra-Community trade); 48–73 (free movement of persons, services, and capital); and 85–94 (rules against distortion of competition). More recently, however, positive integration has often been identified with positive values like social protection and the correction of market failures, negative integration with deregulation and the narrow interests of traders. In fact, economic and other special interests may find it convenient to support measures of positive integration, while fundamental rights and the diffuse interests of consumers are often better protected by measures of negative integration.

The regulatory model of Community policymaking (Majone 1996a) explains why the accumulation of regulatory powers at the European level may owe more to institutional and group interests than to the need to correct various failures of the Single European Market. The starting point of the model is the distinction between regulatory policies and other policies that require the direct expenditure of public funds. Since the real costs of regulations are borne, not by those who make the rules but by those who have to comply with them, budgetary constraints have only a limited impact on regulators. In contrast, the size of nonregulatory, direct expenditure programs is determined by budgetary appropriations and, ultimately, by the level of tax revenues or the borrowing capacity of the government. This structural difference between regulatory policies and policies involving the direct expenditure of public funds is even more important at the European than at the national level, because not only the economic but also the political and administrative costs of implementing European rules are borne, directly or indirectly, by the member states. Free goods tend to be used inefficiently. Hence, it is not surprising that the volume, detail, and complexity of Community regulations are often out of proportion with the benefits they may reasonably be expected to produce. For example, by the early 1990s, the Community was introducing into the corpus of French law more rules than the national authorities themselves. According to some estimates, today only 20–25 percent of the legal texts applicable in France are produced by the parliament or the government in complete autonomy, that is, without any previous consultation in Brussels. Reporting such statistics, the French Conseil d'Etat speaks of normative drift (*dérive normative*) and luxuriating legislation (*droit naturellement foisonnant*), doubting that any government could have foreseen, let alone wished for, such a development. It also points out, however, that the same member states that deplore the 'regulatory fury' of the Brussels authorities are among the major causes of overregulation with their demands for Community interventions in the most varied areas of economic and social regulation (Conseil d'Etat 1993). The fact is that the Commission, being faced by a soft budget constraint as far as its regulatory activities are concerned, finds it easier to give in to such demands than to engage in the politically costly exercise of defining rational regulatory priorities.

The structural difference between regulatory and direct expenditure programs goes a long way toward explaining the regulatory bias of Community policies, but the regulatory model goes beyond this observation, to consider both the supply and the demand side of European regulations. Thanks to its monopoly of legislative initiative, the Commission plays a key role on the supply side. Assuming that its utility function is positively related to the scope of its own competence—an assumption supported by a good deal of empirical evidence—the model shows that the optimal strategy for the Commission is to expand the scope of European regulation: rulemaking puts a good deal of power in the hands of the Brussels authorities in spite of the tight limitations imposed by the member states on the Union budget. It should be kept in mind that the EU budget is quite small in relative terms (slightly over 1 percent of Union gross domestic product, GDP), is largely absorbed by the CAP and by regional aid (structural funds), and must always be balanced. On the demand side of the 'market' for Community rules we find several important actors. Multinationals and other export-oriented firms tend to prefer European to national regulations not only to avoid the costs of meeting different, and often inconsistent, national rules but also to avoid the risk of progressively more stringent regulations in some of the member states. A similar development has been observed in the United States, where, for example, the car industry decided to support federal regulation of air pollution because of the threat posed by different and inconsistent air-pollution standards, and also because it feared the possibility that one state legislature after another, in a kind of political domino effect, would set more and more stringent emission standards.

Demands for Community regulations also come from public-interest organizations, such as environmentalists and consumer-protection groups, particularly those from countries with low levels of health and safety regulation. Such groups hope to get from Brussels the kind of protective legislation that, because of their political weakness, they are unable to get from their own governments. As already mentioned, however, the member states themselves are the most important source of such demands. There are several reasons why a country may want to use European legislation in order to impose on the other member states its own approach to a specific regulatory issue. If successful, such a strategy would minimize the costs of legal and administrative adaptation to new Community rules; it would give a competitive advantage to the national industry, which is already familiar with, and adjusted to, the particular regulatory regime; and, in the case of countries with a high level of environmental and health regulation, it would presumably reduce the cost advantages of countries with lower levels of protection by forcing all member states to adopt the same regulatory standards. Precisely for these reasons other countries may be expected to oppose the proposal. The final outcome will depend not only on the ability of the proposing country to form a winning coalition in the Council of Ministers but also on the congruence of its proposal with the objectives of the Commission. For, if it is true that in a formal sense the Commission proposes and the Council disposes, it is the case that the legislation approved by the Council under QMV usually reflects the policy position of the Commission—a result largely explained by the skillful use of the monopoly of legislative initiative, including the possibility for the Commission to withdraw its proposal at any stage of the policymaking process (see Chapter 3).

7.3   The Limits of Positive Integration

So much for a political economy explanation of the growth of regulatory policies at European level. What the regulatory model cannot provide is a normative assessment of the extent to which these policies actually achieve their stated objectives, and whether they are justified in cost-benefit terms. The evidence presented in Chapter 6 supports the view that EU policies tend to be the by-product of processes largely unrelated to the stated policy objectives. Even though its specialized services may be sincerely devoted to problem-solving, the Commission as a collegial body will never propose a policy that does not contribute, directly or indirectly, to an expansion of EU, and its own, powers—the 'common interest' as perceived in Brussels. Likewise, neither the member states nor the EP will support a proposed solution, however effective, that is unfavorable to their national or institutional interests. Since the organizing principle of the Community is the representation of interests, each European institution sees itself primarily as the bearer of a particular interest, national or supranational, which it strives to protect and promote. Hence, the main theme of political conflict is not the formulation and implementation of policy, but the defense of the respective prerogatives of Council, Parliament, and Commission.

It is true that at the national level also public policy is often made less to solve concrete problems than to serve party-political or other special interests. Most political scientists assume that the main goal of elected politicians is to maximize the probability of being reelected. Hence, politicians tend to care little for actual policy results, and in any case prefer to support distributive rather than efficient policies. Favoring special interest groups or geographical districts appears to be a more promising strategy for achieving their reelection objective than pursuing the public interest, however defined. Yet, recent research has shown that citizens' preferences can constrain legislators' actions, provided issues are framed in a way that allows citizens to reward or punish their representatives for specific policy decisions. If legislators are forced to take public positions on specific programs, voters can hold their legislators accountable for the positions they take and for the effects they produce. Too wide a gap between stated objectives and actual results invites punishment at the polls (Arnold 1990). Unfortunately, no such democratic controls exist in the EU, where suboptimal policies can persist, unscrutinized and unchallenged, for decades.

7.4   The Obsolescence of the Functionalist Approach

According to Tsebelis (1990) the observation of suboptimal policy outcomes indicates that the actors are involved in more than one game. In fact, the examples discussed in the two preceding chapters have shown the main policy actors—Council of Ministers, EP, and Commission—engaging in complex games of domestic and interinstitutional politics rather than in serious problem-solving. Because of its monopoly of policy initiation, the Commission is in a particularly favorable position to pursue several objectives simultaneously: to deal, at least symbolically, with concrete policy problems, and to satisfy powerful interests, but also to advance the process of European integration and expand its own powers, or at least preserve its own prerogatives and the 'balance of powers'. Suboptimal policy outcomes are often the consequence of the unwillingness or inability of EU policymakers to agree on clear policy priorities. The situation was rather different in the early days of the Community, when the overarching goal of market integration meant that policy objectives and integration objectives could be more easily reconciled, and were indeed to a large extent mutually supporting. Also, in those days European policies were often better attuned to the needs of a modern market economy than the corresponding national policies.

For instance, when the Rome Treaty was drafted, only Germany had a well-developed competition policy and an effective competition regulator. The other founding members of the EEC had to develop this policy almost from scratch, largely following European competition rules. At present, however, most member states have competition authorities with a satisfactory level of technical expertise and the power to impose significant remedies. The EU no longer sets the pace in this policy area. The Directorate General for Competition is generally considered the most expert among the Commission services, as well as the one with the strongest treaty-based powers. However, serious doubts about its expertise have been raised when, in 2002, the Directorate suffered three consecutive defeats at the CFI, in high-profile cases over merger decisions. In the *Airtours* case of June 2002, for instance, the CFI in annulling the Commission's decision 'used language that was severely critical both of the Commission's procedure and of its substantive assessment of the alleged collective dominance situation created by the merger' (Goyder 2003: 392). Again, in September 2003 the same court ruled that a heavy fine imposed on a shipping cartel was illegal. This last decision raised fresh doubts, not only over the expertise but also over the procedures used by the European competition authorities. According to a competition lawyer quoted by the *Financial Times* of September 29, 2003, this ruling of the CFI tells the Commission 'that they cannot get away with the shoddy standards of work that they could get away with in the past'.

In fields as varied as telecommunications, environmental protection, and consumer protection, some national policies are significantly more advanced than the corresponding European policies that often cannot go beyond least-common-denominator solutions. The comparative advantage of national governments is even more pronounced in the design and reform of regulatory institutions, not only because of the greater resources available but also because of the freedom from the constraints of the Community method. In addition to greater capacity for institutional and policy innovation, greater resources, and vastly superior implementation capacities, the national level enjoys other significant advantages. Thus, national policymakers have at their disposal instruments that are practically unavailable to European policymakers. For instance, EU environmental policy lacks a vital policy instrument like taxation, and hence finds it difficult to replace the traditional command-and-control approach with more efficient incentives-based schemes (see Chapter 6). Another crucial advantage is the possibility of tailoring policy to specific problems and national preferences. Again, a key criterion of good policy is that a transparent accountability framework and an effective system of remedies be available to the citizens in case of policy failure. Here too the national level enjoys a significant comparative advantage over the European level, where the lack of transparency and the complexity of the policy process tend to reduce accountability to vanishing point. In sum, the welfare costs of positive integration are significant, and it is far from clear that they are compensated by corresponding benefits.

Persistent attempts by the Commission to further increase European competences make the limits of positive integration even more evident. Contrary to the assumptions of the neofunctionalists concerning the expanding authority and jurisdiction of the supranational institutions at the expense of the national governments, the growth of EU powers actually tends to increase the fragility, and reduce the legitimacy, of the supranational institutions. One reason is the unwillingness of the member states to provide the resources necessary to perform effectively the new tasks. In 1987–8, at the start of the Internal Market Program, the national governments rejected President Delors' proposal to raise Community spending to 1.4 percent of Community GDP, granting only 1.2 percent. Similarly, in 1992, there was broad opposition to the 1.37 percent GDP figure (to be reached by 1997) envisaged by the Delors II package. Again, after the failure of the December 2003 IGC to approve the draft Constitutional Treaty, the member states renewed their request that the average EU expenditures in the period after 2006 be stabilized at the present level, in spite of the significant enlargement of the Union. The six countries that are net contributors to the budget even insisted that country contributions should not exceed 1 percent of GDP, instead of the 1.24 percent that the president of the Commission had considered necessary after enlargement. The threat repeatedly made by President Prodi, as by other Commission presidents before him, not to undertake new tasks unless adequate resources are made available is not credible, and hence is not believed by the member states. To 'do less but do it better', as President Santer had promised, would make sense in terms of both policy effectiveness and institutional credibility, but the precept goes against the grain of the functionalist approach. Not surprisingly, the report 'on allegations regarding fraud, mismanagement and nepotism in the European Commission', issued in 1999 by the Committee of Independent Experts, noted the failure 'of any attempt by the Commission to assess in advance the volume of resources required when a new policy was discussed among Community institutions' (cited in Grant et al. 2000: 21).

The mismatch between the EU's highly complex and differentiated regulatory tasks and existing capacities is not only a question of insufficient resources but perhaps even more of insufficient recognition that policy credibility depends crucially on effective implementation. Steeped in the legalistic approach of the Community method, the Commission tends to be more interested in the rewarding task of developing new rules rather than in the thankless and politically costly task of seeing that existing rules are implemented. But regulation is not achieved simply by rulemaking; it also requires detailed knowledge of, and intimate involvement with, the regulated activity. In all industrialized countries this functional need has led, sooner or later, to the creation of specialized agencies, capable not only of rulemaking but also of fact-finding and enforcement. As was argued in Chapter 5, the lack of such administrative infrastructure at European level is a serious obstacle to the effectiveness of EU regulatory policies, and another reason for the progressive obsolescence of the functionalist approach. Our critique of positive integration is not meant to deny the need of some form of regulatory harmonization in an integrated and expanding European market. Rather, the aim is to question the way harmonization has been pursued under the Community method, and to suggest that the rationale for positive integration should be examined more critically than has been done in the past.

As Neil Walker rightly points out, although the EU requires and possesses both legislative and executive capacity, the constitutional logic of the system remains *legislation-centered*. Thus, the key measure of EU competence is legislative; the key basis for the demarcation of the relationship between EU 'supremacy' and national sovereignty is legislative power; the key axis around which the ideological debate between intergovernmental and supranational positions is played out is the legislative act (Walker 2003). By the way, this focus on legislation, rather than administration, is typical of all mixed polities since, as was noted in Chapter 3, the executive function is primarily the responsibility of the corporate bodies that compose the polity. It follows that in all such polities negative law is bound to be more effective, and more predictable in its outcomes, than positive law, which requires administrative implementation.

7.5   Positive Integration, Regulatory Competition, and 'Race to the Bottom'

Many, perhaps most, measures of positive integration in the areas of health, safety, and environmental regulation, are justified by the argument that without EU-level harmonization member states would engage in a socially undesirable 'race to the bottom'. Indeed, not only in the EU but also in most federal states, a standard argument for centralizing social regulation is that it prevents member states from competing for industry by offering environmental or other standards that are too lax relative to the preferences of their citizens. Such competition is said to lower the level of social protection that states would pursue if they did not face international or interjurisdictional competition to attract industry and the additional wages and taxes produced by industry migration. It is assumed that, other things being equal, firms will try to reduce costs by moving to the jurisdiction that imposes the least stringent regulatory requirements.

In order to understand the structure of the race-to-the-bottom argument we take the simplest example of two states that are identical in all relevant aspects, including the level of environmental quality desired by their citizens (Revesz 1992). State 1 initially sets its standard of pollution reduction at the level that would be optimal if it were a completely independent country rather than the member of a federation. State 2 then decides to set a less stringent standard, and industrial migration from State 1 to State 2 will ensue. To recover some of its loss of jobs and tax revenues, the first state then considers relaxing its standard, and so on. The process of adjustment continues until an equilibrium is reached. At the conclusion of the race, both states will have adopted suboptimally lax standards, but will have the same level of industrial activity as before engaging in the race; in equilibrium the two states will not experience any inflow or outflow of industry.

Superficially, such a race to the bottom appears to be an example of the prisoners' dilemma. If the two states could enter into a cooperative agreement to adopt the optimally stringent standard, they could maximize social welfare without engaging in 'unfair' competition for industry. This presupposes, of course, that the agreement is enforceable and that preferences for environmental quality are exactly the same in the two jurisdictions. As long as the jurisdictions are independent states, any cooperative agreement would lack credibility; but the situation is different if they are part of a federal or quasi-federal system. In such a case the suboptimal outcome could be avoided if national environmental standards were harmonized at the higher level, *provided* that the harmonized standards were equal to the standards the two states would find optimal if they were still independent. Article 95(3) EC attempts to offer such a solution, at least for the richer member states of the EU, stating that in proposing harmonization measures concerning health, safety, environmental protection, and consumer protection, the Commission 'will take as a base a high level of protection.... Within their respective powers, the European Parliament and the Council will also seek to achieve this objective.' The proviso about the harmonized standards corresponding to the actual preferences of the member states is crucial. If states have different preferences for environmental protection, then standards that maximize social welfare will be different. Hence, a uniform European standard, even one that sets only a minimal level of pollution control and allows the member states to adopt more stringent national standards, will not be optimal—unless the minimum standard is so low that it is exceeded by all the national standards, precisely the type of minimum harmonization which Article 95(3) is meant to rule out. It is thus quite possible that even if there is a race to the bottom—an assumption that in fact lacks empirical support (see below and also Chapter 9)—a European standard might still reduce aggregate social welfare.

As Revesz (1992) points out, race-to-the-bottom arguments are also incomplete because they fail to consider that there are more direct means of attracting foreign direct investments. The advocates of harmonization implicitly assume that states compete over only one variable, such as environmental quality. Given the assumption of a 'race', however, it is more reasonable to suppose that if harmonization prevents competition on the environmental dimension, states would try to compete over other variables, such as worker safety, minimum wages, or taxation of corporate profits. To avoid these alternative races, the central regulators would have to harmonize national rules, so as to eliminate the possibility of any form of interstate competition altogether. This would amount to eliminating any trace of national autonomy, so that the race-to-the-bottom argument is, in the end, an argument against subsidiarity.

As a matter of fact, the empirical literature finds little evidence of a race to the bottom in social regulation. For example, there is no evidence that industry responds to differences in national environmental laws in significant ways. Knoedgen (1979) surveyed (West) German firms known to have made substantial investments in developing countries since the early 1970s, when Germany began to enforce strict environmental laws. The vast majority of the firms surveyed responded that environmental regulations are totally unimportant in the location of investment. Moreover, 90 percent of the firms claimed to use the same environmental protection measures in developing countries as they used in Germany, essentially for efficiency reasons. More recent international surveys, such as the one conducted by the UN Conference on Trade and Development Program on Transnational Corporations in 1990, confirm Knoedgen's findings.

Thus, most of the 169 respondents to the UN survey claimed that environmental, health, and safety practices overseas are determined by environmental regulations in their home countries. Econometric analyses of trade patterns also fail to find evidence of industrial migration to countries with lower social standards. Levinson (1996) lists several possible reasons for this: corporations doing business in a variety of jurisdictions find it more cost-effective to operate according to the most stringent regulations rather than designing different production processes for each location; environmental compliance costs are too small, relative to other costs, and too similar across countries to weigh heavily in location decisions; multinational corporations believe that most countries are just a few years (less than the lifetime of a factory) behind the most advanced countries in environmental-standards stringency, so that it is better to invest now than be forced to retrofit later. Especially the last reason—the fact that environmental quality is a 'superior' good, the demand for which grows as incomes increase—makes the race-to-the-bottom argument highly implausible within the EU. The assumption, basic to this argument, that firms try to reduce costs by moving to countries with the lowest environmental or social standards lacks also a sound theoretical basis. According to recent surveys of the literature on local public goods (e.g. Wilson 1996) there are no formal models supporting the proposition that competition among states creates a prisoners' dilemma in which states, contrary to their preferences, compete for industry by offering progressively less stringent standards. On the contrary, this body of literature tends to emphasize the fact that interstate competition is not inconsistent with the maximization of social welfare.

Naturally, the fear of a 'race' is not the only rationale for harmonization of environmental and other social standards. A more plausible argument for EU-wide harmonization of social standards is the need to dismantle nontariff barriers to trade within the single market. Even in this respect, however, *ex ante* harmonization may have been pushed too far. Today it is recognized that an initial difference in health, safety, or environmental standards need not distort international trade; rather, it is trade itself that leads to their eventual convergence. The reason, as already mentioned, is that such standards are positively correlated with the standard of living. Hence, as wealth grows as a result of free trade, the endogenous demand for higher social standards grows as well (Casella 1996). It is worthwhile recalling that the Rome Treaty rejected the view, fairly common even then, that differences in social conditions between the member states can represent a form of 'unfair' competition, so that harmonization is needed in order to prevent 'social dumping'. Apart from the condition of equal pay for male and female workers—introduced under French pressure—the treaty never prescribes that social policies be harmonized prior to, or even concurrently with, trade liberalization within the common market. In line with the conclusions of the 1956 Spaak Report, the treaty maintains that harmonization should in general be regarded as a corollary of, rather than a requirement for, market integration. This sequence—free trade first, followed by a more or less spontaneous harmonization of social standards—was generally accepted by European policymakers until the mid-1970s. After a decade of hesitation, a clear shift in the direction of social harmonization occurred in the mid-1980s. Several factors contributed to this shift: the enlargement of the Community, creating large differences in labor costs between member states; high unemployment and stagnating real wages; and, not least, the social activism of the Delors Commission (Sapir 1996). Today the wisdom of *ex ante*, top-down harmonization—positive integration—is again being questioned.

7.6   The Positive Side of Negative Integration

If the necessity of positive integration has too often been overrated, the role of negative integration in legitimating the process of European integration may not have been sufficiently appreciated. Negative integration ('negative law') is not only about removing national restrictions to the free movement of the factors of production but also about limiting monopoly power and market dominance, protecting the diffuse interests of consumers, and about fighting discrimination on grounds of gender, nationality, age, and other factors. The best-known example of negative law in the area of individual rights is Article 119 of the Rome Treaty (now Article 141 EC), which requires application of the principle of equal pay for male and female workers, for equal work or work of equal value. The article itself conferred no positive regulatory power until its amendment by the Amsterdam Treaty. The new paragraph (3) inserted by that treaty extends the scope of the article to positive measures ensuring equality of opportunity and is thus not restricted to measures simply outlawing discrimination. So far, however, the most dramatic results have been achieved by Article 119 in its original, 'negative', formulation.

In the *Second Defrenne* case (*Defrenne v. Sabena*, Case 43/75) the ECJ held that the article is directly enforceable and grants rights to an individual if remedies do not exist under national law. It decided that the policy of the Belgian airline Sabena—forcing stewardesses to change job within the company (at a loss in wages) at the age of forty, but imposing no such requirement on cabin stewards doing the same work—was discriminatory, and required Sabena to compensate Defrenne's loss of income. According to Ellis (1998), the dramatic ruling of the *Second Defrenne* case reveals the Court's frustration with the noncompliance with the article by the member states, and with the weak-willed attitude towards this noncompliance demonstrated by the Commission. In the *Bilka* case of 1986, the Court indicated its willingness, absent a clear justification, to strike down national measures excluding women from any employer-provided benefits, such as pensions. In a later case, the ECJ held that all elements of pay are due to all employees in a particular activity, without regard to the hours worked. At that time, in Germany employees who worked less than ten hours a week for a commercial cleaning company did not receive statutory sick pay. Mostly women were affected by this regulation. The Court saw the regulation as an indirect discrimination against women, hence as a violation of Article 119. Since the discriminatory impact on women of the hours requirement lacked an objective justification—or at least, one was not provided by the German government—the claimant won her case.

The *Barber* case (1990), in which the Court extended the meaning of Article 119 to cover age thresholds for pension eligibility, demonstrates the symmetric effect of this norm. Mr Barber, having been made redundant at age 52, was denied a pension that would have been available immediately to female employees. Instead, he received a lump sum payment. The Court held that this treatment was illegal since pensions are pay and hence within the scope of Article 119. The decision, which required massive restructuring of pension schemes, caused a 'Barber Protocol' to be included in the Maastricht Treaty, to the effect that *Barber* was not to be applied retroactively. Nonetheless, the implications for future pension plans were considerable (Ostner and Lewis 1995). These and other ECJ rulings show the impact negative law can have on national legislation and legal practice by outlawing direct and indirect discrimination both in individual and in collective agreements. It is instructive to compare this direct impact with the uncertain, and often suboptimal, outcomes of many measures of positive integration (see Chapter 6).

7.7   Positive and Negative Rights

The distinction between positive and negative integration is not unrelated to the more traditional one of positive and negative rights. Positive rights, such as the right to education, shelter, or a clean environment, require positive interventions—usually but not necessarily by the state—while negative rights, such as the right to liberty or to freedom of speech, create obligations that consist in refraining from actions harmful to others. While the enforcement of negative rights may involve some costs, for example to pay for a judicial system and a police force, such costs pale into insignificance by comparison with the cost of enforcing positive rights. This asymmetry explains, at least in part, why it is widely thought that, while negative rights can be demanded of every country, this is not the case with positive rights (Bhagwati 1996). Hence the growing acceptance of the principle of 'universal jurisdiction', which allows the prosecution of gross human rights violations even in a country where the crime did not take place. On the other hand, the problem of cost means that not all positive rights can be enforced simultaneously, but have to be prioritized and traded off at the margin. Within democratic nation states such choices are resolved through the political process. A foreign country or an international organization cannot legitimately demand the enforcement of positive rights by another sovereign state, unless they are prepared to cover at least a significant part of the corresponding costs. Thus, while the international community and international law today accept the principle that the protection of basic human rights cannot stop at national borders, the enforcement of positive rights, without adequate aid, is generally regarded as an illegitimate form of intervention in the internal affairs of a sovereign state.

The member states of the EU have pooled some of their internal and external sovereignty at the European level, but this pooling does not make the distinction between positive and negative rights irrelevant from a welfare point of view. Consider the difference between the judicial enforcement of the right not to be discriminated against on the ground of, say, sex, and the promotion of substantive equality, or even of equality of opportunity. The latter objectives are much broader than the simple prohibition of discriminatory practices, and normally require positive interventions. The costs of such interventions will fall on the citizens of the member states affected by the measures, without having been authorized through the normal democratic process. Similarly, positive integration in the form of supranational regulatory measures, for instance in the area of environmental protection, imposes costs that may not adequately reflect national preferences and priorities. This is not an argument against positive integration *per se*, but a suggestion that the loss of welfare resulting from the potential distortion of national priorities should be taken into account in calculating the benefits and costs of positive measures. These difficulties explain the reluctance of the founding treaties to endorse positive rights, and their preference for measures of negative integration. As already noted, positive measures to achieve equality of opportunity only became possible after the Amsterdam Treaty added a new paragraph (3) to Article 141 EC (former Article 119), empowering the Council to 'adopt measures to ensure the application of the principle of equal opportunities and equal treatment of men and women in matters of employment and occupation, including the principle of equal pay for equal work or work of equal value'.

At issue here is not the merit of the objectives of various positive measures, but only whether, or to what extent, they can be legitimately pursued at European level—using the Community method rather than through soft law. For instance, advocates of a stronger role of the Union argue that the concept of nondiscrimination and the resultant negative law are insufficient because they do not tackle the roots of inequality. On the contrary, they are premised on the existing cultural and social divisions to be found in the member states. One example of the static nature of the concept of nondiscrimination cited by the critics is the comment of the ECJ in *Hofmann v. Barmer Ersatzkasse* that the Equal Treatment Directive was 'not designed to settle questions concerned with the organization of the family, or to alter the division of responsibility between parents' (cited in Ellis 1998: 323). This is taken to be too timid an attitude. What is required if real equality of opportunity is to be achieved, social-rights activists argue, is 'law and policy which encourage a degree of social engineering and transform some of the ways in which our lives are presently organized' (ibid.: 324). Of course, such sweeping legal and policy changes are incompatible with the nature of a system like the EU, based on the principles of subsidiarity, proportionality, and enumerated powers, and where national sovereignty in the areas of taxation and social security is still preserved. The activists hope that the EU may evolve into a political union with the legal and financial resources needed to enforce all kinds of positive social rights, but such a vision does not seem to be shared by a majority, or even a significant minority, of EU citizens. Until the federalist vision receives broad popular support, the distinction between positive and negative rights remains relevant. The principle of nondiscrimination may not tackle the roots of inequality, but its forceful enforcement by the ECJ has contributed to a considerable improvement of the quality of the democratic process in the member states.

7.8   Back to Negative Integration?

Approaches that may have been necessary in the early stages of the process—some forty years ago—appear to be either unnecessary or no longer effective today. We have already discussed the progressive obsolescence of the functionalist method, and several manifestations of the erosion of the Community method. A critical reassessment of positive integration could well lead to a more general recognition of the importance of negative integration for the integration process. A return to negative integration—in the original spirit of the Rome Treaty—means that positive integration would be pursued only where it can be shown that, with respect to a certain problem, EU regulations are demonstrably welfare-enhancing. Both fiscal federalism and functional federalism offer a number of criteria for identifying optimal regulatory jurisdictions, such as homogeneous preferences, scope of negative externalities, and similar costs in the provision of public goods. To these functional criteria one should add the normative requirement of an effective framework of accountability—the availability of political and legal mechanisms, which citizens can activate in cases of regulatory failure. In terms of such criteria, the EU appears to be seriously deficient in many important areas of regulation. In Chapter 6, I argued that the EU is probably not an optimal regulatory area with respect to most environmental problems. Risk regulation is another case in point. Since a zero-risk approach is neither practically possible nor logically defensible, regulators can only hope to ensure a level of risk that is socially and politically acceptable. The question is: acceptable to whom? In the Communication on the precautionary principle, which was discussed at some length in Chapter 6, the Commission writes that 'the Community is entitled to prescribe the level of protection, notably as regards the environment and human, animal and plant health, *which it considers appropriate*' (Commission 2000: 12; emphasis added). The claim to be in a position to determine the level of acceptable risk for the entire Union recurs throughout the document.

It is not difficult to understand why at the international level the EU pretends to be able to determine the acceptable level of risk for the citizens of all the member states. In reality, though, all the available evidence suggests that attitudes towards risk vary widely across the Union. Hence, it seems very doubtful that the level of risk chosen by the European institutions in specific cases represents genuine popular preferences—as they would be expressed through the national democratic process—rather than the institutional self-interest of the Commission, or the preferences and priorities of the richer and more risk-averse (or more protectionist) member states. How widely risk perceptions can vary across the Union and between the European and the national levels is shown by the history of the European regulation of genetically modified organisms (GMOs). Under Directives 90/219 and 90/220, eighteen genetically modified crops were approved for import or cultivation, and thousands of research field trials went ahead. A few years later, it was already clear that the risk determinations made in Brussels were rejected by the citizens of many member states. Facing strong public opposition to GMOs, national governments were refusing to approve new applications for GMO release, and no GMO foods were authorized for sale. In June 1999, only nine years after Directive 90/220 was passed, the Council formally suspended all new approvals of GMOs for commercial marketing. Even before the moratorium had been officially proclaimed, some member states took advantage of the safeguard clause, Article 16 of Directive 90/220, not as a basis of temporary measures, but to prevent the licensing of GMO products, even when these products had been approved by the European legislator. It is striking that so shortly after the experience with the GMOs moratorium, the Communication on the PP could refer so glibly to the centralized determination of socially acceptable levels of risk.

Under a negative-integration regime, most regulatory responsibilities would be left with the people who are most directly affected by a given problem, and who have to bear the costs of regulation. The tasks of the European institutions would primarily consist in monitoring closely the behavior of national and subnational regulators to make sure that they do not abuse their autonomy for protectionist purposes, or to violate rights guaranteed by EU law. Where the functional requirements of the Single European Market, or of international trade, require some type of harmonization, this could be achieved by one of the methods discussed in Chapter 5: self-regulation, statutory regulation implemented by networks of independent European agencies, or international standardization. But what about the single market? Is there a danger that the kind of regulatory decentralization envisaged here may lead to market segmentation and, ultimately, to a return to separate national economies? The question of the appropriate relation between positive integration, negative integration, and national regulatory autonomy remains an intensively controversial issue. However, on some points there seems to be fairly general agreement.

First, to repeat a point already mentioned several times, the need of supranational harmonization, which was almost taken for granted in the past, is increasingly questioned today. Especially after the latest enlargement of the Union, it is widely recognized that if citizen preferences, levels of economic development, environmental conditions, and so on vary significantly across jurisdictions, then harmonized rules cannot be welfare-enhancing. Second, as also already mentioned, an extensive body of both theoretical and empirical literature has concluded that harmonization, particularly of social standards, is not necessary for international trade to be 'fair' or undistorted. It is worth emphasizing once more that the Rome Treaty did not mandate that social policies be harmonized prior to, or concurrently with, trade liberalization. Rather, it was expected that a rapid amelioration of living standards throughout the Community would bring about an *ex post* harmonization of social conditions, and this expectation has proved to be largely correct. Finally, market integration is not an absolute value, but a means to increase the welfare of the citizens of the EU. In a series of celebrated cases, starting with *Keck and Mithouard* in 1991 and its progeny, the ECJ has recognized that the regulatory autonomy of the national governments is also a value that deserves protection, so that market integration and regulatory autonomy must be traded off at the margin rather than ordered hierarchically. A few years before—in *Commission v. Denmark*, C 302/86 [1988], the 'Danish Bottles' case—the Court had argued that concern for market integration must be tempered by respect for national concerns to protect the environment from the degradation that may flow from trade. In other policy areas, market integration has been sacrificed to social concerns or to political expediency. As a result, laws on minimum wages, collective bargaining, hiring and firing, duration of the working week, flexible labor contracts, qualifications, and a host of other factors continue to differ among the member states. In the words of Jacques Pelkmans: 'Member States, alone and together, will do everything to protect national labour market regulation, even at the cost of hardening the fragmentation of the EU's labour market' (Pelkmans 1997: 137). But if market integration is not an absolute value, then it follows that the necessity of positive integration should not be assumed, but must be determined in each particular case. One suspects that in the past too many harmonization claims were driven by a political agenda rather than by genuine concerns about the integrity of the Single European Market.

8

Beyond Intergovernmentalism

8.1 The Social Contract, Delegation, and Self-Government

It is time to draw some conclusions from the foregoing critique of various aspects of the Community method. As we saw in Chapters 3 and 4, a key characteristic of this method is the extensive delegation of powers by the member states to the supranational institutions. As social-contract theorists well knew, however, delegation to a third party is not the only mechanism by which a community of free people (or of sovereign states) can solve collective-action problems. A community, once formed by a contract of society, can operate according to different principles. It may be self-governing, without any distinction of ruler and subjects. This was the theory of Rousseau, who excluded categorically any delegation of sovereign (legislative) powers, while allowing delegation of executive powers, but only temporarily and subject to limitations or repeal at the community's pleasure. Again, the community may appoint a fiduciary or trustee government, which it can dismiss for breach of trust on its own interpretation of the nature of the trust. This was the theory of Locke, to which reference was made in Chapter 4. There is a third possibility—the community may transfer every right and every power that it possesses to a sovereign Leviathan: the theory of Hobbes. Thus, whereas Rousseau sets extremely strict limits to the powers that a community may delegate, and Hobbes assumes that the members of the community transfer all their powers to the government, Locke understands that powers may be delegated piecemeal. For him, even the legislative power is only a fiduciary power to act for certain ends, and the members of the community retain the capacity to remove the legislators, or limit the scope of their powers, if they acted contrary to the trust placed in them. In fact, in Chapter 4 and elsewhere, we saw several instances where the community of the member states of the EU revoked or limited some of the powers previously delegated to the supranational institutions.

This is to suggest that certain strands of social-contract theory can provide useful perspectives on the different configurations of European governance. We can of course exclude the Hobbesian strand, since no member state is prepared to surrender the core of national sovereignty and transfer all its rights and powers to a superstate. In contrast, both Rousseau and Locke offer different but complementary perspectives on the nature of European governance. Rousseau's idea of a self-governing community is particularly relevant to the discussion of this chapter. Indeed, in policy fields like foreign affairs and security, where the member states act outside the framework of the Community method, Rousseauian self-government provides a better model than Lockeian delegation of powers to the supranational institutions. In the literature on European integration, self-government by the community of member states is usually called intergovernmentalism, but this label does not really capture the character of policymaking in the crucially important areas where national sovereignty has been preserved essentially intact. As Helen Wallace points out, 'intergovernmentalism' resonates too much of cooperation between governments in international organizations whose role is limited to providing secretariat services and a forum for debate. She suggests a different term, 'intensive transgovernmentalism', to connote those situations where the member states have been prepared to commit themselves to rather extensive engagement and disciplines, but have judged the Community method to be inappropriate or unacceptable. The main institutional characteristics of this mode of non-Community policymaking are the active role of the European Council in setting the overall direction of policy; the predominance of the Council of Ministers in consolidating cooperation; the limited or marginal role of the Commission; and the virtual exclusion of the EP and ECJ from the policy process, together with extensive reliance on networks of national policymakers (Wallace 2000: 33–4). As I argue in Chapter 10, 'confederal arrangements' is not a bad characterization of this mode of policymaking.

The CFSP is the prime example of intensive transgovernmentalism. All measures that the Union adopts under the CFSP originate with the European Council and the Council of Foreign Ministers. The former body defines the principles and general guidelines and decides on 'common strategies'; the latter, adopts 'common positions' and 'joint actions'— operational decisions with financial implications. Before the Amsterdam Treaty the member states enjoyed an exclusive right of agenda-setting in CFSP, whereas they now share this right with the Commission. The Commission is 'fully associated' with the work carried out in this policy area, but the fact that its right of initiative is not exclusive implies that it does not enjoy the other prerogatives associated with that right. Thus, while under the Community method, the Commission can generally amend or withdraw its proposal at any time before the Council has taken a decision, in the non-Community sphere amendment or withdrawal of a proposal has no effect on the manner in which decisions are taken in the Council. What is even more significant is that the creation by the Amsterdam Treaty of the High Representative for the CFSP—with the task of contributing to the formulation, preparation, and implementation of policy decisions in this area—restricts the Commission's ability to influence policy developments. In the future, the role of the Commission will be even more limited by the Foreign Minister of the Union established by the new Constitutional Treaty. As noted in Chapter 3, to the extent that the Commission has a significant role in the CFSP, this is primarily because of its treaty-based powers in relevant areas such as external economic relations, including sanctions, and development policies. As for the other supranational institutions, the Council is entitled to act without seeking the opinion of the EP, and the ECJ has no power of judicial review with respect to decisions relating to the CFSP. The Court's jurisdiction is limited to ensuring that no measure taken in this context detracts from the rights and duties imposed by the treaties.

Monetary policy is another important example of a non-Community method of policymaking that is not adequately characterized by the term 'intergovernmentalism'. It is the sole responsibility of the ECB, which is completely independent from the other European institutions as well as from the national governments. The Commission has been an intermittent player in the process that led to EMU. It made important contributions, first with Roy Jenkins then with Jacques Delors, at key points, but has had little influence on the actual negotiations and little involvement in the implementation of EMU (Tsoukalis 2000). The Commission's controversial role in monitoring national governments' respect of the criteria of the Stability and Growth Pact will be discussed shortly. A future role of the ECB with respect to prudential supervision of financial institutions could provide some opportunity for a less marginal role for the Commission. However, this institution's lack of direct democratic legitimacy means that a real political counterweight to the ECB can only be provided by the Council of Economic and Finance Ministers, or by some other specialized formation of the Council. The EP has so far established only a marginal role in the conduct of monetary policy, while the ECJ is scarcely involved. Both the CFSP and monetary policy follow a non-Community approach to European policymaking, but differ in one important respect. While the CFSP is the outstanding example of self-government by the member states, under monetary union policymaking powers have been delegated to a fiduciary institution, the ECB, which, however, operates outside the framework of the Community method.

8.2   The Possibility of Self-Government

The question we must now examine is whether, or to what extent, the member states will be able to create effective and stable forms of self-government. Given our limited experience with non-Community methods of policymaking, and the ambiguity of the available empirical evidence, we can only reach tentative conclusions based to some extent on a priori theoretical reasoning, or on historical analogy. While the classic Community method rests on the solid foundation of common, legally binding norms, the new modes of governance, including intensive transgovernmentalism, rest on the more elastic, but also more fragile and precarious, foundations of information exchange, networking, collective learning, and reputational mechanisms. Are there reasons to believe that these various methods represent credible alternatives, or at least useful complements, to the traditional approach? On the one hand, some significant results have already been achieved by non-Community methods. After all, the introduction of the single currency—whatever the economic merits of the operation—has been largely the work of an exclusive network of central bankers, economic and finance ministers, and monetary experts. As another important example, the Schengen Agreement has been quite successful in lifting border controls between its signatories, and in expanding its membership even beyond the EU—with Norway and Iceland as associate members—before the Amsterdam Treaty gave it a treaty base. Again, cooperation in JHA, which at the beginning of the 1990s had not yet advanced beyond a range of poorly coordinated intergovernmental groups without decision-making power, legal instruments, and clear objectives, had, by the end of the decade, developed so fast that '[t]here is no other example in the history of integration of an area of loose intergovernmental cooperation having made its way so quickly to the top of the Union's political and legislative agenda' (Monar 2002: 189).

On the other hand, it is easy to find cases where the member states compromised their collective credibility, either by not taking seriously their commitments or by committing themselves to unrealistic objectives.

The so-called 'Lisbon Agenda' may become the classic instance of European hubris. The reform agenda agreed by EU leaders at the Lisbon Summit in March 2000 was driven by two main goals: that the EU should 'become the world's most competitive, knowledge-based economy'; and to 'ensure average annual economic growth of 3 per cent, leading to the creation of 20 million jobs', both goals to be achieved by 2010. These voluntaristic targets, more reminiscent of Soviet-style planning than of agenda-setting by electorally accountable leaders, have become a source of anger and embarrassment to many Europeans. The Commission's Report to the European Council of Spring 2004, *Delivering Lisbon: Reforms for the Enlarged Union* (Commission 2004), shows that far from overtaking its major competitor, the EU is falling further behind the United States in terms of economic growth and productivity, in spite of the good overall performance of a few, mostly small, member states. Per capita GDP in the EU is unchanged since 2003 and is only 72 percent of that of the United States, while the rate of growth of productivity in Europe is falling since the mid-1990s. At present it varies between 0.5 and 1 percent against a rate of growth of 2 percent in the United States. The widening gap in productivity means that Europe will have to struggle just to keep pace with the US economy.

At Lisbon it was also agreed that in order to reach the two main goals, average research and development (R&D) spending should reach 3 percent of total GDP by 2010. However, businesses are deeply skeptical about the EU's ability to meet this goal: the Union is still spending less than 2 percent of total GDP on R&D, compared to about 2.7 percent in the United States and 3 percent in Japan. The Union continues to lag behind these two countries also in terms of total expenditure on information and communications technology, as a proportion of GDP. Another objective of the Lisbon Agenda is to raise private spending on R&D from 55 percent to more than 66 percent of all R&D spending, again by 2010. However, in October 2002 the European Roundtable of Industrialists warned that business R&D spending in Europe was unlikely to increase in the next three years. It also found that its member firms were much more likely to raise their spending levels outside Europe. This failure is summed up by the saga of the Community Patent—an issue that has been under discussion for fourteen years. At Lisbon, EU leaders committed themselves to reaching agreement on the Community Patent by 2001, but member states took until March 2003 to finally reach a broad agreement, which still leaves many technical issues to be resolved. The EU's attempts to stimulate biotechnology research have fared little better. In November 2002, the

Union's Competitiveness Council, which brings together member-state industry ministers, endorsed a new action plan for life sciences and bio-technology with the aim of providing stronger intellectual property rights to biotechnology inventions. At the same time, however, the Commission is beginning infringement procedures against France, Germany, Sweden, and six other member states that have so far failed to implement a 1998 directive designed to protect biotechnology intellectual property rights (Murray 2003). Biotechnology is also one of the priorities of the EU's sixth research framework program, but the continuing de facto moratorium on the development of GM products (see Chapters 6 and 7) casts serious doubts on the success of the program. In the following section, I consider in some detail what at first sight appears to be another clear example of the inability of the member states to credibly commit themselves to long-term goals.

8.3   The Stability and Growth Pact

The short but eventful history of the Stability and Growth Pact—a Euro-pean Council resolution adopted at the Amsterdam Summit in October 1997, together with two implementing Council regulations on multilateral surveillance and on implementation of the excessive deficit procedure—seems to provide ample evidence in support of the cynical view that a commitment that depends on the mutual control of the Council of Min-isters is not believable. In this view, the conflicts about the correct imple-mentation of the pact strongly suggest that there is no viable alternative to the discipline imposed by the Community method. Indeed, in May 2002, just two months after agreeing with the other EU leaders in Barcelona to move to budget parity by 2004, President Chirac decided to cut taxes and increase military expenditures, hoping that the inflated deficit would help secure a majority in the forthcoming June elections. At the same time the interim finance minister announced that France would not reach a bal-anced budget by the agreed deadline. In October of the same year, after the won elections, the new French finance minister, Francis Mer, defied his European colleagues with his refusal to start cutting the budget deficit in 2003. A statement at the end of the meeting of the Eurogroup finance ministers in Luxembourg on October 7, 2002 said that 'all ministers but one' had agreed a program for cutting deficits. Three of the four countries with the most serious deficit problem—Portugal, Germany, and Italy—agreed to cut their structural deficits by 0.5 percent from 2003, but France insisted that it would not start until 2004, so the deadline for budget parity had to be moved to 2006.

Clearly, peer pressure was not sufficient to change Mer's opinion that restoring growth to the French economy (and honoring campaign promises) was more important than honoring France's commitment to fiscal discipline. However, the troubles of the Stability and Growth Pact cannot be blamed only on one country. Portugal was the first member state to break the pact in 2001 with a deficit of 4.1 percent of GDP, but there was special irony in the announcement that Germany would be unable to meet the rules that it itself had devised in order to restrain other, allegedly less virtuous, members of the Eurozone. The German finance minister, who during the campaign for the federal elections of September 2002 insisted that the deficit would be 2.9 percent, admitted a few weeks after the elections what many people—including people in his own ministry—knew all along, namely that Berlin would be unable to keep its budget deficit below 3 percent in 2002.

In spite of these difficulties, it would be wrong to conclude that only closer involvement of the Commission in the process of macroeconomic coordination can give credibility to the member states' commitment to fiscal discipline. For all its 'stupidity'—as the president of the Commission famously described the 1997 agreement, just as the commissioner for monetary affairs was doing his best to enforce it—the pact did seem to influence the behavior of member states. During the late 1990s, most members of the Eurozone used the proceeds of the economic boom to eliminate their deficits and reduce the public debt, to the point that countries like Spain and Belgium became models of fiscal responsibility. The four countries that did not take advantage of the good economic conditions to put their public finances on a sound basis are precisely those that have experienced the greatest difficulties in meeting the criteria. Moreover, all countries seem to be well aware of the loss of credibility that would result from a hasty decision to abandon the pact altogether. Even after the events of November 2003 (see below) the prevalent view seemed to be to wait for economic recovery before undertaking any radical reform of the mechanisms of fiscal discipline. This sense of responsibility is all the more remarkable in light of some facts that are too often forgotten. First, the Stability Pact—formulated at a time of high economic growth—was not freely chosen by the national governments, but rather imposed on them by Germany as a non-negotiable condition of monetary union. At the time, France was the most determined opponent of the German pact, and this may explain in part the defiant attitude of that country. Second, it is important to realize that the budget discipline imposed by the Maastricht Treaty and by the Stability Pact has no equivalent in the majority of federal systems, whose component states are not subject to federal fiscal constraints of similar stringency. It is as if the severity of the legal requirements were meant to compensate for the lack of a convincing economic rationale for monetary union.

A third element to be kept in mind is the weakness of the conceptual foundations of the pact itself. One of the standard arguments is that too high budget deficits increase the interest rates in the Eurozone and put pressure on the ECB to prevent this by loosening monetary policy, thus raising the specter of inflation. Budget deficits, so the argument continues, should be regulated top-down precisely to avoid such an inflationary bias. But as economist Paul De Grauwe points out, in a globalized financial market the real interest rate is not a merely European but an international phenomenon, which cannot be easily influenced by national budget policies. Hence, there is little danger that the ECB can be pressured to compromise on its inflation targets because of the bad budget policies of some member states. On the other hand, too strict budget deficit rules make it impossible for Eurozone countries, which have lost their monetary-policy instruments, to use fiscal policy in order to counter recessions. The risk of default of the national debt is, according to De Grauwe, the only serious argument in support of imposing strict rules on budget deficits. For West European states, however, such risk seems quite remote, so that the stringency of the pact is out of proportion to the objective of avoiding a future debt default of countries like France, Germany, Italy, the Netherlands (which also violated the 3 percent constraint in 2004), or Portugal. The members of the Eurozone have strong enough political institutions to prevent their governments taking the road toward budgetary disaster. De Grauwe concludes that the Stability Pact is, in reality, a vote of no confidence by the Brussels authorities in the strength of the democratic institutions in the member states. It is quite surprising, he writes, that 'EU countries have allowed this to happen, and that they have agreed to be subjected to control by the European institutions that even the International Monetary Fund does not impose on banana republics' (De Grauwe 2002). Seen from this political perspective, the 'nitpicking numerology' applied by the Commission appears to be another manifestation of the paternalism that was discussed in Chapter 6 in connection with EU environmental policy. It should also be remembered that the Commission did not oppose, but actually supported, a 'political' decision concerning the flexible application of the Maastricht parameters, in order to start with a large group of participants in the monetary union. As a consequence, countries like Belgium and Italy, with public debts well over 100 percent of GDP, were allowed to join the EMU from the beginning, against the wishes of Germany and the other members of the 'DM bloc', which intended to start with a small group of countries with sound public finances.

On November 25, 2003, a majority of the members of Ecofin decided to suspend the procedures for excessive deficit initiated by the Commission against France and Germany. Instead, the Council recommended reductions of the structural deficit of the two countries, sufficient to bring the deficit below 3 percent of GDP by the end of 2005. France and Germany promised to do their best to achieve these goals, but this was clearly a political, not a legally binding, commitment. In January 2004, a badly divided Commission decided to bring the decision of the Council before the ECJ. One consequence of the events of November 2003 seems sure: the pact will not be discarded, but it will be significantly modified, in due time, along lines set by the Council rather than by the Commission. This conclusion is not modified by the fact that on July 13, 2004 the ECJ overturned the decision by the finance ministers to suspend the threat of sanctions against France and Germany. The ruling partially vindicated the Commission's decision to go to court to defend the pact, but the Commission lost the second part of its case where it claimed that Ecofin had a duty to adopt its recommendations. A thorough review of the pact is now scheduled for early 2005, and it is very likely that the pact will be made more flexible, along the lines indicated by the Council.

It is important to understand that the real bone of contention was not the pact as such, but rather the future of economic governance in the Eurozone. The conflict between the Commission and Ecofin was about the issue of which institution should be responsible for the coordination of macroeconomic policy at European level. 'Flexibility' is a key word here. While the president of the Commission was saying that the pact is stupid because it is not flexible enough—and sticking to his statement despite all the uproar caused by his choice of words—the monetary affairs commissioner kept repeating that the rules are flexible as well as rigorous. The contradiction was more apparent than real, however. Commissioner Solbes was referring to the text of the pact, which does indeed provide some leeway in the interpretation of the key parameters—for example, in the precise definition of 'close to balance', or of a 'serious recession' that would warrant a public deficit greater than 3 percent of GDP. On the other hand, Prodi did not really object to the text of the pact, which he had defended on many occasions; rather, he seemed to be reacting to the rejection by Ecofin of the Commission's proposal to allow national governments to discuss directly with Brussels the adoption of discretionary measures of economic and budgetary policy. In other words, a more flexible and intelligent interpretation of the pact required, according to the Commission's president, greater centralization of economic policy coordination, with the Commission, rather than the Council, providing the political counterweight to the ECB. Ecofin's 'November revolution' has apparently settled the matter: in the future, economic governance in the Eurozone will be provided by the Council, not by the Commission. Whatever the risks, this solution has at least the advantage of clarity, since responsibility for the coordination of national economic policies will rest squarely with the finance ministers.

In sum, the empirical evidence does not allow any firm conclusion concerning the viability of self-government by the member states. In part, this is due to a lack of experience with the new non-Community methods, so that the situation could improve with time, as learning takes place. It is also important to keep in mind that the problems the new approaches attempt to solve are particularly difficult from a political viewpoint, hence it is highly unlikely that the Community method, even if it were extended to these new policy areas, could achieve better results there. Since the evidence is ambiguous, we turn to some of the theoretical and historical reasons suggesting the possibility of self-government by the community of national governments.

8.4   Transgovernmentalism as a Polycentric Process

The level of information available to the members of a group about each other's preferences is one of the key variables determining the capacity of the group for self-government. Some years ago Miles Kahler advanced an 'arc-of-information' hypothesis, according to which 'decentralized institutional evolution and design is most likely when levels of information among governments and societies are low (and an initial confidence-building role is awarded to institutions) and again when information about the preferences of other governments is plentiful. Europe's highly centralized institutions may seem less necessary as economic integration and political understanding produce an increasingly information-rich environment' (Kahler 1995: 122–3). In other words, when levels of information are low, centralized institutions are impossible; when they are high, such institutions are unnecessary. Hence, the information-rich environment in which the Council of Ministers of the EU operates today would explain why deeper economic and political integration does not entail the greater centralization that many expected or feared, but rather tends to favor various strategies of institutional and decisional decentralization.

Kahler's hypothesis is an empirical generalization from several examples considered by the author. Michael Polanyi's model of *coordination by mutual adjustment*, on the other hand, provides a theoretical underpinning to the insight that information exchange and adaptive behavior can, under some conditions, replace central coordination. Polanyi shows that a group of people can perform a collective task without a central coordinator, provided that each individual adjusts himself or herself to the state of affairs resulting from the actions of the other members of the group. This requires that information about the state of affairs in question is available to each member of the group. *Polycentricity* is the property of a set of autonomous decision centers that coordinate their actions by each center adjusting its actions to the results achieved by all other centers in the set. A *polycentric task* is the problem of balancing or coordinating a number of such centers. The proper method of managing a polycentric task, according to Polanyi, is not by collecting all the data at a central coordinating authority. Rather, the desired result is achieved by each individual center reacting to the whole range of signals that reach it from all the parts of the system which it takes into account. Each center evaluates the joint significance of the signals, and thus guided all centers collectively produce a solution to the polycentric task, or achieve, at any rate, a measure of success in this direction.

Rather than reproducing the formal analysis supporting this conclusion, it may be more useful to quote one of Polanyi's examples of coordination by mutual adjustment. Suppose we have to piece together a large jigsaw puzzle, which it would take a person several days or even weeks to complete. In order to save time we hire a team of helpers and the polycentric task is: how should we organize them? A moment's reflection shows that central direction would not work, since each helper would have to wait for directions from the center and all would have to wait until a decision is taken at the highest level. All participants except the one acting as central coordinator would cease to make any appreciable contribution to the piecing together of the puzzle, so that the benefit of cooperation would be close to zero. The only way to finish the job quickly, argues Polanyi, is to let each helper be free to follow his or her own initiative. The helper would then watch the situation as it is affected by the progress made by all the others and would set himself or herself new problems in accordance with the latest outline of the completed part of the puzzle. The tasks undertaken by each would closely dovetail into those performed by the others. Consequently, the joint efforts of all would form a closely organized whole, even though each helper would follow entirely his or her own independent judgment. It is clear, then, that the possibility of solving polycentric tasks depends on two crucial conditions: that each suggested new step can be readily judged as to its correctness or otherwise; and that each new step is rapidly brought to the attention of all participants and taken into account by them when they make their own next move (Polanyi 1951: 35–6).

Unlike the jigsaw puzzle, there is no preformed or generally accepted pattern for the end state of the process of European integration. Polanyi's notion of coordination by mutual adjustment is nevertheless relevant because it suggests that information exchange can not only prevent negative policy externalities—the function usually emphasized by students of international policy coordination—but can also facilitate a decentralized and yet coordinated approach to collective problem-solving by the member states of the EU. This is what the OMC and related 'new governance' approaches aim to achieve. As we saw in Chapter 3, the OMC has been pushed by the European Council in order to favor some convergence of national policies in areas, such as social policy, employment, and pension reform, that are too politically sensitive to be handled by the centralized Community method. OMC has been conceived as a learning process that, by means of information exchange, benchmarking, evaluation, and peer review of the results, should lead to policy coordination through mutual adjustment.

The view of EU governance as a polycentric process has not only some empirical and theoretical support but is also deeply rooted in the history of our continent. The European states system as it developed between the peace of Westphalia and the French Revolution had many of the properties of polycentricity discussed by Polanyi. Its key characteristic was that changes in one component of the system affected the others: it was a multicell organization with a built-in ability to replace its local losses and regenerate itself. The polycentric task was to maintain a balance of power, which had the latent function of strengthening the system and bringing about an autonomous growth in it. In this way, as the British historian E. L. Jones has brilliantly shown, the European states system realized not only the benefits of competitive decision-making but also some of the economies of scale expected of a centralized empire. This achievement was facilitated by the fact that Europe shared in important respects a common culture and not too dissimilar lifestyles, and formed something of a common market. Coordination by mutual adjustment worked because 'European states were similar enough *and informed enough about each other*, to learn to solve problems precisely because they could see that some other member of the system had solved them. Competitiveness and diversity helped to generalize best practices by the movement of capital and labour, by the continuous flow of ideas, and by the spirit of imitation and emulation' (Jones 1987: 122–3; emphasis added). Thus history provides additional evidence that polycentric tasks can indeed be managed, even on a continental scale.

8.5 New Strategies of Commitment

In the final analysis, the viability of self-government at European level depends on the credibility of the member states' commitment to common strategies. Delegation of powers to the supranational institutions has been until now the main 'technology of commitment', but increasing reliance on decentralized modes of governance implies that other methods will have to be relied on in the future. In general terms, credibility requires finding a way to prevent going back on one's promises or threats. To make a strategic move credible, it is necessary to take a supporting action, typically by limiting one's discretionary choices. Such a supporting action is called a *commitment*, and it should be clear that delegating powers to an agent or fiduciary is only one of a number of possible devices for achieving credible commitments. Here I consider three other devices that seem to be particularly useful in a context of self-government: building and using a reputation; developing credibility through teamwork; and breaking down large commitments into smaller ones (Dixit and Nalebuff 1991).

Reputation can arise only in a context of repeated interactions, which create a link between current and expected future decisions. If the future is long enough, or important enough, short-run temptations to renege one's promise to do the *ex post* optimal thing today can be resisted. This is because doing the optimal thing today entails not only current benefits but also future costs, which reduce the incentive to renege. In a context of repeated interactions one can distinguish between two different methods of building and using a reputation (Milgrom and Roberts 1992). The first method applies when, although it is not possible to specify in advance what to do in any specific situation ('incomplete contracting', in the terminology of Chapter 4), the parties themselves have enough information to evaluate each other's past behavior. When the latter condition does not hold—for example, because the situation is ambiguous and thus open to different and conflicting interpretations—a system of reputations can work, if at all, only with the help of independent third parties. In the limiting case, legal institutions replace the system of reputations altogether. Parties who rely on the legal system count on the threat of a lawsuit, rather than on reputational mechanisms, to ensure compliance with the original agreement. Thus we arrive by a different route to the same conclusion reached in the preceding section: centralized institutions are not needed, except perhaps in exceptional situations, among members of a team who are sufficiently informed about each other to be able to interpret correctly their present and past actions. In turn, this information, which is a basic requirement of any system of reputations, is an important by-product of repeated interactions.

The application of this theory of reputation to the problems of European governance is straightforward. The frequent meetings of the Council of Ministers—at least once a month for major Councils like General Affairs, Agriculture, and Economic and Financial Affairs—create a situation of repeated interactions where reputation can become a very valuable asset. Students of the European Council seem to agree on the significance of reputational factors also for this body, even though it meets less frequently than the Council of Ministers. Fiona Hayes-Renshaw, for example, writes: 'With so much attention focused on the President-in-office, it has become a point of pride for the outgoing office-holders to be viewed by their colleagues as having conducted a "good presidency".' Among the criteria used in forming such judgments this author mentions: whether Council business was dealt with efficiently and impartially; whether the main objectives outlined in the presidency program were achieved; and 'whether unpredictable events were dealt with calmly, efficiently, and effectively' (Hayes-Renshaw 2002: 60). Even in the case of EPC, which for twenty years represented a 'working model of intergovernmental cooperation without formal integration' (Forster and Wallace 2000: 466), early accounts pointed to the development of an *esprit de corps* among key policymakers, leading gradually to the Europeanization of national foreign policies (Joergensen 2002).

Reputation seems to be quite important even below the ministerial level. Indeed, because of the more frequent interactions at the lower levels, reputation may be an even more valuable asset there. To quote Hayes-Renshaw again: 'A certain *esprit de corps*, similar to that perceptible in Coreper [the Committee of Permanent Representatives of the national governments] . . . is noticeable among the members of the working groups that meet on a regular basis. The personal relations forged through continuous interaction between individuals in the group (many of whom may be long-serving members) eventually fosters an appreciation of differing points of view and a desire to reach agreement by consensus, in an attempt to keep everyone on board' (Hayes-Renshaw 2002: 55). According to Lewis (2002: 280), the members of Coreper 'exemplify a brand of diplomacy based on thick bonds of mutual trust, understanding, responsiveness, and a willingness to compromise'. The norm of thick trust is 'reconfirmed weekly through the normal cycle of meetings, trips, and lunches'. There is also a norm of mutual responsiveness that is best described as a shared purpose to understand each other's problems. Finally a 'culture of compromise' favors a self-restraint in the calculation and defense of interests (ibid.: 291).

A second strategy is based on the observation that teamwork can be used to enhance credibility. Although people may be weak on their own, they can build resolve by forming a group. Any member of the group is open to peer pressure and thus places himself or herself in a situation where pride and self-respect are lost when commitments are broken (Dixit and Nalebuff 1991: 158). Some of the evidence quoted above also shows the importance of peer pressure in a setting like the Council of Ministers. It is peer pressure that makes it so difficult for a minister to oppose the opinion of a large majority of his or her colleagues, even under the unanimity rule. What is true of individuals in a team can also apply to organizations forming a network. As was suggested in Chapter 5, for instance, a European regulatory agency that sees itself as part of a transnational network of institutions pursuing similar objectives and facing similar problems is more motivated than an isolated agency to defend its policy commitments and/or professional standards against external influences. Unprofessional, selfish, or politically motivated behavior would compromise its international reputation and make cooperation more difficult to achieve in the future. Thus, the function of a network is not only to diffuse information but also to act as an extended peer group, enhancing the effectiveness of the social mechanisms of reputation enforcement. This is one reason why networks are such a pervasive feature of intensive transgovernmentalism.

The third path to credibility—moving in small, frequent steps—should be followed whenever a large commitment is infeasible and hence not credible. The method consists in breaking down the total commitment into a number of small steps such that the scale of commitment of each is sufficiently reduced to be credible. The commitment made at the Lisbon

Summit of March 2000—to become the world's most competitive economy by 2010—is not credible because, given the rigidity of most national
economies, a decade is not long enough to permit breaking down such an
ambitious goal into a number of smaller, credible commitments. In general, however, the strategy of moving in small steps has been applied
frequently in the EU, not without success.

Consider, for instance, the many incremental steps that, from the
launching of EPC at the Hague summit of December 1969, led to the
creation of the position of High Representative for CFSP at the Helsinki
Summit of December 1999, and to the creation by the Constitutional
Treaty of a Minister for Foreign Affairs combining the responsibilities of
the High Representative and of the Commissioner for external relations.
Intermediate steps include the 1981 London Report, attempting to promote closer political cooperation following the Soviet invasion of
Afghanistan, and the much more ambitious Genscher–Colombo Plan;
the 1986 SEA that brought together the EPC and the EC under the
common roof of the European Council; the establishment of the CFSP
pillar by the TEU in 1992; the Petersberg Declaration committing the
Western European Union to peacekeeping and peacemaking tasks in the
same year, and the embedding of these tasks in the 1997 Amsterdam Treaty.
In the area of JHA, one can trace the various steps from the creation of the
Trevi Group (as part of EPC) by the Rome European Council of December
1975; the first Schengen Agreement in 1985 and its subsequent incorpor-
ation in the Amsterdam Treaty; the transformation of JHA into a fundamental treaty objective, also at Amsterdam; up to the Tampere European
Council of October 1999—a landmark for both the policy and institutional
development of JHA.

The case of EMU is particularly instructive. Before the final decision to
proceed with full monetary integration in 1999—a quantum jump whose
long-term implications and risks are still uncertain (see Chapter 6)—this
major area of non-Community policymaking also generally exhibited the
same strategy of small steps as CFSP and JHA, with one significant exception. The Rome Treaty contained very little in terms of binding commitments in the field of macroeconomic policy. At the Hague Summit of
December 1969, however, the political leaders of the Six adopted, for the
first time, the target of full EMU. This premature commitment to monetary union turned out to be infeasible, especially in the situation of monetary instability following the collapse of the Bretton Woods System in
1971. As Tsoukalis (2000: 152) writes: 'EMU became the biggest non-event
of the decade. ... Very senior west European politicians had made

political commitments but had not by and large translated them into the appropriate economic policies. Finally they gave way under market pressure.'

After this serious setback, the strategy of small steps was followed pretty consistently for about two decades. After 1972 what was left of the over-ambitious plan for EMU was the 'snake', a fixed exchange-rate regime including, in addition to Germany, the Benelux countries, as well as Denmark, Austria, and Switzerland—in practice, a DM bloc. Although the 'snake' was short-lived, it was 'a decisive step in the process of ever closer cooperation among European central bankers, thus laying the ground for more ambitious initiatives to come' (ibid.). The European Monetary System (EMS)—a system of fixed, but periodically adjustable, exchange rates between EC currencies—was established in March 1979. The early years of the EMS were still characterized by high inflation rates and persisting divergences between the national economies, but from the early 1980s and especially during the 1990s the downward convergence of inflation rates became pronounced. In turn, price convergence, coupled with the growing credibility of stability-oriented policies, brought about the gradual convergence of nominal long-term interest rates. The decision to liberalize capital movements, taken in 1988 as part of the single market program, was another important step on the road leading gradually from an extensive coordination of national policies to the centralization of monetary policy at EU level.

The strategy of small, credible steps came to a sudden halt with the reunification of Germany in 1989 and the disintegration of the Soviet Union. For many people in Paris, Rome, and Brussels the transformation of the geopolitical context called for a deepening of the integration pro-cess and a strengthening of the ties binding the new, larger Germany to its European partners. As a result, the economic and political desirabil-ity of EMU was not seriously questioned during the negotiations leading to the Maastricht Treaty. The matter was supposed to have been already settled. The doubters, of which there were quite a few, kept a low profile, preferring to concentrate on specific problems instead of challenging the main principles and objectives. As a result, the decision to move to a single currency and an ECB by January 1, 1999 left a number of crucial issues still unresolved (see Chapter 6). During the treaty negotiations member states were unable to achieve a consensus on such matters as the external mon-etary policy, and the mechanisms by which exchange rate policy was to be formulated. In the words of an American analyst: 'Prudence might have counseled that the European Union take certain steps well before the creation of the euro area: namely, fill in the holes in the external monetary policymaking machinery and operationalize those parts that were addressed by the treaty. Even several months after the event, however, many basic institutional questions remained unresolved' (Henning 2000: 36). They are still unresolved at the time of writing (May 2004). After Maastricht, the only attempt to meet widespread concerns about the insufficient coordination of the fiscal and economic policies of the members of the Eurozone was the Stability and Growth Pact. Shortly after its introduction, Wim Duisenberg, the first president of the ECB, argued that the existence of the pact had made a centralized budget unnecessary (McNamara 2002). In fact, subsequent developments have demonstrated the urgent need of clarifying which institution should be responsible for macroeconomic coordination in the Eurozone.

8.6   Complementary Approaches to Integration

No single method, however powerful, can match the complexity of European governance. The real problem facing the member states today is not how to choose between 'self-government' and delegation to the supranational institutions, but how to combine the two approaches optimally. The advantages and limitations of intensive transgovernmentalism— broadly understood to include the various 'new governance' methods— are in a sense the reverse of those of the Community method. Flexible, respectful of national autonomy, and sustained by the legitimacy of democratically elected leaders, transgovernmentalism can achieve results that are precluded to the traditional approach. On the other hand, the price of operating free of the constraints of the Community method is a loss of legal certainty and the opaqueness of the process. These differences, which are partly explained by the differences in the policy areas to which the two methods are applied, suggest a useful complementarity, rather than mutual exclusiveness. Embedded in an information-rich environment and supported by suitable strategies of commitment, intensive transgovernmentalism will continue to be a viable and increasingly effective method for driving forward the process of European integration in areas close to the core of national sovereignty. The available empirical evidence, when carefully examined, does not support any a priori reason why 'self-government' by the member states cannot work, or why it should be only a second-best alternative to the Community method. On the contrary, the evidence suggests that centralized coordination or a greater role for the Commission are not adequate responses to the problems of EMU or CFSP, which have other sources.

On the other hand, the Single European Market still needs the legal certainty that only the Community method, with its binding rules and independent supranational institutions, can provide. But as was suggested in Chapter 7, legal certainty is better ensured by 'negative' law—preventing the member states, and the European institutions themselves, from engaging in discretionary behavior—than by measures of positive integration, which often produce uncertain and suboptimal outcomes. The situation in Europe has changed radically since the late 1950s. A reform of the Community method is certainly needed, but not along the lines indicated in the White Book on European governance and in subsequent documents by the Brussels authorities, which would transform the Commission into a full-fledged 'government of Europe'. The truth is that the method is too rigid to be easily adapted to new situations and new tasks, while a fragile legitimacy base prevents its expansion into some crucially important policy areas. Restricting the scope of the Community method can only enhance its credibility and democratic legitimacy, while its generalization would weaken, perhaps fatally, the process of European integration.

International Economic Integration, the Nation-State, and Democracy: An Impossible Trinity?

9.1 The 'Diminished Democracy' Syndrome

In this chapter we go back to some issues already discussed in Chapter 2, but the present treatment is more general in two respects. First, the central issue—the tension between economic integration, national sovereignty, and democracy—is examined not only in relation to European integration but in the more general context of an integrating world economy. In this broader setting, Europe's deep economic integration represents a limiting case against which the theses advanced by the critics of globalization can be usefully tested. Second, this chapter probes, rather more deeply than the previous discussion, into certain aspects of democratic theory dealing with the transformations of democracy, and its adaptation to fit the realities of the new transnational societies.

It has been well said that political power has determined frontiers while economic power has the freedom of the world. As markets grow beyond national boundaries it becomes increasingly difficult to evade the question: can markets become international while politics remains national or even local? It is clear that international economic integration tends to erode the effectiveness of some traditional policy instruments. For example, the greater the degree of openness of a national economy, the less effective Keynesian demand management will be as an instrument of domestic stabilization policy. This is because some portion of any additional government expenditure will be spent on imports from the rest of the world, so that some of the demand-creating effect of the expenditure is dissipated abroad. The obsolescence of some policy instruments does not imply, however, that democratic polities are no longer able to satisfy the demands of their citizens. From the perspective of democratic theory the question is whether deepening economic integration will result in a more constrained national agenda, and thus in fewer channels for the expression of people's preferences; or whether integration may, on balance, enrich the national agenda and improve the quality of the democratic process. We may note, for example, that a good deal of the work of international bodies such as the OECD, the Food and Agriculture Organization, and the WHO, is aimed at influencing the national agendas by raising the level of public awareness of global problems such as environmental degradation. Sometimes the aim is not simply to raise certain issues but even to change the priorities of the decision agenda—as in the case of the AIDS epidemic in Africa, or the need to coordinate public-health measures on a global scale. A significant influence is exercised also by transnational nongovernmental organizations (NGOs) particularly on issues of poverty and the protection of human rights.

Greater interdependence among nations may improve the quality of policymaking by, among other things, making national leaders more aware of the international impacts of their decisions, more willing to engage in international cooperation, and more sensitive to international comparisons. Another indirect benefit of greater economic integration is the added incentive to make the political and bureaucratic systems of trading nations more open and accountable, as well as more efficient. In fact, the demand of greater transparency in public decision-making, the search for new forms of accountability, and the growing reliance on persuasion rather than on traditional forms of governmental coercion can be shown to be related to the process of growing economic and political interdependence among nations (Majone 1996b).

A heuristically useful starting point for an analysis of the relations between economic integration and democracy is provided by a familiar result of international economics known as the Mundell–Fleming theorem or, more informally, the 'impossible trinity' or 'open-economy trilemma'. According to the Mundell–Fleming theorem, countries cannot simultaneously maintain an independent monetary policy, capital mobility, and fixed exchange rates. If a government chooses fixed exchange rates and capital mobility, it has to give up monetary autonomy. If it chooses monetary autonomy and capital mobility, it has to go with floating exchange rates. Finally, if it wishes to combine fixed exchange rates with monetary autonomy, it has to limit capital mobility. Harvard economist

Dani Rodrik has argued that the standard open-economy trilemma can be extended to what he calls the political trilemma of the world economy (see Fig. 9.1). The elements of Rodrik's political trilemma are: integrated national economies, the nation-state, and 'mass politics', that is, a democratic system characterized by a high degree of political mobilization and by institutions that are responsive to mobilized groups. The claim, as in the standard trilemma, is that it is possible to have at most two of these things.

To quote Rodrik (2000: 180):

> If we want true international economic integration, we have to go either with the nation-state, in which case the domain of national politics will have to be significantly restricted, or else with mass politics, in which case we will have to give up the nation-state in favor of global federalism. If we want highly participatory political regimes, we have to choose between the nation-state and international economic integration. If we want to keep the nation-state, we have to choose between mass politics and international economic integration.

Democratic politics would not necessarily shrink under global federalism since economic power and political power would then be aligned: all important political and policy issues would be treated at the global level. However, a world government is not in the domain of the politically possible, now or in the foreseeable future. Hence, the price of maintaining national sovereignty while markets become international is that politics has to be exercised over a much narrower range of issues: 'The overarching goal of nation-states ... would be to appear attractive to international markets. ... Domestic regulations and tax policies would be either harmonized according to international standards, or structured such that

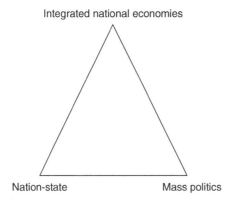

Fig. 9.1 Rodrik's trilemma

Source: Rodrik (2000: 181)

they pose the least amount of hindrance to international economic integration. The only local public goods provided would be those that are compatible with integrated markets' (ibid.: 182). In essence, this is the 'diminished democracy' thesis, which has found wide acceptance among critics of international (or even regional) economic integration.

The core of this thesis is an argument about the declining ability of democratic policymakers to produce public policies that depart from market-conforming principles. Typical of this school of thought is the assertion that 'European economic integration has significantly reduced the range of policy instruments available, and the range of policy goals achievable, at the national level. To that extent, the effectiveness as well as the responsiveness of government, and hence democratic legitimacy, are seen to have been weakened' (Scharpf 2001: 360). However, several studies cast serious doubts on the accuracy of any simple correlation, much less of any causal link, between increasing economic integration and a 'diminished democracy' syndrome, not only in Europe but in all advanced democracies. Thus, a recent econometric analysis using annual data from 1964 to 1993 for sixteen OECD countries finds little evidence that international capital mobility exerts systematic downward pressure on the public sector, the welfare state, and the provisions of public goods (Swank 2001). Another set of data on total social expenditure in twenty-one advanced democracies between 1980 and 1997 shows that a race to the bottom in welfare provision did not take place. Average social spending as a percentage of GDP increased from 19.2 in 1980 to 23.8 in 1997. The increase in social expenditure was particularly significant in countries like Finland, Greece, Italy, and Portugal, indicating that social expenditure dynamics have been driven by catch-up, as well as by rising unemployment and population aging. Overall, welfare spending across nations converged in the period considered (OECD 2000).

These and similar findings (see Section 9.2) must appear counterintuitive to many critics of the globalization of trade, but they are quite understandable once we realize that the rules of the world trading system do not restrict the autonomy of national policymakers in any significant way. Thus the critics claim that under WTO rules a government cannot protect from import competition those domestic industries that have to bear the costs of environmental or other social regulations not applied by other countries. As Roessler (1996) has convincingly shown, however, WTO rules do permit member states to take a domestic regulatory measure raising the cost of production in combination with subsidies or tariffs that maintain the competitive position of the domestic producers who have to bear these costs. The only restriction is that if the compensatory measures adversely affect the interests of other WTO members, procedures designed to remove the adverse effects of those measures on third countries must be observed. A striking demonstration of the autonomy of national policymakers in politically sensitive matters is provided by the WTO Agreement on SPS measures (see Chapter 6). Under this agreement each signatory has the right to set its own standards in the health field. This presumption of national autonomy can be challenged only by showing that a measure lacks a scientific justification. If a health measure has a scientific basis there is little other countries can do to oppose it. The combination of rigid rules with flexible safeguards has permitted the liberalization of international trade to proceed so far without any domestic policy harmonization. This subtle compromise makes possible the coexistence of the two apparently opposing principles of domestic policy autonomy and the globalization of trade (Roessler 1996).

9.2   Shallow Versus Deep Integration

The arguments presented so far could be judged insufficient to challenge Rodrik's pessimistic scenario or to disprove the 'diminished democracy' hypothesis. It may be objected that the liberalization of capital and goods markets is a form of 'shallow' integration—integration limited to measures for removing controls and barriers that block exchange at national borders. As international economic integration progresses, however, such measures would no longer be sufficient. Issues of 'deeper' integration emerge on the international agenda. These issues concern behind-the-border policies and institutions that had previously not been subjected to international scrutiny (Kahler 1995). Domestic regulatory regimes, in particular, may have to be replaced by internationally harmonized rules that cannot be tailored to national preferences. Hence, it is concluded, the real threat to the autonomy of democratically accountable policymakers comes from the harmonization bias of deeper integration, or, to use Rodrik's terminology, from *true* international economic integration.

An example of this line of reasoning is provided by the received view of international tax competition. According to this view, because of increasing economic integration capital becomes more footloose and countries begin to compete to attract it by cutting their tax rates. The process may reach a point where a country is forced to provide a lower level of public services than its citizens would otherwise wish. Given this scenario, tax harmonization seems a reasonable proposition. At a minimum, if tax cutting is matched by all nations, no country gains a comparative advantage. Thus, international tax harmonization would resemble price-fixing cartels among firms—a very attractive strategy to all negotiating parties. In fact, one observes relatively little tax harmonization, even among countries whose economies are undergoing a process of deep integration, like the members of the EU.

It has often been predicted that a failure to harmonize taxation in the EU would result in a destructive competition among member states that would ultimately undermine Europe's generous welfare systems, but no such 'race to the bottom' has been observed so far (see also Chapter 7). While barriers to trade and to capital mobility have been falling almost continuously since the late 1950s, EU countries have not experienced any significant degree of tax competition and consequent fall of tax rates. In fact, the average tax rates have been climbing since the mid-1960s both in the original member states—the Benelux countries, Germany, France, and Italy, and in the countries of the European 'periphery'—Spain, Portugal, Greece, and Ireland. Moreover, tax rates have always been higher in the richer than in the poorer countries, showing that the growing integration of Europe did not make the richer members of the Community feel constrained by tax competition from low-wage countries. Since the late 1970s the difference between the tax rates of these two groups of countries has narrowed. However, this narrowing has gone in the opposite direction to that predicted by the tax-competition view, with average tax rates in the less prosperous countries approaching those of the richer countries. The member states of the EU seem to have engaged in a race to the top, rather than to the bottom, in taxation. There are also few signs that a race to the bottom in the provision of public services is taking place in the Union. Rather, as in the case of taxation, the race has been in the other direction, with the southern countries upgrading to northern levels of expenditure on service provision (Barnard 2000). This is precisely what one should expect, since we know from Chapter 5 that the level of social standards is positively correlated with the standard of living. Thus, as wealth grows as a result of market integration, the endogenous demand for higher social standards grows as well.

In sum, it is not at all evident that international economic integration must necessarily reduce the capacity of democratically elected policy-makers to provide the public goods the voters demand. Even in a deeply integrated EU, 'the nation-state is still the principal site of policy change, and there remains ample scope for political choice...if institutional arrangements and policy mixes are suitably modified, then the core principles of the European social model can be preserved and in many respects enhanced in their translation into the real worlds of European welfare' (Ferrera et al. 2001: 164). Of course, to say that the rules of the world trade regime, the liberalization of capital markets, and even 'deep' integration need not significantly reduce the autonomy of national policymakers is not to suggest that domestic policies do not have to be adapted to constantly changing economic, political, social, and technological conditions. Everywhere welfare states face serious problems, but the causes of the current difficulties are mostly related to factors that have little to do with the growing integration of the national economies: the impact of demographic changes, growing domestic opposition to high tax rates, the failure of traditional social policies to respond to new needs and new risks generated by technical change, and ideological and political shifts reflecting all these factors.

9.3   Europe's Impossible Trinity

Thus the experience of the EU seems to refute Rodrik's trilemma: it is after all possible to integrate national economies without eliminating the nation-state, and preserving (perhaps even enhancing) the quality of democratic processes at national level. In the EU the problem is not a diminution of democracy at the national level. At issue, rather, is a 'democratic deficit' at the supranational level, that is, the absence or incomplete development of democratic institutions and processes that the citizens of the Union take for granted in their own country. The immediate cause of this deficit was discussed in Chapter 2: while the majority of the citizens of the EU support deep economic integration because of its obvious advantages in terms of consumer choice and the free movement of people, goods, and services, there is no evidence that even a sizeable minority are in favor of establishing a European superstate. Hence the strategy of integration by stealth adopted by the supranational institutions. But let us assume, for the sake of argument, that national leaders in a moment of self-denying Euro-enthusiasm decided to create a United States of Europe (USE), and that the national parliaments duly ratified the new federal constitution. Naturally, this constitution would effect a significant transfer of powers to the European level. In addition to the regulatory and monetary powers that the EU already possesses, the USE would need, at a minimum, an independent power to tax and spend, and exclusive competences in foreign and security matters. Such transfer of powers would entail a severe loss of sovereignty for the member states, but sovereignty is not the issue with which we are concerned here. Rather, the aim is to explore the implications of the federalist hypothesis for the viability of participatory democracy at the transnational level (see Fig. 9.2).

According to Rodrik's argument, a European federation should permit 'mass politics' to flourish at the supranational level. Politics would simply relocate there, just as in the United States the most contentious political battles are fought not at the state level, but at the federal level (Rodrik 2000: 183). But US-type federalism is hardly a useful model for Europe. As Buchanan (1990: 6) has written: 'It is mockery to use "federalism" or "federal union" in descriptive reference to the United States...which is, of course, simply a very large nation-state.' In fact, in US political discourse 'national' is identical with 'federal'—Madison's 'invention' of an American People distinct from, and superior to, the peoples of the separate states (see Chapter 2) has materialized, *ex post*, with a vengeance. Directly or indirectly, the US government can regulate or control most of the activities of the state or local governments, but it is highly unlikely that something like this will ever be possible in Europe.

Any federal union in Europe would have to respect the historical, cultural, and institutional diversity, which is the hallmark of the old continent. In particular, it would have to respect what a distinguished historian has called the most fundamental peculiarity of European society—the absolute primacy of the territorial state over all competing principles of social cohesion (McNeill 1974). It is worth remembering that the idea of the primacy of the territorial state has the same origin as the idea

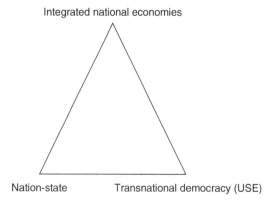

Fig. 9.2 Europe's trilemma

of democracy, namely in the Greek polis. Cleisthenes (about 570–508 BC) is regarded as the founder of Athenian democracy. His most important innovation was the basing of individual political rights and duties on citizenship of a locality rather than membership in a clan. In this way, Cleisthenes brought the territorial principle to triumph over the kinship principle or other possible principles of social organization. This explains why, even today, it is still so difficult to think about democracy outside the framework of the nation-state and why, therefore, the very notion of transnational democracy appears so problematic.

As discussed in Chapter 2, democracy presupposes a territorially based demos, but there is no European demos, let alone a European nation. The absence of a European demos—in the sense of 'a collectivity in which the identification of members with the group is sufficiently strong to override the divisive interests of subgroups in cases of conflict' (Scharpf 2001: 364)— implies, *inter alia*, that a basic criterion for the democratic process could not be satisfied at the European level. This is the criterion of *final agenda control*, which Dahl (1989: 113) formulates as follows: 'the *demos* must have the exclusive opportunity to decide how matters are to be placed on the agenda of matters that are to be decided by means of the democratic process.' If this criterion (which, incidentally, is radically violated by the Commission's monopoly of agenda-setting) cannot be satisfied at European level, then, *pace* Rodrik, the 'diminished democracy' thesis—the argument about the declining ability of democratic policymakers to provide the public goods the citizens demand—is more likely to be true in the case of a European federal state than at national level.

It is important to understand clearly why the criterion of final agenda control cannot be satisfied in a federation composed of states deeply divided along cultural, social, institutional, and economic lines. Observe, first, that like the democratic process itself, the majority principle presupposes the existence of a fairly homogeneous polity. Only in such a polity are majority decisions considered legitimate and hence accepted also by the outvoted minority. In fact, empirical research has shown that in polities divided into virtually separate subsocieties with their own political parties, interest groups, and media of communication, the majority principle is often rejected in favor of nonmajoritarian institutions (Lijphart et al. 1993). This research is clearly relevant to the EU—and a fortiori to a would-be European federation. Nonhomogeneous polities find it particularly difficult to pursue redistributive and other policies with clearly identified winners and losers. Redistribution of income and wealth is a zero-sum game since the gain of one group in society is the loss of another group. Public decisions concerning redistribution can only be taken by majority vote because any issue over which there is unavoidable conflict is defeated under more inclusive rules. It follows that in a transnational federation all such policies would have to be excluded from the public agenda as being too divisive. This is, in fact, the main reason why redistributive social policy plays such a small role even in the present EU.

It is true that the funds allocated to regional redistribution have grown considerably in recent years, reaching about 30 percent of the total Union budget. However, in the EU, regional aid is less an instrument of social policy than a side payment to induce the poorer member states to accept deep economic integration. There is an important distinction between reducing inequality among individuals (the main objective of social policy at the national level) and reducing disparities among regions. Since most regions contain a mix of rich and poor people, a policy aimed at redistributing resources to a poor region may be implemented in such a way as to favor mostly rich individuals within that region. The problem of targeting regions to achieve a better distribution of personal income is particularly difficult in federal systems. Even in the United States, where the federal government pays three-quarters of the cost of welfare assistance, states insist on defining the standards of need and setting the benefit levels. As a consequence, the level of welfare assistance among American states varies widely, more so than interstate disparities in wage rates or cost of living (Peterson and Rom 1990). In Europe too the countries that benefit most from regional aid are strongly opposed to individualized transfers of EU funds. Attempts to circumvent national governments in the management of regional policy by establishing direct links between subnational actors and the supranational level have largely failed. In sum, whatever the merits of EU regional policy, it cannot be considered a form of European social policy.

The delicate value judgments about the appropriate balance of efficiency and equity, which social policies express, can be made legitimately only within polities where the principle of final agenda control by the people is generally accepted. Hence it is difficult to see how politically acceptable levels of income redistribution could be determined centrally. The inclusion of income redistribution in the public agenda of a transnational federation where majoritarian principles can only play a limited role would not improve its democratic legitimacy, but only increase the level of conflict among its constituent states. Even the democratic legitimacy of a popularly elected federal parliament would be questioned. This is because the parliament, which is supposed to represent a nonexistent transnational demos, would be unable to respond to demands from citizens whose interests are rooted at the national level. Hence the federal parliament would be considered largely irrelevant as a representative institution, and could even be viewed as an instrument of centralization. It is interesting to note that back in 1862 Lord Acton analyzed the intrinsic limitations of parliamentary representation in imperial Austria in similar terms. The conclusion of the great liberal historian was that 'in those countries where different races dwell together... the power of the imperial parliament must be limited as jealously as the power of the crown, and many of its functions must be discharged by provincial diets, and a descending series of local authorities' (Acton 1967: 156).

Which policies, then, could be legitimately included in the agenda of a European federal state? Aside from foreign and security policy, the public agenda would mostly include efficiency-enhancing, market-preserving policies—a combination of liberalization and negative-integration measures to remove obstacles to the free movement of people, services, goods, and capital within the territory of the federation. Unlike redistribution—a zero-sum game—efficiency issues may be thought of as positive-sum games where everybody can gain, provided the right policy is adopted. Hence, efficiency-enhancing policies do not need a strong normative foundation: output legitimacy (accountability by results) is generally sufficient. In contrast, redistributive policies can only be legitimated by majority decisions and hence place too heavy a burden on the fragile normative foundations of a transnational polity.

9.4   Market-Preserving Federalism

Returning to Fig. 9.2, I have argued that in order to be viable, a European federal state would require such a constrained public agenda that the criterion of full agenda control could not be satisfied. Hence, democracy would be seriously diminished—at the federal rather than at the national level. It should be noted that this conclusion remains true even if a majority of the citizens of the transnational federation support a given measure, as long as the opponents of the measure are concentrated in a few member states where they are a majority of the voters. In a federation of polities sharply divided along linguistic, political, and institutional cleavages—and lacking the sense of solidarity generated by shared historical memories—any measure by the central government that differentially damages (or favors) the citizens of the separate states or regions within its territory, creates serious constitutional and legitimacy problems.

For these reasons, the only kind of federalism that would be viable in today's Europe is the one Barry Weingast calls 'market-preserving federalism'. A federal system is market-preserving if it satisfies three conditions: (1) member states have primary regulatory responsibility over the economy; (2) a common market is ensured, preventing the national governments from using their regulatory authority to erect trade barriers against the goods and services from other member states; and (3) the member states face a hard budget constraint, meaning that they have neither the ability to print money, nor access to unlimited credit (Weingast 1995). The author uses theoretical arguments and historical evidence to show that this type of federalism is conducive to economic development. The restrictions on the central government's regulatory power combine with competition among lower jurisdictions to imply that no government has monopoly control over economic regulation. This should prevent interest groups and rent-seeking coalitions, limited in their influence over lower-level governments because of competition, from transferring their influence to the federal level. Weingast's conditions for market-preserving federalism are largely satisfied in the present EU, except for the current emphasis on positive rather than negative integration (see Chapter 7). Thus, leaving aside the issue of foreign and security policy, to which I return in Chapter 10, a federal Europe could not do more than what the Union is already doing—in fact, it should do less if it wants to stimulate economic growth and avoid serious legitimacy problems.

9.5   Democracy and its Transformations

We have reached the conclusion that democracy as we know it—a system of government responsive to the wishes of the citizens—could not thrive in a European federation, or in any other transnational polity whose component units are deeply divided by various cleavages. The absence of a strong feeling of solidarity means that social and other policies, which historically have legitimated the national welfare state, could not be transferred to the higher level of governance. In short, transnational democracy would be, at best, a diminished democracy. Before discussing the broader implications of this conclusion it is important to remember that the theory and practice of democracy have changed dramatically in history. Dahl (1989) identifies three crucial transformations. The first transformation took place during the first half of the fifth century BC, when several Greek city-states that had been governed by monarchs, aristocrats, or tyrants were transformed into systems in which a substantial number of citizens were entitled to participate in governing. Political decisions came to be taken by a majority vote preceded by free public debate. Direct citizen participation, not only in law-making but also in administration, was such an essential element of the Greek idea of democracy that Greeks found it very difficult to conceive of representative government, much less to accept it as a legitimate alternative to direct democracy.

While one cannot exaggerate the significance of the Greek experience for human civilization, for the purpose of the present discussion it is necessary to point out the limitations of classical democracy. From a contemporary perspective, one crucially important limit of Greek democracy was that citizenship was highly exclusive, both internally and externally. Within the city-state, a large part of the adult population (women, long-term residents and their descendants, slaves) were denied full citizenship. Externally, the exclusiveness of classical democracy is revealed by the fact that genuine federal systems—as distinct from leagues or confederacies, often under the guidance and control of a hegemonic city—failed to develop in Greece. Every attempt to establish a true federation 'was shipwrecked on the inability of the Polis to moderate its love of autonomy and fit itself into a larger whole' (Ehrenberg 1969: 118–19). The face of the polis, as Ehrenberg writes, was almost completely turned inwards. Because Greek democracy lacked the means and the desire to extend the rule of law beyond the narrow limits of the city-state, in their external relations the city-states lived in a situation of almost continuous warfare—until peace was forced on them by a foreign power, first Macedonia and then Rome.

The exclusiveness of Greek democracy had serious consequences also in the area of *individual* rights. It is a much-discussed question to what extent the freedom of the polis included the freedom of the individual. At any rate, it meant freedom *within* the state and not freedom *from* the state. This is why nineteenth-century liberals like Benjamin Constant argued that the modern conception of liberty—as a private sphere of choice protected by individual rights—differs radically from the ancient conception of liberty as citizens sharing in public decision-making and the exercise of power. A fortiori, Greek democracy failed to acknowledge the existence of universal claims to freedom, equality, or human and political rights. Only after the breakdown of the polis in the second century AD did a new conception of universal individual rights emerge. In place of a law rooted in the tradition of a single city-state, the Stoic philosophers proposed a law for the 'city of the world'. In place of the exclusiveness of Greek democracy, they advanced the new conception of a worldwide human brotherhood, the idea that men are by nature equal, despite differences of race, rank, and wealth (Sabine 1960). Thus Stoicism revised the political ideas of the city-state to fit the reality of the new transnational societies created by the Hellenistic monarchies and the Roman empire.

The second democratic transformation took place 2,000 years after the first one. It resulted from the union of democracy with representation—the possibility that a legislative assembly might legitimately consist not of the entire body of citizens but only of their elected representatives. Incidentally, representation was not a democratic invention, but developed instead as a medieval institution of monarchical, aristocratic, and mixed government, and of the Conciliar movement in the Church. This is not the only case of nondemocratic institutions being adopted in order to extend and improve the practice of democracy. Another important example is constitutionalism (see below), which, in its modern form, was first theorized by predemocratic theorists like Bodin (1530–96) and Althusius (1557–1638).

Through the institution of representation, it became possible to extend the idea of democracy to the large domain of the nation-state. To quote Dahl (1989: 30):

Thus the idea of democracy, which might have perished with the disappearance of city-states, became relevant to the modern world of nation-states. Within the far larger domain of the nation-state, new conceptions of personal rights, individual freedom, and personal autonomy could flourish. Moreover, important problems that could never be solved within the narrow limits of the city-state . . . might be dealt with more effectively by a government capable of making laws and regulations over a far larger territory. To this extent, the capacity of citizens to govern themselves was greatly enhanced.

Representative democracy presents another important advantage: it makes possible the existence of a civil society separate from the state and independent from it. As already noted, direct democracy as practiced by the Greeks meant citizen participation not only in law-making but also in administration. Such total devotion to public affairs was possible only in a society founded on slave labor; hence the paradox, pointed out by Rousseau in Book III of *Social Contract*, that perhaps liberty can be maintained only on a basis of slavery: 'extremes meet!' Because life in the polis was so completely politicized, it was impossible for the citizens to carve out a sphere of private values and beliefs. By contrast, the separation of state and civil society, in particular of politics and economics, became one of the cornerstones of liberal representative democracy.

Thus, the second transformation simultaneously contracted and expanded the limits of democracy. Direct participation by the demos in the making and implementation of laws was no longer possible, but it became feasible to extend democracy and the rule of law to an entire nation-state. The sense of community nurtured by repeated interactions in face-to-face assemblies was lost, but the individual gained protection and security against the discretionary power of an omnicompetent majority. It became impossible to assume a widely shared conception of the public interest, but the democratic nation-state could accept a much greater diversity of groups and interests than the polis, and prove that such diversity need not be destructive of the polity.

We are now in the midst of a dramatic change—a third transformation—in the scale of decision-making as more and more policy competences are transferred from the national to the transnational level, or are exercised jointly by the two levels. In the remainder of this chapter, I suggest that the implications of the third transformation for the theory and practice of democracy will likely be quite different from those of the second transformation. The challenge for democrats today is less to build full-fledged democratic institutions at the transnational level—an impossible task in the absence of a transnational demos, as I have argued—than to use the higher level in order to improve the quality of democracy at national and subnational level. The experience of the EU shows that a rule-based system of cooperation and dispute resolution can not only civilize relations among sovereign states by eliminating the excesses of narrowly conceived national interest but, by protecting the rights of citizens even against their own government, such a system strengthens the foundations of liberal democracy that have been eroded by decades of discretionary executive power. In this sense, the 'virtuous trinity' of Fig. 9.3 may represent the third transformation of democracy in an increasingly interdependent world.

9.6 Transnational Constitutionalism

Contemporary western democracies are constitutional democracies, but 'democracy' and 'constitutionalism' are, both historically and conceptually, distinct ideas. While a constitution is an instrument to limit, control, and divide the power of governments, democracy—at least in its populist version—tends to concentrate potentially unlimited power in the hands of the current majority. According to the populist model, majorities

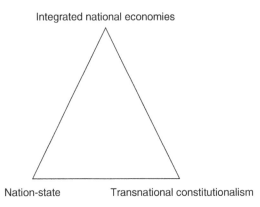

Fig. 9.3 The virtuous trinity

should be able 'to control all of government—legislative, executive and, if they have a mind to, judicial—and thus to control everything politics can touch' (Spitz 1984, cited in Lijphart 1991: 485). By contrast, constitutional rules are exempted from the majoritarian controls that govern ordinary legislation, and are enforced by those quintessentially nonmajoritarian institutions, the constitutional courts. The effect of constitutional rules is to remove certain decisions, for example concerning fundamental rights, from the electoral process and thus to tie the hands of the current majority.

It is not difficult to understand why some democrats consider the expression 'constitutional democracy' an oxymoron—a combination of contradictory ideas. Yet, a moment's reflection shows why a constitution-ally unconstrained democracy is not only more unstable but also less efficient than a liberal, constitutional democracy. Like other constraints, constitutional rules are not only limiting but also enabling. It is only an apparent paradox that Jean Bodin, the first modern theorist of sovereignty and absolutism, was also one of the first political philosophers to point out that limited power is more powerful than unlimited power, and that by closing off some options a ruler can open up others. By allowing his power to be restricted in certain specific ways, a sovereign increases the likeli-hood of social compliance with his wishes. This is indeed the central paradox of Bodin's theory of sovereignty: less power is more power. He says this explicitly in Book IV of *République*: 'The less the power of the sovereign is (the true marks of majesty thereunto still reserved) the more it is assured' (cited in Holmes 1995: 115). In particular, Bodin understood perfectly well the value of nondiscretionary monetary policy. He wrote:

'The prince may not make any false money, no more than he may kill or rob, neither can he alter the weight of his coin to the prejudice of his subjects, and much less of strangers, which treat with him and traffic with his people, for that he is subject to the law of nations, unless he will lose the name and majesty of a king' (cited ibid.: 114). This, comments Stephen Holmes, is a perfect illustration of a self-imposed restriction. To achieve his objectives a king must cultivate a reputation for trustworthiness, and this requires him to play by the rules. By committing himself in advance to coins of fixed value, the king can successfully resist pressures to depreciate, cultivate the confidence of creditors, and retain better control of the economy. In similar fashion, constitutional constraints improve the efficiency of the modern sovereign—the sovereign people—by guaranteeing property and basic civil rights, limiting arbitrary executive discretion, and enhancing the credibility of long-term policy commitments.

Bodin's lesson is forgotten in recent times. Constitutional scholars have written about the 'eclipse of constitutionalism' in twentieth-century Europe (Matteucci 1993). During this period, the need to tax, spend, and borrow to finance two world wars and extensive welfare provisions greatly increased the economic role of the state. The constitutional consequence was to strengthen the executive branch of government. The assumption of macroeconomic responsibilities by the 'Keynesian state' further extended the already wide discretionary powers of the executive. In the end, it was inevitable that an old constitutional truth would be rediscovered: that discretionary powers can be abused and that the prevention of such abuse is, to a large extent, a matter of institutional and constitutional design (Harden 1994). In Europe the rediscovery of the virtues of constitutionalism has been greatly facilitated, perhaps even made possible, by the process of economic integration. Keynesian policies require not only extensive discretionary powers to 'fine-tune' the economy but also the separateness of the national economies. The creation of a common European market and the attendant rules of market liberalization and negative integration meant that governments could no longer pursue protectionist policies within the EC, or continue to protect public and private monopolies within the national borders. The discipline imposed on state subsidies and on the criteria of public procurement further reduced the discretionary powers of the national executives—and the various forms of rent-seeking and political corruption that usually accompany administrative decisions in these areas. The rules and institutions of monetary union, whatever their problems, are meant to be another constitutional limitation on the unconstrained discretionary policies of the past.

Note that the impact of supranational constitutionalism on the national level is not limited to the economic sphere, as was shown in Chapter 7. Through the principle of 'direct effect' and in other ways, the ECJ has progressively extended the rights of individuals under EC law, and the duties of national courts to protect those rights, even against the decisions of national governments. Nothing as powerful as the ECJ exists at the international level, but significant progress in the constitutionalization of international economic relations has been made in the framework of multilateral institutions, especially the GATT/WTO. Trade disputes under the WTO are now subject to binding adjudication in an institution that looks more and more like an international court. Today's situation is a striking contrast to the early days of the GATT, when the 'working parties' set up to report on disputes between member states were really a forum for encouraging negotiation, not a third-party investigation for the purpose of coming to objective conclusions on the merits of the case. An example of how the present system may protect the smaller members of the international community is the dispute known as the *Sardine* case. This dispute involved an EC regulation reserving the name 'sardine' to certain fish species (*Sardina pilchardus*, to be found in the Mediterranean) to the exclusion of others (such as the Peruvian *Sardinops sagax*), thus precluding Peru from marketing its sardines under the name 'sardines' in the territory of the EU. The WTO Panel found that the European regulation violated Article 2.4 of the Agreement on Technical Barriers to Trade (TBT) since it was not based on the relevant international (Codex) standard. This standard laid down common marketing rules for preserved sardines and it covered twenty sardine species, including both *Sardina pilchardus* and *Sardinops sagax*. The fact that the Codex recognized both species as 'sardines' meant that the Peruvian product also should be allowed to be marketed in Europe under that name.

9.7   Transnational Constitutionalism and the Third Transformation

The constitutionalization of the EC/EU and the evolution of dispute-resolution mechanisms in the GATT/WTO are notable examples of what, in spite of occasional lapses, appears to be a general trend: the transition from a power-oriented to a rule-oriented approach in international economic relations. Under the former approach, international disputes are settled by negotiations where the relative bargaining power of the parties inevitably counts a great deal, with unilateral action as the limiting case. Failure to reach agreement would involve the use of all instruments of retaliation—economic, political, possibly even military—available to the more powerful country. Understandably, a small country would hesitate to oppose a large one on whom its trade and international position depend. Under a rule-oriented approach, on the other hand, disputes, such as the one between Peru and the EU, are resolved by reference to norms that both parties have agreed upon. The current movement towards a rule-based system of international relations in a sense recapitulates the process of progressive constitutionalization of democratic governments during the last two centuries. As was already emphasized in Chapter 2 with reference to the EU, transnational constitutionalism is unlikely to be in itself a prelude to transnational democracy, but it can improve the quality of democracy at the national level. Thus, while a power-oriented approach favors the use of executive discretion and the secrecy of traditional diplomacy, a rule-based system facilitates democratic accountability, citizen participation, and public debate. This is because international rules—not only the rules of GATT/WTO or other international organizations but also treaties dealing with environmental protection, human rights, or regional integration—have to be ratified by national parliaments, may be subject to popular referenda, and are open to the scrutiny of courts, interest groups, NGOs, and scholarly opinion.

In sum, the contribution of transnational constitutionalism to the idea and practice of democracy consists, to paraphrase Weiler (1999: 341), in affirming the values of the liberal nation-state by policing its boundaries against abuse. Perhaps the main lesson of European integration, from this point of view, is that supranational rules can be reasonably effective even without the traditional state monopoly of coercive power. The recent strengthening of the WTO as an organization suggests that this lesson has been learned by the international community. In order to realize this democratic potential of transnational systems of rules, however, national parliaments must devise more effective ways of enforcing public account-ability at the international or supranational level. Concretely, this means that national legislatures should assume an active role in areas tradition-ally reserved to the executive branch of government. The domain of foreign affairs has historically been regarded as a core executive function over which parliaments have had difficulty in extending their control. Even the 'sovereign' British parliament has failed to establish full control over foreign affairs and treaty-making—historically both aspects of the royal prerogative. In an age of growing interdependence among nations, however, any sharp distinction between 'domestic' and 'foreign' is becoming increasingly difficult to maintain.

Also in this respect, the EU shows clearly the nature of the problem, and suggests possible solutions. According to widespread opinion, European integration has weakened the position of national parliaments to the benefit of political executives, represented in the Council of Ministers, and of the supranational institutions. However, some parliaments have reacted more forcefully than others to the challenge of supranational law and policymaking (Harlow 2002). The most stringent control is through mandate, and the Danish parliament, on accession to the EU, has extended to the supranational level its constitutional power to mandate its ministers in European policymaking. No other member state has adopted the mandate model, but everywhere mechanisms are put in place to ensure better control of European policymaking by the national parliaments. Thus, the French Assembly, although handicapped by the exceptionally strong position of the president of the Republic in foreign affairs, and by a constitutional limit on the number of parliamentary committees that could be appointed, was able to circumvent the latter constraint by setting up *délégations* of eighteen members, selected along party lines, which would report on EU matters to their respective chambers. The *délégation* of the Chamber of Deputies now meets regularly and scrutinizes EU legislation systematically. It has also insisted on the right to be informed and comment on the proceedings of IGCs—a concession first granted in 1996.

In the United Kingdom, the House of Commons in 1980 established the 'parliamentary reserve', prohibiting British ministers in the EU Council of Ministers from giving assent to any proposal subject to scrutiny or awaiting consideration by the House. The principle of parliamentary reserve has been adopted by several other European parliaments, including the French one. Thus, five national parliaments were recorded as placing a reserve on Council discussion of the European arrest warrant in 2002. The House of Lords, with a greater degree of autonomy from government, has reacted to the challenges of European integration even before the House of Commons. The House of Lords Select Committee on the ECs, established in 1972 with a wide mandate to consider policy as well as draft legislation, concentrates on prior control of policy, preferably at an early stage in the debate. Its expert reports on a wide range of topics are widely circulated in Brussels, and extensively used by academic specialists on European integration, and by many NGOs. In sum, to use the words with which Harlow

(2002: 91–2) concludes her informative survey of the contribution of national parliaments to EU law-making, 'a picture emerges of national parliaments increasingly on the alert, anxious to participate in EU affairs and keen to strengthen machinery for scrutiny of government.' The indispensable role of national parliaments in European governance is acknowledged also by the new Constitutional Treaty—an open admission of the failure of the EP to provide a sufficient basis of legitimacy to EU governance.

To conclude, it seems likely that the third transformation of democracy—its adaptation to the new conditions created by an increasingly integrated world economy—will not consist in a mechanical extrapolation of domestic principles and institutions to areas and levels of governance where democracy, as we know it, cannot flourish. Rather, an essential feature of the transformed democracy will be its ability to extend the scope of democratic accountability to areas that representative institutions had previously abandoned to executive prerogative.

The Future of the Union: Montesquieu Versus Madison

10.1 *Quo Vadis Europa?*

'Where are you going Europe?' asked Joschka Fischer in a controversial speech given at Berlin's Humboldt University on May 22, 2000. The title of the speech, 'From Association of States to Federation: Reflections on the Finality of European Integration', indicates the main thrust of the argument. For the German foreign minister (speaking in a private capacity) the only possible answer to his question is: forward, to full political integration. Indeed, he asked rhetorically, how is it possible that states which have irrevocably committed themselves to monetary union and deep economic integration fail to ensure their common security by making a united front against external threats? The launch of a common security and defense policy at the Helsinki Summit of the European Council of December 1999 is only the first step in that direction. There is only one, simple solution to the security and other problems facing the newly enlarged EU: a federal parliament and a federal government with full legislative and executive powers. *Herr* Fischer is of course aware that Europeans still pledge their highest political allegiance to their own nation-states with their distinct historical, linguistic, and cultural traditions. Hence, he rejects what he sees as the still prevailing model of a sovereign European federation eventually replacing the old nation-states.

For Fischer, the federalist project has a chance of becoming reality only if national institutions are not only preserved but in fact become active participants in the integration process. The German political leader envisages a division of sovereignty between Europe and the nation-states. Divided sovereignty entails a bicameral federal parliament that would represent both the Europe of the nation-states and the Europe of the citizens, thus bringing together the national political elites and the different national populations. In order to avoid potential conflicts, the lower house of the federal parliament would be composed of directly elected representatives who are at the same time members of the national parliaments. The upper house, representing the member states, could be organized either as a directly elected senate (the US model), or as a council whose members are appointed by the member states (the German model). Also for the federal executive there are two possible models. Either the European government evolves from the present European Council, meaning that it would be formed with members of the national governments; or it is derived from the present Commission, with a directly elected president enjoying wide executive powers.

All of this presupposes a constitutional treaty establishing which matters are to be regulated at the federal level and which ones at the national level. The treaty would transfer to the federation the 'core sovereign powers' (including, presumably, the power to tax and spend), and competence over what must necessarily be regulated at European level; all other competences would remain with the member states. At this point *Herr* Fischer introduces what is arguably the most original element of his analysis, and clearly differentiates his position not only from that of older federalists à la Hallstein (see Section 10.2), but also from those who, like former Commission President Prodi, advocate the generalization of the Community method as the only adequate answer to the increasing complexity of European governance. For Fischer the crisis of the Community method is evident, hence the federal vision cannot possibly be realized by trying to drive forward the integration process by dint of policies designed by remote supranational institutions. The method itself is one of the problems confronting the Union today since, in spite of its past successes, it has proved unable to achieve the political integration and democratization of Europe. For this reason, whenever a group of member states decided to move forward along the integration path, as with monetary union or the Schengen Agreement, they had to do so outside the framework of the traditional method. In an enlarged and necessarily more heterogeneous Union differentiation will be unavoidable. This then is the alternative approach proposed by the German leader: the member states that are willing to deepen their political integration would sign a new treaty, the nucleus of a federal constitution. The hope is that this coalition of the willing would become an 'integration magnet' able to attract, eventually, most, if not all, other member states.

The irrevocable commitment to a federal union would be preceded by a period of enhanced intergovernmental cooperation in such policy domains as environmental protection, crime control, immigration and asylum, and of course foreign affairs and security. What distinguishes this proposal from the traditional functionalist approach? First, supranational institutions appear to have no significant role in such enhanced cooperation, which would be primarily the responsibility of the national governments. Second, the aim of the various types of enhanced cooperation should be openly political—integration by stealth is rejected. Still, the new method runs into some of the same difficulties of the old functionalist approach: there is no guarantee that enhanced cooperation would lead automatically to the final goal of a federal union. Like the old method, it could in fact lead to the abandonment, in practice, of the final goal. Fischer is aware of this problematic aspect of his proposal, but in the end he can do no more than appeal to an act of political will to produce a new constitution for a federal Europe.

10.2   A Federalist Bias

Fischer's plan is the latest expression of the federalist aspirations of a long line of distinguished German statesmen, high-level bureaucrats, and legal experts. Indeed, nowhere the idea of a future European federal state has been cultivated as assiduously as in Germany. The title of a book published by Walter Hallstein in 1969, two years after his resignation as first president of the European Commission—*Der Unvollendete Bundesstaat* (The Incomplete Federal State)—is indicative of what Ipsen (1972) has called the German 'federalist bias'. It must be admitted that, overall, this bias has not been particularly helpful either to clear thinking (see Section 10.3), or to the cause of European integration—as exemplified by the vicissitudes of the Hallstein Commission. From the beginning of his presidency, Hallstein, a former state secretary in the German Foreign Office who worked closely with Jean Monnet to bring about the ECSC, used every opportunity to push European integration along federalist lines. He sought to turn the Commission into an embryonic European government, often referring to himself as the equivalent of a 'European prime minister'. His federalist rhetoric and provocative actions put him on a collision course with French President Charles de Gaulle, who opposed any extension of the Commission's powers. The showdown came in 1965, when the Commission president proposed to link completion of the financial arrangements of the

CAP with greater budgetary powers for the EP and executive authority for the Commission. The institutional bulimia of the Brussels authority, with all the resulting legitimacy problems (see Chapter 2), may be traced back to its first head. Hallstein's federal ambitions eventually led to the so-called Empty Chair Crisis, when de Gaulle announced that French officials would no longer participate in the work of the Council of Ministers. The real issue at stake, however, was not so much agricultural policy or budgetary authority, but the planned move to QMV in the Council on January 1, 1966, which de Gaulle saw as an unacceptable assault on national sovereignty, and the Commission president, like other presidents after him, as indispensable to the integration process.

The fact that among the six original founders of the EC Germany was the only country with a federal constitution explains in part the federalist bias of a number of its political and intellectual leaders. If for Hallstein the EEC was 'a construct with federal tendencies', according to Carl Friedrich Ophuels—the Permanent Representative of the German government in Brussels during the formative years of the EC—'anybody familiar with the early history of the Communities knows that their institutions have been established according to a federalist model' (cited in Ipsen 1972: 190; my translation). Statements such as these are based partly on wishful thinking, partly on the kind of analogical reasoning that has been criticized in Chapter 2. At the institutional level it is indeed easy to draw analogies between the Council of Ministers and the German *Bundesrat*—both institutions being composed of ministers of the member states (or *Laender*) who represent territorial interests and take an active part in the lawmaking process at the 'federal' level. Similarly, the Commission, the EP, and the ECJ may be said to prefigure the executive, legislative, and judicial organs of a full-fledged federal state, while the similarity between the ECB and the Bundesbank seems only too obvious. The direct effect and supremacy of Community law (at least from the ECJ's perspective) apparently clinch the federal analogy. The question, though, is whether such analogies provide any useful insights into the nature of the EC/EU or, what is more important, into the limits of what the would-be federation could actually do for its citizens. The answer can only be negative. Much more important than superficial institutional analogies is the fact that the supposedly 'pre-federal' EC/EU has no inherent powers—it possesses only the powers conferred on it by the member states—and hence lacks *Kompetenz-Kompetenz*, the sovereign authority to define the limits of its own competence. Article I-9 of the new Constitutional Treaty reaffirms that: 'The limits of Union competences are governed by the principle of

conferral. . . . Competences not conferred upon the Union in the Constitution remain with the Member States.'

Of course, a federalist bias is by no means an exclusive characteristic of
the German school. It seems fair to say that, apart from those few who
oppose *any* form of European integration, a majority of academic writers
on EU affairs share this bias to a greater or lesser extent, just as so many
students of environmental problems share a commitment to environmental values. A similar commitment to federalist values may explain the
contrast—so noticeable among old and new federalists alike—between
the attention paid to the details of institutional architecture and the lack
of concern about what a European federal state should, or could in fact, do.

10.3   The Federalist Dilemma

In Chapters 2 and 9, I indicated some of the inherent limits of a full-fledged
European federation. The issue of what could be reasonably expected
from such a federation is so important for my general argument that it
deserves to be reviewed and further elaborated. Concerning its normative
resources, it was pointed out that federalism never enjoyed broad popular
support in Europe, and even elite support seems to be eroding in both the
old and the new members of the Union. Indeed, the low turnout at the
latest European elections—particularly in the new member states—and
the growth of Euro-skeptic parties indicate a lack of support not just for
the federal vision but for the integration process itself. Another clear
indication of the limited appeal of federalist ideas was mentioned in
Chapter 2: nothing like the 1952 Political Community Treaty—not even
the draft TEU inspired by the federalist Spinelli Plan and approved by the
EP in 1984—has ever been seriously considered by the national governments. Fischer's federalist ideas, which appeared so daring when he first
presented them, are actually a good deal less ambitious (or more realistic)
than previous proposals, as shown by his rejection of the supranational
Community method, the limited powers attributed to a future federal
government, and especially by the recognition of the indispensable role
of national institutions in European governance.

Public opinion can change, however. If we assume that at some time in
the future a majority of Europeans could be in favor of a full-fledged
federal union, then the really important question becomes: what could
be included in the public agenda of a federation composed of states deeply
divided along cultural, social, institutional, and economic lines? Only by

asking this question is it possible to appreciate the limits of a European federation by comparison with existing federal states like the USA, Germany, Australia, or even Canada and Switzerland with their multicultural traditions. In these, as in most other known federations, the institutions of the federal government are embedded in a constitutional framework that presupposes the existence of a 'constitutional demos' by whose ultimate authority the particular constitutional arrangement has been established. Hence the reference to an 'American People', distinct from, and superior to, the peoples of the thirteen former colonies in the Preamble to the US Federal Constitution of 1787 (see Chapter 2). In Europe the presupposition of a constitutional demos does not hold. As Weiler (2001: 57) writes: 'Europe's constitutional architecture has never been validated by a process of constitutional adoption by a European constitutional demos, and hence the European constitutional discipline does not enjoy the same kind of authority as may be found in federal states where their federalism is rooted in a classical constitutional order. European federalism is constructed with a top-to-bottom hierarchy of norms, but with a bottom-to-top hierarchy of authority and real power.'

The absence of a constitutional demos, or of a European demos *tout court*, has far-reaching consequences not only at the constitutional level but also at the level of legislation and policymaking. As we saw in Chapter 9, the majority principle presupposes the existence of a fairly homogeneous polity. Only in such a polity are majority decisions considered legitimate and hence accepted also by the outvoted minority. This is the reason why societies that are divided into virtually separate subsocieties, with their own political parties, interest groups, and media of communication, rely extensively on nonmajoritarian instruments of governance and cleavage management. In particular, a federation of sharply divided polities—thus lacking the sense of solidarity generated by shared historical memories—would find it difficult to pursue redistributive and other policies with clearly identified winners and losers. Hence, as already noted, such policies would have to be largely excluded from the federal agenda for being too divisive.

Again, many forms of state intervention that may be considered useful in parts of the federation at a relatively low level of development could turn out to be harmful in other, more developed parts, or vice versa. Similar problems are not unknown at national level, but they are made less troublesome by the relative homogeneity, the common tradition, and the sense of solidarity of the people of a nation-state. In fact, Hayek (1948: 264) has suggested that existing sovereign nation-states 'are mostly of such dimensions and composition as to render possible agreement on an amount of state interference which they would not suffer if they were much smaller or much larger'. Much smaller states would not be viable, while if sovereign states were much larger than they are today, it would be a good deal more difficult to impose costs on the inhabitants of one region in order to help the inhabitants of a very distant region who might differ from the former in language, traditions, and in almost every other respect.

People will be especially reluctant to accept majority decisions when the majority that controls the government is composed of people of different nationalities and different traditions. It follows that (ibid.: 265)

[T]he central government in a federation composed of many different people will have to be restricted in scope if it is to avoid meeting an increasing resistance on the part of the various groups which it includes.... There seems to be little possible doubt that the scope for the regulation of economic life will be much narrower for the central government of [such] a federation than for national states.

In line with my analysis of positive and negative integration in Chapter 7, Hayek concludes that a very inhomogeneous federation 'will have to possess the negative power of preventing individual states from interfering with economic activity in certain ways, although it may not have the positive power of acting in their stead' (ibid.: 267).

In sum, a European federal state would require not only an irrevocable transfer of national sovereignty but also a highly constrained public agenda. It would be unable to pursue precisely those policies that characterize and legitimate the modern welfare state: social redistributive policies and, more generally, all policies favoring particular socioeconomic groups or jurisdictions, at the expense of other identifiable groups or jurisdictions. Because of the opposition of the losers, such policies can only be enforced by majority rule, but as we saw, the majority principle lacks legitimacy in a deeply segmented polity. We also noted that a serious legitimacy problem arises even if a large majority in the federation is in favor of a given policy, as long as the opponents of that policy are concentrated in a few jurisdictions or states, where they form the majority. But a European federation unable to provide the variety of public goods (including income redistribution) that citizens of modern welfare states take for granted would be unable to attract and retain sufficient popular support. The national governments would remain, for their people, the principal focus of collective loyalty and the real arena for democratic politics. Democratic life would continue to develop in the framework of the nation-state, while the federation, far from correcting the democratic deficit of the present EU, would actually make it worse because of the disappointed expectations of those who had envisaged something like a European welfare state. In turn, this loss of legitimacy would prevent the federal government from acting energetically even in areas, such as foreign policy and defense, where the nation-states do need to pool their sovereignty in order to play a more incisive role on the international scene. This, then, is the basic dilemma that committed federalists have always been unwilling to face: on the one hand, European integration has advanced so far that a further pooling of sovereignty in a number of key policy areas seems unavoidable; on the other hand, for the reasons stated above, a European federal state would lack democratic legitimacy. Even the extension of the classic Community method to foreign and security policy, and to other domains close to the core of national sovereignty, has been rejected. A confederation of sovereign states—Montesquieu's *république fédérative*—seems to offer the only feasible solution to this dilemma.

10.4   The Confederal Option

It will be recalled that confederations are associations of independent states that, in order to secure some common purpose, agree to certain limitations on their freedom of action and establish some common machinery of deliberation and decision. The confederal model is also called 'compact federalism' to stress that the confederation is brought into existence not by the act of a sovereign people but by a compact among sovereign states. It is interesting to note that from the end of World War II to this day, the significance of confederation as a possible goal of the European integration process has been systematically overlooked. Thus, after the collapse of the plans for a federal Political Community in the 1950s, many European leaders turned not to confederation but to functionalism as the alternative road to an ultimate federalist end. Since that time, the integration debate has been largely conducted in terms of 'supranationalism' and 'intergovernmentalism', rather than in the more traditional, and clearer, language of federation and confederation. This is rather paradoxical since a confederal tendency is embedded in the institutional architecture designed by the Rome Treaty (see Section 10.8). It is as if one wished to ignore the fact that a significant change in the finality of integration had taken place between the federally biased Paris Treaty, which in 1951 established the ECSC, and the 1957 Rome Treaty.

Part of the explanation of the lack of interest for the confederal option was, and still is, the widespread opinion that confederal arrangements are inadequate to solve the problems of modern political economies, and hence that federalism can only mean federal state (Elazar 2001). It is of course true that most confederations of the past have lacked institutions strong enough to ensure the economic integration of the component polities. Thus the Articles of Confederation that preceded the US Federal Constitution of 1787 established a Congress of the Confederation as a unicameral assembly of state representatives, each possessing a single vote. Although the Congress was given authority in important areas such as foreign affairs, defense, and the establishment of coinage and weights and measures, it lacked both an independent source of revenue and the institutional means to establish a common market among the former colonies. Similarly, the constitution of the Swiss Confederation of 1815 proved unable to create a common market out of the local economies of the twenty-two cantons. Economic integration was achieved only by the stronger federal constitution of 1848. Also the other confederation created by the Congress of Vienna, the German *Bund*, proved unable or unwilling to bring about the economic integration of the German states. This was rather the achievement of the customs union (*Zollverein*) sponsored by Prussia as a way of reducing the influence of Austria on the German confederation.

Another plausible explanation of the absence of the confederal option from the discourse on European integration is that in the past the main reason for establishing federal compacts (confederations or leagues) among sovereign states was the search for collective security. In post-war Western Europe, however, collective security was placed in the hands of NATO, not of the ECs. Instead of collective security, economic integration became the rationale for a new form of association among sovereign states, based on law and on strong common institutions. According to a well-known student of federalism, the late Daniel Elazar, by the late 1960s the EC had begun to build what were, in effect, confederal arrangements, based on the integration of specific economic functions, rather than on a general act of confederation establishing an overarching general government, however limited its powers. Elazar viewed the present EU as being essentially complete as a confederation, although the member states and their citizens do not share this sense of completeness partly because integration has taken place piecemeal, but especially because of the assumption that integration means federation, and federation means a federal state (Elazar 2001). Indeed, according to the definition of confederation given above, even 'intensive transgovernmentalism' (see Chapter 8) could be considered a confederal arrangement. Be that as it may, it seems clear that to a number of contemporary European leaders the EU appears to be a good deal closer to the confederal than to a full-fledged federal model—even if they carefully eschew the language of confederation. Jacques Delors is generally considered a federalist, but his notion of a 'federation of nation-states' has an unmistakable confederate ring. The title of Fischer's speech at Humboldt University explicitly refers to federation as the 'finality' of European integration, but most of his concrete proposals are more in the spirit of confederation than of a full-fledged federation. Again, Tony Blair's often expressed vision of Europe—Superpower, not Super-state: the title of a speech given in Warsaw in Fall 2000—seems to suggest a Montesquieuian *république fédérative*, capable of playing a significant role in international affairs without undermining the sovereignty of the *états confédérés*.

The main reason for the deliberate exclusion of the confederal option from the discourse on European integration, however, is the statist tradition, which has such deep roots in continental Europe. A confederation is not a state, but the 'state' is what Europeans have known for at least four centuries. Scholars may try to describe the EU as a system of 'governance without government', but to citizens and political leaders alike this is only a combination of contradictory ideas, an oxymoron. As Elazar (2001: 43) put it: 'Once statist premises are accepted it is very difficult to avoid viewing the EU as an anomaly, something that has to be turned into a state, even a decentralized one, very soon.' Since the end of World War II, moreover, the statist tradition has derived new strength from the development of the welfare state. The idea that in the age of international economic integration the welfare state can only be rescued by the creation of a world, or at least a European, federation has influential advocates (see Chapter 9). But as explained above, a European, and a fortiori a world, federation would be unable to pursue precisely those policies that characterize and legitimate national welfare states.

If it is true that the confederal option—the limited ends of confederation rather than the comprehensive ends of a full-fledged federal union—offers the only way out of the dilemma of supranational federalism, then it is important to examine more closely the normative and conceptual foundations of the confederation model. This is an appropriate time to revive intellectual and political interest in this model, and to revisit the old, but still relevant, arguments raised by the American anti-Federalists in the course of the debate on the US Constitution. Elazar is not alone in thinking that the EU, as a novel but nonetheless recognizable and (according to him) highly developed confederation, has perhaps more in common with the US Confederation of 1781 than with the modern US federation. This is especially true after the agreement reached by the member states of the EU on the new Constitutional Treaty, which, I will argue, has significantly accentuated the confederal tendencies of the European integration process.

10.5   Montesquieu's Confederate Republic

Modern scholarship has shown that Montesquieu's model of the confederate republic provided the theoretical underpinning of anti-Federalist thought, and of the successors of the states' rights school of constitutional interpretation (Beer 1993). The French political philosopher is known as the discoverer of the principle of separation of powers but in fact he was an advocate of mixed government—a mode of governance which, as we saw in Chapter 3, rejects separation of powers in favor of institutional balance. In reality, Montesquieu was referring to a separation of functions rather than separation of powers in the sense of organs of the state. Moreover, his notion of checks and balances—which was wholeheartedly adopted by James Madison and, through him, shaped so decisively the federal constitution of the United States—has to be interpreted, in accordance with the underlying philosophy of mixed government, as a balance between the socioeconomic interests represented in the polity. In light of these misunderstandings it is only an apparent paradox that the real disciples of Montesquieu in the United States were not the Federalists led by Madison, but the anti-Federalists who wanted to preserve the sovereignty of the thirteen states, while recognizing the need of forming a confederation for the purpose of defense against external threats. Indeed, I suggest below that confederation may be viewed as the extension of mixed government to the international level.

Montesquieu's model of the confederate republic has two main elements. The first, derived from Machiavelli and from classical political philosophy, is the small-republic theory, according to which in a small republic the public interest is more obvious, better understood, and more within the grasp of citizens, than in a large republic. The second element, and Montesquieu's principal contribution to the theory of confederation, was his solution to the dilemma of scale by means of compact federalism. According to the French philosopher, diversity in the body politic leads to conflict, and so disrupts popular government, while homogeneity, which is fostered by small scale—'small' in terms of population or area, or of both parameters—improves the prospects of self-government. However, small republics are easily dominated by large states, unless they protect their collective security by forming a confederation. In a confederation the various member states have their separate, internally determined interests, which the common institutions are supposed to defend, but not to modify or regulate. The confederates bargain over the exchange of benefits that are useful to their respective purposes, but this exchange is purely utilitarian, and not constitutive of the interests being served (Beer 1993). As in neorealist accounts of European integration, national preferences remain essentially unchanged.

Like the French philosopher, the American anti-Federalists—who, as we saw in Chapter 3, also favored mixed government—believed that democracy and liberty could flourish only in fairly homogeneous polities, while a federation of the type Madison envisaged would lead, eventually, to excessive centralization. For both Montesquieu and the anti-Federalists, smaller government meant less danger from overpowerful bureaucrats wielding authority commensurate with their great competences. A key tenet of their common philosophy is that the political process tends to be divisive, hence cannot reduce diversity. Therefore, if lawmaking is to approach agreement, it must start as nearly as possible from homogeneous preferences. Within the member states of the confederation, homogeneity is favored by their relatively small scale. In the government of the confederate republic, agreement is made easier by the narrow scope of policy, which often is limited mainly to defense. Defense is a matter on which the member states can fairly easily agree since it involves no internal regulation of the diverse interests of the confederates, but only the external protection of their territory. In general, confederation is government by agreement, and this form of collective governance is possible only if the confederation is not required to act in fields where true agreement cannot be achieved. For Montesquieu it is right that power should remain largely within the member states since they are the true political communities. Among the important consequences of basing the confederate republic on a treaty or contract among the member states was the idea of secession as a fully acknowledged right. As we read in Book 9, Chapter 1 of *Spirit of the Laws*, 'the confederacy may be dissolved and the confederates preserve their sovereignty'.

These were also the positions defended by the American anti-Federalists. The purpose of the confederation, they argued, is merely to preserve the state governments, not to govern individuals. Hence the Preamble of the Constitution should start with the words 'We the States' rather than 'We the People' of the United States. They admitted that some strengthening of the confederation was needed, but its powers should be as few as possible and should be narrowly, not broadly, construed. In their opinion, the supremacy clause of Article VI: 'This Constitution, and the Laws of the United States which shall be made in the Pursuance thereof . . . shall be the supreme Law of the Land', and the 'necessary and proper' clause of Article I, Section 8: 'The Congress shall have the power to . . . make all Laws which shall be necessary and proper for carrying into Execution the foregoing Powers, and all other Powers vested by this Constitution in the Government of the United States, or in any Department or Officer thereof' simply went too far.

As Samuel Beer has shown, Madison's theory of the extended republic, set out in classic form in *The Federalist*, numbers 10 and 51, was framed in reaction to the model of the confederate republic and to the Montesquieuian argument which supported it. His intellectual critique was reinforced by a demonstration of the failures of the Confederation of 1781: internationally, the weakness of the new republic abroad; domestically, the inability of the Continental Congress to prevent the member states from creating obstacles to interstate trade or from discriminating in favor of foreign goods and services. The proposed solution consisted in replacing the model of a 'government over governments' (Madison's expression) by one in which the authority of the government of the United States extended to individuals as well as to states. As we saw in Chapter 2, in order to justify such a drastic centralization of power the Federalists needed a new legitimacy, and this was provided by Madison's 'invention' of the sovereignty of the people of the United States as a whole, which alone could stand superior to the people of any single state. Thus Madison envisioned a federal government resting for its authority not on the states, not even on the people of the several states considered separately (as in the case of the EU), but on 'an American people . . . who constituted a separate and superior entity that would necessarily impinge on the authority of the states' (Morgan 1988, cited in Beer 1993: 254).

The Madisonian solution to the problem of legitimizing a centralized federal government is simply unavailable to the political leaders of the EU (see Chapter 2). In fact, Europe may be said to have explicitly rejected the Madisonian solution and, with it, the model of the federal state. Starting with the Rome Treaty, all European Treaties refer to 'an ever closer union among the peoples of Europe', so that, in Weiler's words 'even in the

eventual promised land of European integration, the distinct peoplehood
of its components was to remain intact—in contrast with the theory of
most, and the praxis of all, federal states which predicate the existence of
one people' (Weiler 2001: 57). What remains, then, is the confederal option. As has already been pointed out, confederations have typically failed
because of their inability to integrate the separate markets of their component units. However, far-reaching, and probably irreversible, integration of the national markets of the member states is the great achievement
of the Community method and 'negative' law. Building on this solid
foundation it should be possible to establish confederal structures that
are both stable and effective. The Constitutional Treaty agreed to by the
member states in June 2004 may turn out to be a crucially important step
in this direction.

10.6   The Right to Secede

What is arguably the single most important element of compact federalism in the new Constitutional Treaty has attracted very little public attention. This is Article I-59 on 'Voluntary withdrawal from the Union',
according to which: 'Any Member State may decide to withdraw from
the European Union in accordance with its own constitutional requirements.' The procedure is spelled out in the second paragraph:

A Member State which decides to withdraw shall notify the European Council of its
intention; the European Council shall examine that notification. In the light of the
guidelines provided by the European Council, the Union shall negotiate and
conclude an agreement with that State, setting out the arrangements for its withdrawal, taking account of the framework for its future relationship with the Union.
That agreement shall be concluded on behalf of the Union by the Council, acting
by qualified majority, after obtaining the consent of the European Parliament.

The Constitution ceases to apply to the State in question from the date of
the entry into force of the agreement or, failing that, two years after
notification of the decision to withdraw from the Union. To appreciate
the significance of these provisions, one should keep in mind that the
possibility of secession is a crucial element distinguishing the confederal
from the federal model, being inherent in the contractual nature of the
confederate pact. As already mentioned, in Montesquieu's model of
the confederate republic, secession is a fully acknowledged right of every
member. The view of the confederate pact as a formal contract among

sovereign states was fundamental also to John C. Calhoun's constitutional theory, justifying secession from the Union and nullification of its laws at the time of the American Civil War. It has even been argued that '[w]ithout an implicit acceptance of an ultimate right to secede, to opt out, to exercise the exit option, the constitutional agreement hammered out in Philadelphia in the hot summer of 1787 would never have come into being' (Buchanan 1990: 5). The refusal of the federal government to accept secession as a solution was of course the immediate cause of the Civil War.

The founding Rome Treaty was silent on this point, but most legal commentators think that secession would be illegal under European law. When the possibility of voluntary withdrawal was first proposed by Giscard d'Estaing, president of the Constitutional Convention, in October 2002, concerns were expressed that it could be a recipe for chaos, with Euro-skeptic parties in member states provoking secession crises for short-run political advantages. This is unlikely to be a serious problem in practice. The advantages of economic integration are such that a *credible* secessionist threat could emerge only if the EU should pursue policies that seriously violate the sovereign rights of some member states, or systematically discriminate against their citizens or regions. As long as the policies of the Union satisfy the basic requirements of subsidiarity and proportionality, and are in the general interest of all the citizens, an argument for secession would not be credible and hence not believed.

10.7   The Emerging Confederal Model for Collective Security

The exit option is only one, albeit a particularly significant one, of a number of features that give the Constitutional Treaty a recognizable confederal complexion. In institutional terms, the Constitutional Convention had to choose among three possibilities: (1) to continue with the present arrangements, whereby the executive function at the European level is effectively divided between the Council of Ministers and the Commission, with one institution more in the lead on some policy issues and the other on other issues; (2) a Commission-led executive; and (3) an executive led by the European Council (Wallace 2003). Following the arguments of the 'Feasibility Study' (code name Penelope) contributed by the Commission to the debate on the Constitutional Treaty, a Commission-led executive would have meant: a generalization of the Community method, including of course the Commission's monopoly of legislative initiative, codecision for the Parliament, and generalized QMV in the Council; strong Commission powers in all policy domains, including EMU and the CFSP; a 'Secretary of the Union', responsible for external relations, enjoying a special status but integrated into the Commission; a Commission President elected by the EP and confirmed by the European Council; abolition of the unanimity rule even for future constitutional amendments, the only exception being the admission of new member states. Implicit in this institutional architecture is the restriction of the role of the Presidency of the European Council to the general guidance and coordination of the activities of the Union.

The final agreement reached by the member states moved definitely beyond the status quo, and just as definitely rejected the model proposed by the Commission, in favor of a European executive led by the European Council. Whereas the Commission wanted to deny the Council the status of a European institution, now Article I-18 of the Constitutional Treaty lists it among the institutions of the Union, along with the EP, the Council of Ministers, the Commission, and the ECJ. The European Council, consisting of the heads of state or government of the member states, together with its President and the President of the Commission, provides the Union with the necessary impetus for its development, and defines its general political directions and priorities. It meets quarterly and decides by consensus, except where the Treaty provides otherwise. Its President is elected by QMV of the Council, for a term of two-and-a-half years, renewable once. He, or she, drives forward the work of the Council, ensuring proper preparation and continuity, and the external representation of the Union on issues concerning its CFSP, without prejudice to the responsibilities of the Minister for Foreign Affairs. This foreign minister of the EU—who is appointed by the European Council by QMV, with the agreement of the President of the Commission—is another significant innovation. He or she will assume the responsibilities of both the High Representative for the CFSP (Javier Solana in 2004) and of the Commissioner for External Affairs (Chris Patten in the Prodi Commission), thus putting an end to the dichotomy of the EU's diplomacy. The new position amounts to an unprecedented fusion of policy development and policy execution at EU level, as he or she is also one of the vice presidents of the Commission, but carries out the common foreign, security, and defense policy as mandated by the European Council. This dual allegiance may blur the line of accountability, but will likely increase independence by comparison to both the High Representative and the Commissioner for External Affairs. The Minister's special status is emphasized by the considerable resources at disposal. Whereas the current High Representative for the CFSP has a budget of only €45 million and a staff of about 270 functionaries and diplomats, the Foreign Minister will have a budget of more than €6 billion and a staff of some 600 functionaries coming from the Commission Directorate for External Relations, and head a real diplomatic service, rather than the Commission's 'delegations' abroad as today. In addition, he or she will manage the European Armaments, Research and Military Capabilities Agency established by Article I-40, which is supposed to be fully operational by December 31, 2004. The Commission has a representative in the Agency, which, however, is exclusively accountable to the Council.

Thus Articles I-39 and I-40 of the Constitutional Treaty—on 'Specific provisions for implementing the common foreign and security policy' and 'Specific provisions for implementing the common European security and defence policy', respectively—lay the foundations of a European confederal model in the area of collective security, which is the traditional concern of the confederations and leagues of the past. According to Article I-39, the European Council identifies the strategic interests of the Union, and determines the objectives of its CFSP. In turn, the Council of Ministers frames this policy within the framework of the strategic guidelines established by the European Council. The CFSP is implemented by the Union's Minister for Foreign Affairs *and* by the member states, using national and Union resources. Before undertaking any action on the international scene or any commitment that could affect the Union's interests, each member state must consult the others within the Council or the European Council. European decisions on CFSP are adopted by the European Council and the Council of Ministers *unanimously*, as a rule. The European Council and the Council act on a proposal from a member state, from the Minister for Foreign Affairs, or, on certain matters, from the Minister with the Commission's support. 'European laws and framework laws are excluded', while the EP is only consulted on the main aspects and basic choices of the CFSP, and is kept informed on how the policy evolves.

The common security and defense policy, which is an integral part of the CFSP, is supposed to provide the Union with an operational capability, drawing on civil and military assets that the Union may use on missions for peace-keeping, conflict prevention, and strengthening international security in accordance with the principles of the United Nations Charter. Article I-40(2) states: 'The common security and defence policy shall include the progressive framing of a common Union defence policy. This will lead to a common defence, when the European Council, acting unanimously, so decides.' The Union's policy in the area of security and defense will respect the obligations of the member states that are members

THE FUTURE OF THE UNION

of the NATO, as well as the specific character of the security and defense policy of those that are not members of the organization. The objectives of the European Armaments, Research and Military Capabilities Agency are spelled out in Article I-40(3): 'to identify operational requirements, to put forward measures to satisfy those requirements, to contribute to identifying and, where appropriate, implementing any measure needed to strengthen the industrial and technological base of the defence sector, to participate in defining a European capabilities and armaments policy, and to assist the Council in evaluating the improvement of military capabilities.'

Decisions on the implementation of the common security and defense policy are to be adopted by the Council acting unanimously on a proposal from the Minister for Foreign Affairs or from member states. Under both Articles I-39 and I-40, the role of the Commission is minimal, being restricted to supporting the Minister's proposals 'where appropriate'. Far from generalizing the Community method, the treaty effectively excludes it from these crucially important policy areas even more completely than the previous treaties. For example, the Commission is no longer 'fully associated with the work carried out in the common foreign and security policy field' (Article 27 EC), and while the EP has to be regularly consulted on the main aspects and basic choices of the CFSP, and kept informed on the evolution of the policy, the Council President is no longer required to 'ensure that the views of the European Parliament are duly taken into consideration' (Article 21 EC).

10.8   Conclusion: a Failed Federation, a Model Confederation

The history of European integration provides ample evidence of the failure of the federalist project: a Europe united on the model of existing federal states. The new Constitutional Treaty is the latest proof of the lack of support for such a model. This book has argued that the federalist project was doomed from the start, because—absent a European demos—a European federation would lack the material and normative resources to provide the public goods people have come to expect from the state, whether unitary or federal. As was noted at the beginning of this chapter, and in the Preface, federalists have always been reluctant to face squarely this problem, indulging instead in the much easier task of designing alternative institutional architectures for the would-be federation. In the current atmosphere of Euro-skepticism such academic exercises are no longer sufficient. Federalists will have to explain in detail how a supranational federal state could establish and maintain its own legitimacy despite its inability to fulfill the basic functions of a modern welfare state. Integration by stealth is no longer a viable strategy. The latest European elections have shown that the efficiency and legitimacy costs of the traditional approach have become so high that popular hostility to the very idea of integration is no longer a phenomenon limited to a few member states of the Union.

The present tide of disillusionment and skepticism cannot be stemmed by means of worn-out formulas such as 'we need more Europe'. What is needed, rather, is less ambiguity about ultimate goals, a clearer distinction of means and ends, and greater honesty about the costs, as well as the benefits, of integration. At the same time, it is important for Europeans to realize that integration, in one form or another, is less an option than a common destiny. Economically, geopolitically, culturally, our continent has always cooperated on a scale and with an intensity unknown in other parts of the world. 'Unity in diversity' and 'competition with cooperation' are not slogans newly minted in Brussels; they are the essential traits of European history (Jones 1987). Hence the failure of the federal project certainly should not entail the failure of the integration process. The various ambiguities, pitfalls, and outright failures analyzed in this book are largely due, not to the process as such, but to underhand efforts to steer it in the direction of full political union.

In Section 10.4 reference was made to Elazar's view that by the late 1960s the EC had begun to build what were, in effect, confederal arrangements, based on the integration of specific economic functions or sectors, rather than on a general act of confederation. In fact, our analysis suggests that such arrangements were already built into the 1957 Rome Treaty. In Chapter 3 it was shown that the institutional architecture designed by the treaty is nothing else than a latter-day version of the old form of governance known as mixed government. According to the philosophy of mixed government, the general polity is composed, not of individual citizens but of corporate bodies ('estates') governed by mutual agreement rather than by a political sovereign. Each estate was supposed to take care of its own members, hence there was no direct link between the central government and the individual members of the estates. The function of the central institutions was limited to preserving the balance between the different political and economic interests and protecting the rights and privileges of the estates—their corporate 'liberties'. The protection of corporate, rather than individual, liberties is one criterion by which confederations may be distinguished from federations. As Elazar has pointed out, federations are communities of both individuals and polities and are committed to protect the liberties of both, but with a greater emphasis on the liberties of individuals than on the liberties of the constituent polities. Confederations, on the other hand, place greater emphasis on the liberties of the constituent polities, since it is the task of each polity to protect individual liberty, more or less as each defines it, within its own borders. In other words, Montesquieu's confederate republic is simply the application of the model of mixed government to contractual relations among sovereign states for the purpose of producing 'club goods' such as collective security or, nowadays, economic integration. In this sense, the major shift from the Paris Treaty to the Rome Treaty was indeed the change from a pre-federal to a confederal tendency.

Viewing the EC as a confederation, we can see that it succeeded where most confederations of the past had failed, namely in integrating the economies of a group of advanced countries, by peaceful means and respecting their national sovereignty. Because of this achievement—largely obtained, let us not forget, by market liberalization and by negative, rather than positive, integration—the EU is today the leading model of the post-modern confederation designed to prepare the economies of its component polities to the challenges of globalization. It is a striking fact that as globalization advances, the number of regional associations—ranging from free trade areas to common markets and various types of commonwealths—grows at an even faster pace. Few states seem to be willing to give up the core of their sovereignty, but almost all recognize the necessity of joining transnational functional associations, and are willing to do so as long as they can preserve their 'liberties', and take part in the common governance. The truly historical significance of the EU is as the paradigm of post-modern confederation, not as a poor copy of one of the existing federal states.

References

Acton, J. E. E. (1967). 'Nationality', in W. H. McNeill (ed.), *Essays in the Liberal Interpretation of History*. Chicago, IL: The University of Chicago Press, 131–59.

Alesina, A. and Grilli, V. (1994). 'The European Central Bank: Reshaping Monetary Politics in Europe', in T. Persson and G. Tabellini (eds.), *Monetary and Fiscal Policy*, Vol. 1. Cambridge, MA: The MIT Press, 247–78.

Arnold, R. D. (1990). *The Logic of Congressional Action*. New Haven, CT: Yale University Press.

Barker, E. (1962). 'Introduction', in E. Barker (ed.), *Social Contract: Locke Hume Rousseau*. New York: Oxford University Press, vii–xliv.

Barnard, C. (2000). 'Social Dumping and the Race to the Bottom: Some Lessons for the European Union from Delaware?', *European Law Review*, 25/1: 57–78.

Beer, S. H. (1993). *To Make a Nation: The Rediscovery of American Federalism*. Cambridge, MA: The Belknap Press.

Bhagwati, J. N. (1996). 'The Demands to Reduce Domestic Diversity among Trading Nations', in J. N. Bhagwati and R. E. Hudec (eds.), *Fair Trade and Harmonization*, Vol. 1. Cambridge, MA: The MIT Press, 9–40.

—— and Hudec, R. E. (eds.) (1996). *Fair Trade and Harmonization: Prerequisites for Free Trade?*, 2 vols. Cambridge, MA: The MIT Press.

Bogert, G. T. (1987). *Trusts*, 6th edn. St. Paul, MN: West Publishing Company.

Buchanan, J. M. (1965). 'An Economic Theory of Clubs'. *Economica*, 32, February: 1–14.

—— (1990). 'Europe's Constitutional Opportunity', in Institute of Economic Affairs, *Europe's Constitutional Future*. London: Institute of Economic Affairs, 1–20.

—— and Tullock, G. (1962). *The Calculus of Consent: Logical Foundations of Constitutional Democracy*. Ann Arbor, MI: The University of Michigan Press.

Casella, A. (1996). 'Free Trade and Evolving Standards', in J. N. Bhagwati and R. E. Hudec (eds.), *Fair Trade and Harmonization*, Vol. 1. Cambridge, MA: The MIT Press, 119–56.

Clark, R. C. (1985). 'Agency Costs Versus Fiduciary Duties', in J. W. Pratt and R. J. Zeckhauser (eds.) *Principals and Agents: The Structure of Business*. Boston, MA: Harvard Business School Press, 55–79.

Commission of the European Communities (2000). *Communication from the Commission on the Precautionary Principle*, COM(2000) 1. Brussels.

—— (2001). *European Governance*. Luxembourg: Office for Official Publications of the European Communities.

—— (2002). *Communication from the Commission: The Operating Framework for the European Regulatory Agencies*, COM(2002) 718 final. Brussels.

—— (2004). *Delivering Lisbon: Reforms for the Enlarged Union*. http://www.europa.eu.int/index_en.htm.

Conseil d'Etat (1993). *Report of the Conseil d'Etat 1992*. Paris: Documentation Française.

Craig, P. and de Búrca, G. (2003). *EU Law: Text, Cases, and Materials*, 3rd edn. Oxford: Oxford University Press.

Curtin, D. (1993). 'The Constitutional Structure of the Union: A Europe of Bits and Pieces', *Common Market Law Review*, 30/1: 17–69.

Dahl, R. A. (1989). *Democracy and its Critics*. New Haven, CT: Yale University Press.

Dashwood, A. (1983). 'Hastening Slowly: The Communities' Path towards Harmonization', in H. Wallace, W. Wallace, and C. Webb (eds.), *Policy-Making in the European Community*, 2nd edn. Chichester, UK: Wiley, 177–208.

—— (1996). 'The Limits of European Community Powers', *European Law Review*, 21: 113–28.

de Búrca, G. and Scott, J. (2000). 'The Impact of the WTO on EU Decision-making', *Harvard Jean Monnet Working Paper 6/00*.

De Grauwe, P. (2002). 'Europe's Instability Pact', http://www.ft.com, July 24.

Dehousse, R. (2002). 'Misfits: EU Law and the Transformation of European Governance', in R. Dehousse and C. Joerges (eds.), *Good Governance in Europe's Integrated Market*. Oxford: Oxford University Press, 207–29.

Derthick, M. (1974). *Between State and Nation: Regional Organizations of the United States*. Washington, DC: The Brookings Institution.

de Schoutheete, P. (2002). 'The European Council', in J. Peterson and M. Shackleton (eds.), *The Institutions of the European Union*. Oxford: Oxford University Press, 21–46.

Dixit, A. K. and Nalebuff, B. J. (1991). *Thinking Strategically*. New York: W. W. Norton.

Duchesne, S. and Forgnier, A.-P. (1995). 'Is there a European Identity?', in O. Niedermayer and R. Sinnott (eds.), *Public Opinion and International Governance*. Oxford: Oxford University Press.

Easterbrook, F. H. and Fischel, D. R. (1991). *The Economic Structure of Corporate Law*. Cambridge, MA: Harvard University Press.

Ehrenberg, V. (1969). *The Greek State*. London: Methuen.

Elazar, D. J. (2001). 'The United States and the European Union: Models for Their Epochs', in K. Nicolaidis and R. Howse (eds.), *The Federal Vision: Legitimacy and Levels of Governance in the United States and the European Union*. Oxford: Oxford University Press, 31–53.

Ellis, E. (1998). *EC Sex Equality Law*, 2nd edn. Oxford: Clarendon Press.

Epstein, D. and O'Halloran, S. (1999). *Delegating Powers*. Cambridge: Cambridge University Press.

European Council (2000). Lisbon European Council (http://europa.eu.int/council/off/conclu/mar2000/index.htm).

Ferrera, M., Hemerijck, A., and Rhodes, M. (2001). 'The Future of the European "Social Model" in the Global Economy', *Journal of Comparative Policy Analysis*, 3/2: 163–90.

Forster, A. and Wallace, W. (2000). 'Common Foreign and Security Policy', in H. Wallace and W. Wallace (eds.), *Policy-Making in the European Union*, 4th edn. Oxford: Oxford University Press, 461–91.

Gillingham, J. (1991). *Coal, Steel, and the Rebirth of Europe, 1945–1955*. Cambridge: Cambridge University Press.

Golub, J. (1999). 'In the Shadow of the Vote? Decision Making in the European Community', *International Organization*, 53/4: 733–64.

Gormley, L. and de Haan, J. (1996). 'The Democratic Deficit of the European Central Bank', *European Law Review*, Vol. 21.

Goyder, D. G. (2003). *EC Competition Law*, 4th edn. New York: Oxford University Press.

Graham, J. D., Green, L. C., and Roberts, M. J. (1988). *In Search of Safety*. Cambridge, MA: Harvard University Press.

Grant, W., Matthews, D., and Newell, P. (2000). *The Effectiveness of European Union Environmental Policy*. London: Macmillan.

Greenwood, T. (1984). *Knowledge and Discretion in Government Regulation*. New York: Praeger.

Haas, E. B. (1958). *The Uniting of Europe: Political, Social and Economic Forces, 1950–1957*. Stanford, CA: Stanford University Press.

Harden, I. (1994). 'The Constitution of the European Union', *Public Law*, Winter: 609–24.

Harlow, C. (2002). *Accountability in the European Union*. Oxford: Oxford University Press.

Hartley, T. C. (1991). *The Foundations of European Community Law*, 2nd edn. New York: Oxford University Press.

Hayek, F. A. (1948). *Individualism and Economic Order*. Chicago, IL: The University of Chicago Press.

Hayes-Renshaw, F. (2002). 'The Council of Ministers', in J. Peterson and M. Shackleton (eds.), *The Institutions of the European Union*. Oxford: Oxford University Press, 47–70.

Henning, C. R. (2000). 'U.S.-EU Relations after the Inception of the Monetary Union: Cooperation or Rivalry?', in C.R. Henning and P. C. Padoan (eds.), *Transatlantic Perspectives on the Euro*. Washington, DC: The Brookings Institution, 5–63.

Hix, S. (1999). *The Political System of the European Union*. London: Macmillan.

Holmes, S. (1995). *Passions and Constraint: On the Theory of Liberal Democracy*. Chicago, IL: The University of Chicago Press.

Horn, M. J. (1995). *The Political Economy of Public Administration*. Cambridge: Cambridge University Press.

Ipsen, H. P. (1972). *Europäisches Gemeinschaftsrecht*. Tuebingen: J. C. B. Mohr (Paul Siebeck).

Jacqué, J. P. (1991). 'Cours Général de Droit Communautaire', in A. Clapham (ed.), *Collected Courses of the Academy of European Law*, Vol. 1, Book 1. Dordrecht, The Netherlands: Martinus Nijhoff Publishers, 247–360.

Joergensen, K. E. (2002). 'Making the CFSP Work', in J. Peterson and M. Shackleton (eds.), *The Institutions of the European Union*. Oxford: Oxford University Press, 210–32.

Joerges, C. (1997). 'Scientific Expertise in Social Regulation and the European Court of Justice: Legal Frameworks for Denationalized Governance Structures', in C. Joerges, K.-H. Ladeur, and E. Vos (eds.), *Integrating Scientific Expertise into Regulatory Decision-Making*. Baden-Baden, Germany: Nomos.

—— (2001). 'Law, Science and the Management of Risks to Health at the National, European and International Level: Stories on Baby Dummies, Mad Cows and Hormones in Beef', *Columbia Journal of European Law*, 7: 1–19.

—— Schepel, H., and Vos, E. (1999). *The Law's Problems with the Involvement of Non-Governmental Actors in Europe's Legislative Processes: The Case of Standardisation under the 'New Approach'*. EUI Working Papers, Law No. 99/9. Florence: European University Institute.

Jones, E. L. (1987). *The European Miracle: Environments, Economies and Geopolitics in the History of Europe and Asia*, 2nd edn. New York: Cambridge University Press.

Kahler, M. (1995). *International Institutions and the Political Economy of Integration*. Washington, DC: The Brookings Institution.

Kay, A. (2003). 'Path Dependency and the CAP', *Journal of European Public Policy*, 10/3: 405–20.

Kelemen, R. D. (2003). 'The Structure and Dynamics of EU Federalism', *Comparative Political Studies*, 36/1–2: 184–208.

Knoedgen, G. (1979). 'Environment and Industrial Siting'. *Zeitschrift fuer Umweltpolitik*, Vol. 1, December.

Landis, J. M. (1966). *The Administrative Process*. New Haven, CT: Yale University Press (originally published in 1938).

Lenaerts, K. (1990). 'Constitutionalism and the Many Faces of Federalism', *American Journal of Comparative Law*, 38: 205–63.

—— (1993). 'Regulating the Regulatory Process: "Delegation of Powers" in the European Community', *European Law Review*, 18: 23–49.

—— and Van Nuffel, P. (1999). *Constitutional Law of the European Union*. London: Sweet and Maxwell.

Lequesne, C. (2000). 'The Common Fisheries Policy', in H. Wallace and W. Wallace (eds.), *Policy-Making in the European Union*, 4th edn. Oxford: Oxford University Press, 345–72.

Levinson, A. (1996). 'Environmental Regulations and Industry Location: International and Domestic Evidence', in J. N. Bhagwati and R. E. Hudec (eds.), *Fair Trade and Harmonization*, Vol. 1. Cambridge, MA: The MIT Press, 429–57.

Lewis, J. (2002). 'National Interests: Coreper', in J. Peterson and M. Shackleton (eds.), *The Institutions of the European Union*. Oxford: Oxford University Press, 277–98.

Lijphart, A. (1991). 'Majority Rule in Theory and Practice: the Tenacity of a Flawed Paradigm', *International Social Science Journal*, 129: 483–94.

—— Rogowski, R., and Weaver, R. K. (1993). 'Separation of Powers and Cleavage Management', in R. K. Weaver and B. Rockman (eds.), *Do Institutions Matter?* Washington, DC: The Brookings Institution, 7–35.

Lindberg, L. N. (1963). *The Political Dynamics of Economic Integration*. Oxford: Oxford University Press.

Lindley, D. (1971). *Making Decisions*. New York and London: Wiley-Interscience.

Locke, J. (1965). 'The Second Treatise of Government', in P. Laslett (ed.), *Two Treatises of Government*. New York: The New American Library, 299–477.

Lodge, J. (ed.) (1989). *The European Community and the Challenge of the Future*. London: Frances Pinter.

Lucas, N. J. D. (1977). *Energy and the European Communities*. London: Europa Publications.

MacCormick, N. (1999). *Questioning Sovereignty: Law, State, and Nation in the European Commonwealth*. New York: Oxford University Press.

McCubbins, M. D. and Noble, G. W. (1995). 'The Appearance of Power: Legislators, Bureaucrats, and the Budget Process in the United States and Japan', in P. F. Cowhey and M. D. McCubbins (eds.), *Structure and Policy in Japan and the United States*. New York: Cambridge University Press, 56–80.

—— Noll, R.G., and Weingast, B.R. (1987). 'Administrative Procedures as Instruments of Political Control', *Journal of Law, Economics, and Organization*, 3: 243–77.

McNamara, K. R. (2002). 'Managing the Euro: The European Central Bank', in J. Peterson and M. Shackleton (eds.), *The Institutions of the European Union*. Oxford: Oxford University Press, 164–85.

McNeill, W. H. (1974). *The Shape of European History*. New York: Oxford University Press.

Magnette, P. (2001). 'Appointing and Censuring the Commission: The Adaptation of Parliamentary Institutions to the Community Context'. *European Law Journal*, 7/3: 292–310.

Majone, G. (1996a). *Regulating Europe*. London: Routledge.

—— (1996b). 'Public Policy and Administration: Ideas, Interests and Institutions', in R. E. Goodin and H.-D. Klingemann (eds.), *A New Handbook of Political Science*. Oxford: Oxford University Press, 610–27.

—— (1998). 'Europe's "Democratic Deficit": The Question of Standards', *European Law Journal*, 4/1: 5–28.

—— (2001). 'Two Logics of Delegation: Agency and Fiduciary Relations in EU Governance'. *European Union Politics*, 2/1: 103–22.

—— (2002). 'Delegation of Regulatory Powers in a Mixed Polity', *European Law Journal*, 8/3: 319–39.

—— (ed.) (2003). *Risk Regulation in the European Union: Between Enlargement and Internationalization*. Florence: European University Institute.

Mannori, L. and Sordi, B. (2001). *Storia del Diritto Amministrativo*. Bari and Rome: Laterza.

Mashaw, J. L., Merrill, R. A., and Shane, P. M. (1998). *Administrative Law*, 4th edn. St. Paul, MN: West Group.

Matteucci, N. (1993). *Lo Stato Moderno*. Bologna: Il Mulino.

Matthews, D. and Pickering, J. (1997). 'Directive 80/778 on Drinking Water Quality: An Analysis of the Development of European Environmental Rules', *International Journal of Biosciences and the Law*, 1: 265–99.

Mendeloff, J. M. (1988). *The Dilemma of Toxic Substance Regulation*. Cambridge, MA: The MIT Press.

Milgrom, J. and Roberts, P. (1992). *Economics, Organization and Management*. Englewood Cliffs, NJ: Prentice-Hall.

Moe, T. M. (1990). 'Political Institutions: The Neglected Side of the Story', *Journal of Law, Economics, and Organization*, 6 : 213–53.

Monar, J. (2002). 'Institutionalizing Freedom, Security, and Justice', in J. Peterson and M. Shackleton (eds.), *The Institutions of the European Union*. Oxford: Oxford University Press, 186–209.

Moravcsik, A. (1993). 'Preferences and Power in the European Community: A Liberal Intergovernmentalist Approach', *Journal of Common Market Studies*, 31/4: 473–522.

Morgan, E. S. (1988). *Inventing the People: The Rise of Popular Sovereignty in England and America*. New York: W. W. Norton.

Mueller, D. C. (1989). *Public Choice II*. New York: Cambridge University Press.

Murray, A. (2003). *The Lisbon Scorecard III: The Status of Economic Reform in the Enlarging EU*. London: Centre for European Reform.

O'Kelley, C. R. T. and Thompson, R. B. (2003). *Corporations and other Business Associations*, 4th edn. New York: Aspen Publishers.

Organization for Economic Co-operation and Development (2000). *Social Expenditure Database, 1980–1999* (CD-ROM). Paris: OECD.

Ostner, I. and Lewis, J. (1995). 'Gender and the Evolution of European Social Policies', in S. Leibfried and P. Pierson (eds.), *European Social Policy: Between Fragmentation and Integration*. Washington, DC: The Brookings Institution, 159–93.

Otsuki, T., Wilson, J. S., and Sewadeh, M. (2000). 'Saving Two in a Billion: A Case Study to Quantify the Trade Effect of European Food Safety Standards on African Exports'. The World Bank (mimeo).

Payne, D. C. (2000). 'Policy-making in Nested Institutions: Explaining the Conservation Failure of the EU's Common Fisheries Policy', *Journal of Common Market Studies*, 38/2: 303–24.

Pelkmans, J. (1997). *European Integration*. New York: Longman.

Peterson, P. E. and Rom, M. C. (1990). *Welfare Magnets*. Washington, DC: The Brookings Institution.

Poehl, K. O. (1990). 'Towards Monetary Union in Europe', in Institute of Economic Affairs, *Europe's Constitutional Future*. London: Institute of Economic Affairs, 35–42.

Poggi, G. (1978). *The Development of the Modern State*. Stanford, CA: Stanford University Press.

Polanyi, M. (1951). *The Logic of Liberty: Reflections and Rejoinders*. London: Routledge and Kegan Paul.

Poli, S. (2003). 'The Emerging EU Regulatory Framework on Genetically Modified Organisms: Dilemmas and Challenges', in G. Majone (ed.), *Risk Regulation in the European Union: Between Enlargement and Internationalization*. Florence: European University Institute, 79–124.

Pollack, M. A. (1997). 'Delegation, Agency, and Agenda Setting in the European Community', *International Organization*, 51: 99–134.

Previdi, E. (1997). 'The Organization of Public and Private Responsibilities in European Risk Regulation: An Institutional Gap Between Them?', in C. Joerges, K.-H. Ladeur, and E. Vos (eds.), *Integrating Scientific Expertise into Regulatory Decision-Making*. Baden-Baden, Germany: Nomos.

Rakove, J. N. (1997). *Original Meanings*. New York: Vintage Books.

Revesz, R. L. (1992). 'Rehabilitating Interstate Competition: Rethinking the "Race-to-the-Bottom" Rationale for Federal Environmental Regulation', *New York University Law Review*, 67: 1210–54.

Rieger, E. (2000). 'The Common Agricultural Policy', in H. Wallace and W. Wallace (eds.), *Policy-Making in the European Union*, 4th edn. Oxford: Oxford University Press, 179–210.

Rodrik, D. (2000). 'How Far Will International Economic Integration Go?', *Journal of Economic Perspectives*, 14/1: 177–86.

Roessler, F. (1996). 'Diverging Domestic Policies and Multilateral Trade Integration', in J. N. Bhagwati and R. E. Hudec (eds.), *Fair Trade and Harmonization*, Vol. 2. Cambridge, MA: The MIT Press, 21–56.

Rogoff, K. (1985). 'The Optimal Degree of Commitment to an Intermediate Monetary Target', *Quarterly Journal of Economics*, 100: 1169–90.

Ryle, G. (1949). *The Concept of Mind*. New York: Barnes & Noble Books.

Sabine, G. H. (1960). *A History of Political Theory*, 2nd edn. New York: Holt, Rinehart and Winston.

Sapir, A. (1996). 'Trade Liberalization and the Harmonization of Social Policies: Lessons from European Integration', in J. N. Bhagwati and R. E. Hudec (eds.), *Fair Trade and Harmonization*, Vol. 1. Cambridge, MA: The MIT Press, 543–70.

Sbragia, A. M. (2000). 'Environmental Policy', in H. Wallace and W. Wallace (eds.), *Policy-Making in the European Union*, 4th edn. Oxford: Oxford University Press, 293–316.

Scharpf, F. W. (2001). 'Democratic Legitimacy under Conditions of Regulatory Competition: Why Europe Differs from the United States', in K. Nicolaidis and R. Howse (eds.), *The Federal Vision: Legitimacy and Levels of Governance in the United States and the European Union*. Oxford: Oxford University Press, 355–74.

Scott, J. and Trubek, D. M. (2002). 'Mind the Gap: Law and New Approaches to Governance in the European Union', *European Law Journal*, 8/1: 1–18.

—— and Vos, E. (2002). 'The Juridification of Uncertainty: Observations on the Ambivalence of the Precautionary Principle within the EU and the WTO', in R. Dehousse and C. Joerges (eds.), *Good Governance in Europe's Integrated Market*. Oxford: Oxford University Press, 253–86.

Sedelmeier, U. and Wallace, H. (2000). 'Eastern Enlargement', in H. Wallace and W. Wallace (eds.), *Policy-Making in the European Union*, 4th edn. Oxford: Oxford University Press, 427–60.

Shaw, J. (2003). 'Flexibility in a "Reorganised" and "Simplified" Treaty', in B. de Witte (ed.), *Ten Reflections on the Constitutional Treaty for Europe* (E-book). Florence: European University Institute, 183–202.

Sidjanski, D. (1992). *L'avenir fédéraliste de l'Europe*. Paris: Presses Universitaires de France.

Spitz, E. (1984). *Majority Rule*. Chatham, NJ: Chatham House Publishers.

Spruyt, H. (1994). *The Sovereign State and Its Competitors: An Analysis of Systems Change*. Princeton, NJ: Princeton University Press.

Stewart, R. B. (1975). 'The Reformation of American Administrative Law', *Harvard Law Review*, 88: 1667–813.

Swank, D. (2001). 'Mobile Capital, Democratic Institutions and the Public Economy in Advanced Industrial Societies', *Journal of Comparative Policy Analysis*, 3/2: 133–62.

Symes, D. and Crean, K. (1995). 'Historic Prejudice and Invisible Boundaries: Dilemmas for the Development of the Common Fisheries Policy', in G. Blake, W. Hildesley, R. Pratt, R. Ridley, and C. Schofield (eds.), *The Peaceful Management of Transboundary Resources*. London: Graham and Trotman.

Tsebelis, G. (1990). *Nested Games: Rational Choice in Comparative Politics*. Berkeley and Los Angeles, CA: University of California Press.

Tsoukalis, L. (2000). 'Economic and Monetary Union', in H. Wallace and W. Wallace (eds.), *Policy-Making in the European Union*, 4th edn. Oxford: Oxford University Press, 149–78.

Vaubel, R. (1995). *The Centralisation of Western Europe: The Common Market, Political Integration, and Democracy*. London: Institute of Economic Affairs.

Walker, N. (2003). 'Freedom, Security and Justice', in B. de Witte (ed.), *Ten Reflections on the Constitutional Treaty for Europe* (E-book). Florence: European University Institute, 159–82.

Wallace, H. (2000). 'The Institutional Setting', in H. Wallace and W. Wallace (eds.), *Policy-Making in the European Union*, 4th edn. Oxford: Oxford University Press, 3–37.

—— (2003). 'Designing Institutions for an Enlarging European Union', in B. de Witte (ed.), *Ten Reflections on the Constitutional Treaty for Europe* (E-book). Florence: European University Institute, 85–106.

Weatherill, S. (1995). *Law and Integration in the European Union*. Oxford: Clarendon Press.

—— (2003). 'Competence', in B. de Witte (ed.), *Ten Reflections on the Constitutional Treaty for Europe* (E-book). Florence: European University Institute, 45–66.

Weiler, J. H. H. (1999). *The Constitution of Europe*. Cambridge: Cambridge University Press.

—— (2001). 'Federalism without Constitutionalism: Europe's *Sonderweg*', in K. Nicolaidis and R. Howse (eds.), *The Federal Vision: Legitimacy and Levels of Governance in the United States and the European Union*. Oxford: Oxford University Press, 54–70.

Weingast, B. R. (1995). 'The Economic Role of Political Institutions: Market-Preserving Federalism and Economic Development', *The Journal of Law, Economics, and Organization*, 11/1: 1–31.

Williams, S. (1991). 'Sovereignty and Accountability in the European Community', in R. O. Keohane and S. Hoffmann (eds.), *The New European Community: Decisionmaking and Institutional Change*. Boulder, CO: Westview Press, 155–76.

Williamson, O. E. (1985). *The Economic Institutions of Capitalism*. New York: The Free Press.

Wilson, J. D. (1996). 'Capital Mobility and Environmental Standards: Is There a Theoretical Basis for a Race to the Bottom?', in J. N. Bhagwati and R. E. Hudec (eds.), *Fair Trade and Harmonization*, Vol. 1. Cambridge, MA: The MIT Press, 393–427.

Wood, G. S. (1998). *The Creation of the American Republic, 1776–1787*. Chapel Hill, NC: The University of North Carolina Press.

Index

Lightning Source UK Ltd.
Milton Keynes UK
UKOW06f0750190416

272526UK00001B/40/P